Kim Hunter

Loose in the Kitchen

Kim Hunter

Loose in the Kitchen

DOMINA BOOKS

North Hollywood, California

To the dear persons, unknown to me, who invented paper towels, the electric mixer, the slotted spoon, Teflon, and the tomato.

the Contents

LOOSE IN THE KITCHEN

Janet Cole is the name I was born with. I was a quiet, unobtrusive child. Shy. Obedient. By rights, I should have grown up to be a nice, normal, wifely person . . . a natural in the kitchen . . . married and dutifully settled down with husband, home, and offspring, like my mother before me. I didn't.

That quiet exterior should have been a tip-off that everything would go wrong, but nobody caught it until it was too late.

The truth was, I didn't clamor for attention from family or peers because I'd found a much more enticing life elsewhere. I spent most of my childhood having an absolutely marvelous time in fantasy worlds of my own creation. Living out one exciting role after another.

In fact, I enjoyed my fantasies so thoroughly, that eventually I saw no reason why I shouldn't bring them into the real world.

My first attempt came at age nine. I learned a song, "Shuffle Off To Buffalo." We lived in Detroit, and radio station WXYZ broadcast a weekly Amateur Hour that I listened to regularly. One day I finagled my older brother into driving me to the station and presented myself as a contestant.

I botched it. The shyness did me in. I sang my song so softly no one could hear it. When the Master of Ceremonies coaxed me to sit on his lap, the better to hear me, my voice got even softer. It's possible he never even knew what song I was singing. I was rejected as a contestant. But I knew in my heart that if I had been one, I would have outshone all the others and become a *STAR*.

I was very discouraged for at least an hour, then decided I'd turn my talents to an easier field, writing. I wrote half a dozen plays before I was twelve. I never got them put on, not even a garage production, but the fantasies *they* hatched led me to discover something I really could do. Act.

My determination was more fruitful this time. I worked with a teacher, and after three years or so, actually got on a stage. And I could be heard. I never lost the shyness, but the drive to create my own reality got sturdier and sturdier and I actually became an actress.

A few years later, the actress was given a name . . . Kim Hunter. And Kim Hunter went on to become rather good, a star of stage, screen, and television, as they say. Yes, a STAR. Hey-hey! (To some it may seem that she specializes in pregnant Southern women and chimpanzees. Not true. She's played everything from queens and witches to poets and tarts.)

1

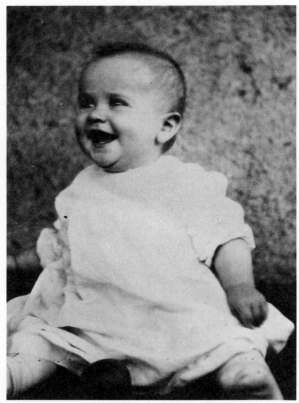

"Lights! Camera! Action!" — The author at eight months

She never became a *SUPERSTAR*, however . . . though she always thought she would like that. One problem was all those *other* fantasies whirling inside that busy little head.

I wanted everything. I wanted to be an actress, a *STAR* . . . famous and acclaimed, with long fingernails and an entourage of servants and lawyers, managers and fur stoles. I also wanted the gentle pleasures of the NEST . . . a home, with a loving husband, children, house-plants and footstools. And on top of that, I wanted to be master of my own canoe . . . a LONER, down the rapids, guiding my own destiny. I wanted attention paid to all several of me.

It was a problem. The fantasies conflicted. And the one area that should have been the most natural, by upbringing, was the one I least understood in practice. The *NEST*.

My first attempt to realize that dream was a whopping flop. But I was no more willing to give up that aspiration than I was to give up the career. And, at last, I made it! I found my loving husband, children, home . . . and, after twenty-three years, it's still a reality.

There have been ups and downs in all my worlds, but I have quite a bit to show for each of them. Publicly, I've had a long and healthy career, and I expect to make a few more noises before I'm through. In private, I'm my own person, whoever she may be. And I've been blessed with an understanding husband whom I adore, two children who survived my experiment in motherhood and grew up into admirable people, and a very pleasant home that I enjoy living in and that friends enjoy visiting. And yes, I'm a damn good cook. A godawful housekeeper, but I make up for it in the kitchen.

Not to cop a plea, but really, I was ill-prepared in childhood for the domestic life. I kept escaping to that fantasy world instead of paying attention to a mother who was expert at homemaking. I observed, in a detached way, but none of it ever "took."

Of course, eventually I had to make a stab at learning everything. Even sewing and knitting, for God's sake. All to realize my fantasy image of the ideal wife and homebody. Frankly, I found most of it a bore. Particularly general housekeeping. I never managed more than the bare basics, and to this day I avoid cleaning and scrubbing with a touch of deviousness.

Cooking, however, was different. Learning to cook was hellish hard in the beginning, but gradually I caught on. I even became aware of a certain talent. Then pleasure. And, as in acting, the terrors and struggles finally bore sweet fruit.

In fact, cooking has become the other side of my acting coin.

That youthful, rather daring urge to make some of my private world public, was a shy girl's need for a creative outlet. I found it in acting. And luckily, I was a "natural" (who gradually developed a craft). I was never a "natural" homemaker. Without the protective covering of make-believe, the NEST was far from an outlet for self-expression. It was an avalanche of *experience* . . . anxiety, joy, confusion, riding the waves, ups and downs. I've spent my life improvising and hoping for the best, relying on the work periods to release some of the tensions.

Until the joys of cooking entered my life. At last! A second creative outlet when and where I needed it. I actually became a dandier wife and a more relaxed parent.

In the kitchen, just as on the stage, the fun is in the exploring, the doing. I do the best I can, with loving care, and then face the fact that everything is ultimately in the hands of the gods anyway.

A note about the recipes. Some are my own concoctions, but most have been inherited, given, solicited, or stolen . . . from family and friends. They run the gamut . . . a personal hodgepodge from which I really cook. The Collection *has proved very satisfying to my household. May it add pleasure to yours.*

Antonios Zamouzakis

My first "Hollywood" portrait

4

PEANUT BUTTER, JELLY, AND DAVID O. SELZNICK

My first genuine accomplishment in the kitchen was achieved at a very early age . . . the peanut butter and jelly sandwich. It was my most frequent concoction until I was a teenager, and I got rather good at it. I don't claim that my version is absolutely original, but I have yet to encounter one made in exactly the same way. I offer it with some pride, and one caution. Being an open-faced sandwich, it's pretty goopy. For example, I don't recommend it for picnics.

It's also seductive, habit forming, and about *three hundred and fifty* calories. And was responsible for my goofing the first assignment I ever had from David O. Selznick.

I'd always been roundish, but not fat, so I never gave calories much thought. I'd certainly never been on a diet. Until Selznick put me under contract. He was convinced the camera added ten pounds to the look of one's weight, and said the "chub" had to go.

It was my first meeting with a Big Hollywood Producer, and I was the innocent of all time. I fully expected a probing discussion of my acting qualifications and careful consideration of what type roles I might best play.

Nothing like that. He had me stand up, remove my suit jacket, turn around, walk to the sofa and back. That was it.

"Thank you, Miss Cole. I'll get in touch with your agent."

I was politely ushered out, feeling terribly let down, and convinced that this was "Shuffle Off To Buffalo" all over again.

It wasn't. Selznick did call my agent. He bought the merchandise, changed its label from Janet Cole to Kim Hunter, and ordered it streamlined before he marketed it to various other studios.

In the two years I was under contract to D.O.S., I made five films . . . all of them "loan-outs." I spent exactly two days on camera at Selznick's Vanguard Studios . . . the back of my head substituting for the back of Ingrid Bergman's head while Alfred Hitchcock screen-tested various chaps for minor roles in "Spellbound."

For my streamlining I was sent to a doctor who gave me a complete physical and sent me home with a low-calorie diet and two huge bottles. One was filled with thyroid pills. The other was benzedrine.

I tried to follow the diet. Truly I did. But I also took the pills. What did I know? In those days the only things known as "uppers" were pajama tops.

I must have had a gland loose, because instead of the pills killing my appetite, they made me high as a kite and absolutely ravenous. A food freak. I kept flying (literally) into the kitchen to cheat on the

5

diet with *Peanut Butter and Jelly Sandwiches*. I did make them on little bitty saltines. But who was I kidding?

I didn't lose an ounce. What I gained was my first sense of guilt about food, and my mother telling me how vivacious I'd become. Vivacious? I was stratospheric.

The weight came off eventually . . . without bennies . . . but I lost neither my taste for peanut butter and jelly nor the guilt. The P. B. & J. is still forbidden fruit. And I'll still cheat, but not often enough to gain much more than a delicious sense of sinning.

Peanut Butter and Jelly Sandwich   *349*

David O. Selznick

The forbidden has always attracted me. I think that's why I'm so crazy about movies. When I was a child in Detroit they were almost taboo, at least for us Coles. My father had something against them. Just what, I was never sure. But while he was alive he'd made it clear that he disapproved of anyone, particularly a child, spending time in picture houses. I think he felt it eroded the intellect.

Daddy died when I was three, but Mother faithfully stood by his set of rules. Oh, she did relent when I was ten or so and took me to see "The Sign of the Cross." I suppose she felt the moral uplift would outweigh the intellectual erosion.

Well, you can't see just one movie. The Christian Martyrs were followed by Tarzan, and by the time I saw Frankenstein I was a goner. Hooked on film.

For most of my childhood, though, I found my entertainment around the house, in my room, in the backyard, or in the kitchen. I spent hours in the kitchen. Watching my mother cook was the best show on the block. She was as much the artist, the star in her kitchen, as Myrna Loy ever was at Grauman's Chinese. Not that I learned much about cooking. I was simply enthralled by her magic act.

I remember that kitchen vividly. It had all the usual accoutrements of the period . . . the enameled stove, standing high on legs, with its old-fashioned eye-level oven; a true ice box, to which the iceman cameth and lifted huge blocks of ice into place with lethal-looking tongs; and the best feature of all, an enormous rectangular wooden table in the center of the room. Mother scrubbed it daily with a stiff brush and soap suds, while I watched, mesmerized by the ever-changing patterns the bristles drew in the suds, and her uncanny talent for getting the edges of the table as spotless as the center without a drop of water ever touching the floor.

Once I did prevail on her to teach me a recipe. Naturally, I picked my favorite dessert . . . *HER CAKE*. It was Mother's version of the old-fashioned 1-2-3-4 Butter Cake, simple, versatile, and delicious.

Well, we started. And before my eyes that sweet, huggable woman turned into a grim, relentless tyrant. Mother Legree. An uncompromising perfectionist. She had me beating that batter till I thought I'd go through life with a revolving arm.

It was a long, hard pull . . . but my determination survived, and I won her nodding approval. It was worth it. And to this day, it only hurts when I wave.

That year Mother married Bliss Stebbins, a dear man with a delightful sense of life and humor. My brother Gordon called him "the Governor." I shortened it to "Govie," and the nickname stuck.

We moved to Govie's home in Miami Beach, and Daddy's theories about "the cinema" got lost in the shuffle. I became a regular patron of all the local movie houses . . . thoroughly addicted. And "Mom-in-the-Kitchen" went down the drain as entertainment value.

I made a couple of culinary forays on my own, though. Govie very nearly became the father I'd never really known, and I thrived on his approval. I remember taking over the kitchen one day, wanting to do something special for him. Mother was out shopping, and Govie was in his den, busy with paper work.   I'd make him *HER CAKE*.

I opened Mother's recipe book and got side-tracked to the *Gingerbread* recipe instead. That would be much more daring, since I'd never baked it before. With Mother's training for *HER CAKE*, and a lot of beginner's luck, the *Gingerbread* came out of the oven like a dream.

Bursting with pride and delight, bearing my grand accomplishment before me, I rushed into his study like a colt, and skidded on the tile floor.

We married Govie and moved into his home in Miami Beach — **Govie, Mother, Gordon and me**

The gingerbread went up and I went down. I can still see in slow-motion that flying gingerbread's trajectory from my hands to Govie's desk. God knows what went through his mind at the moment of impact.

He helped me salvage as much as possible, and through my tears I accepted his twinkling complicity. We served the fragments that night, the damage camouflaged with whipped cream, and Govie fibbed a little, to put my sanitary-minded mother at ease. My ruptured dessert was a triumph. How I loved that man.

In the summer, Govie would take us to a resort hotel he owned in northern Michigan . . . at Grand Lake. It was a sprawling complex of main lodge and lakeside cottages in the midst of a forest of birch, cedar, beech and pine trees.

Movies weren't available, so there was no competition for the wonders of the great outdoors. I explored it all. I was also ravenous day and night.

We ate most of our meals in the hotel dining room with the guests, but once in a while Mother would tackle the huge iron stove

**Mother's favorite
portrait of Govie**

9

in our cottage. It was fueled with wood, and pretty tricky for city folks to manage, but Mother got onto it, and would turn out some masterpieces.

For instance, a *Strawberry Shortcake* I defy you to duplicate today. The biscuits baked in the oven of that storybook wood stove. Country cream skimmed from the top of those five-gallon tins of fresh farm milk and whipped into clouds. Add the wild strawberries, tiny and poignant, that I had picked myself in the woods where they abounded. Those were the days.

HER CAKE (Grace Stebbins)	*366*
Chocolate Frosting	*388*
Chocolate Sauce I and II	*388, 389*
Butterscotch Sauce	*389*
Vanilla Sauce	*387*
Gingerbread (Grace Stebbins-Jeannette Obenauer)	*374*
Whipped Cream Sauce	*387*
Strawberry Shortcake (Grace Stebbins)	*368*

Daddy died when I was three — **Donald Cole in his World War I uniform**

Govie died the year I entered high school. It wasn't really sudden . . . he'd been ill for several months. But losing him was hard to come to grips with. Years later, in psychoanalysis, I would still be studying the disappearing of fathers, trying to convince my subconscious that they didn't do it on purpose.

An abundance of teenage activity was some sort of solace. High school had brought me out of solitary and into the joys and agonies of a social life. Dating. Golly! What do you talk about while he sneaks his arm across the back of your seat? Who'll teach me "the Shag?" Life was rich with very important stuff.

And that was only half of it. At the same time, I had joined the acting classes of Charmine Lantaff Camine (sic), a true gem of a dramatics teacher, when you consider the rhinestones who usually teach acting. Mrs. Camine was good. We learned basic acting techniques, and gradually lessons in singing, fencing, and dancing were added to the schedule.

This double life carried on for the rest of my school years. And any agonies I had in high school . . . with boy friends, or geometry, or the peach strapless that wouldn't stay up even with scotch tape . . . any of these tribulations was easier to bear, knowing I had my "I'll-show-them-all" world of acting to escape to.

Each acting class brought me a notch closer to the crazy dream . . . the dream that movies were now stimulating regularly, in spite of Mrs. Camine's purer guidance. She held, stubbornly, that the stage was my only worthy ambition. And to a certain extent she won. But the movies always promised a very special glamour of their own.

Mother thought I should go to college, but there'd already been the lead in a Little Theatre production of "Penny Wise," and a co-starring part in our Senior Class play, "What A Life!" Even a one-girl performance in General Assembly . . . Dorothy Parker's "The Waltz." I didn't want a college, I wanted a THEATRE.

Mrs. Camine conveniently provided the first one that summer after graduation. She'd turned an abandoned grist mill in North Carolina into The Old Mill Playhouse, and hired The Vagabond Players from Baltimore to perform a season of stock. As her protégé, I had a sizeable part in nearly every production.

Back in Miami Beach, I struck out on my own. I wormed my way into several productions of winter stock at the Gant Gaither Theatre. And later in the season, auditioned for the Theatre of the Fifteen in Coral Gables. My timing was perfect. Their resident ingénue was getting married and had just given her notice, leaving

11

them with no "Cecily" for their upcoming production of "The Importance of Being Earnest." I spent the next fourteen months with The Fifteen, drawing grand parts, much experience, and no pay. Thank God I had a family who could afford to subsidize me.

When the urge came to try the "Big Time," my eye was on New York. I'd fight my way into the legitimate "theatah" the way I'd seen Kate Hepburn do it in the RKO movie "Stage Door." At the last moment I was spared by a wire from Hale McKeen, a director I'd worked with in stock, inviting me to detour slightly through the Pasadena Playhouse in California.

My first job in stock was at the Old Mill Playhouse. My visiting friend — Neva Ennis.

There I played Peggy in Hale's production of "The Women," and a few months later, the ingénue in "Arsenic and Old Lace," with Raymond Burr playing the heavy. (Many years later, both came back into my life. "The Women," via a glamorous Broadway revival in 1973, this time starring as Mary Haines . . . and dear Ray Burr, via a couple of segments of "Ironside," who was now tracking down villains instead of playing them.)

In those days, Pasadena Playhouse was a showcase for studio scouts. Selznick's people discovered me, and the Great Man signed me to a seven-year movie contract, filled with options. All his, of course. But . . . I was out of the bush league into the majors.

Cooking? Oh, no. I was being "groomed for stardom, darling." Mother finally got the idea that Wellesley would have to get along without me. She sold the Florida house, and we took an apartment in "HOLLYWOOD!"

Through the Looking Glass into the Moooooooovies! I was agog. Selznick rented me out to RKO to star in my first film, "The Seventh Victim," a "B" horror opus. It was a "first" for director Mark Robson, too. He'd just moved up from film editing. I'd moved up from stock. It was exciting for both of us. And not a little terrifying for me.

I was learning about all the demands of the camera . . . the close-up, the long-shot, those devilish things called "marks." I can still be tyrannized by those tapes on the floor that tell you just how far to move in a scene, or all is ruined for the lighting and camera.

Acting at *all* in front of a camera seemed abnormal and distracted. The deathly silence after the director said "Action!" was so loud all my concentration disappeared. I could hear my own pulse, and feel the eyes of an entire crew glued to my every twitch. "Don't twitch!" They told me the camera exaggerated every movement of every facial muscle, and one degree too much came out pure distortion.

"Cut!"

"Did I twitch?!"

"No, not one twitch. In fact, you're behaving like you're embalmed. Try it again."

Somehow with Mark's help, I got through it all and wasn't fired.

I was drawing my first weekly paychecks, and that was pretty thrilling in itself. My first outlay was the down payment on a car . . . a Ford business coupe, the smallest they made. I zipped up to Sunset and parked proudly in front of my agent's office.

"Take it back," he said. "Don't you know you must have a Cadillac? When you're a famous star, *then* drive a Ford business coupe. They'll say you're eccentric. Now all it says is you're nobody!"

I gulped, but on my salary I figured I'd have to risk anonymity. I kept the coupe.

RKO didn't hold my little Ford against me. They rented me again from Selznick for a second picture, "Tender Comrade," this one a first-class "A" production, starring Ginger Rogers. I'd moved up in the world.

I had a principal part but this time the whole film wasn't on my shoulders. And the schedule was leisurely. There was time to observe and learn from the pros around me . . . Ginger, Bob Ryan, Ruth Hussey, Patricia Collinge. And time for director Edward Dmytryk to rise to the challenge of my naiveté. I was all of 21, but slightly retarded in certain respects. When I was having a hard time understanding the nature of the grin he wanted for the "morning after my wedding night" scene, he brilliantly suggested I use the image of a luscious two-scoop, hot fudge sundae. "Print!"

The pervasive make-believe of Hollywood took over my personal life as well. One afternoon I was posing for publicity stills on the set when a group of servicemen on R. and R. (Rest and Recreation) came through on a tour of the studio. I was introduced to Captain William Baldwin of the Marine Air Corps, a handsome and persuasive chap. He talked me into a date that led to a whirl-wind romance and my first marriage.

Without realizing it, I was living my own movie. World War II was the background. My brave war ace sharing with me his brief moment out of danger. The bittersweet gaiety of love in the face of an ominous future. Hold me. There's no tomorrow.

All serious thoughts were banished. We romped through the days and nights . . . the glorious merry-go-round of Ciro's, the Mocambo, Earl Carroll's, the Coconut Grove . . . the Brave and the Beautiful, dancing, laughing . . . always people, lots of people.

There was another woman who'd also fallen in love with Bill. My mother. Actually, she fell in love with the whole Marine Corps. The first party she gave for Bill and his friends was a knockout. Literally. She served a drink they'd never had before, and disarmed half a squadron singlehanded. God knows where this gentle woman had learned to make it, but with a smile it just took your head off.

Bill named it the *Stebbins Stinger*. It's as delicious as it is deadly, and oddly enough, there's no hangover.

Stebbins Stinger (Grace Stebbins)   *200*

14

In the midst of this impetuous courtship, I was summoned once again to Selznick's office. This time it was different. Being an old veteran of two whole movies I was one professional meeting another.

We discussed the work I'd been doing. He wanted to know if I was happy at RKO, said he'd had good reports on my acting, and he set up an appointment with Margaret Ettinger, a top public relations woman in Hollywood, to launch a publicity build-up.

I was delighted and grateful at this indication of his faith in me, and I was telling him so when I realized that I'd been backing away from him but that he wasn't any further away.

No. No, this wasn't happening. It was just a coincidence. I must be *imagining* that he was following me around his desk and seemed to be accelerating. Could it be true? I tried to invent casual conversation, but all I could think was, "My God . . . I'm being chased around this room by the man who made *Gone With The Wind!*" I found myself at a 45-degree angle, leaning backwards over the desk, saying, "But Mr. Selznick! I'm in *LOVE!*"

That stopped him. The look in his eye made me think it might not have been the first time he'd met resistance, but the shade of utter astonishment suggested it had never happened quite this way before. He straightened up and said, "Of course. Why didn't you tell me? Are you planning to be married?"

I had to confess that Bill hadn't proposed yet, but that if he didn't soon, I would, and Mr. Selznick would be the first to know. That seemed to please him. I was gallantly released and shown out of his office.

Bill did ask me to marry him shortly after that, and as promised, D.O.S. knew everything. In fact, once our plans were settled . . . date, church, etc . . . he took over as completely as any Father of the Bride. It isn't every girl that can have her church wedding produced by David O. Selznick.

This was early 1944, and I was still caught up in the wonder of Hollywood's glamorous sheen. The premieres, the fabulous parties given by famous people, attended by photographers and more famous people . . . (and me). And the publicity agent who was spreading the name of Kim Hunter across the pages of the world's press. Fantastic.

When Margaret Ettinger and her organization went to work for you, it was noisy. Your face and your name began to appear everywhere. There were interviews with newspapers, periodicals, and fan magazines, photographic sessions tied in with fashion, with beauty, and God knows what. Pure fiction went out in press releases as fact. I was being Ettingerized.

That was their job . . . to create a familiar public personality, and any similarity between that creature and your own true identity was irrelevant. It was fascinating to read in the papers what a colorful life I was living. It came as quite a surprise that I had been born in a lighthouse off the Florida Keys, and that my favorite hobby was diving for coral.

Before Bill and I were engaged, Hedda and Lolly detailed my romantic attachments and detachments in their columns. My name was linked with all sorts of people (most of whom I didn't know), and cute items described my lively activities (few of which I would have conceived doing, much less done). I sounded to me like someone I'd really like to meet.

At first I giggled at the inaccuracies, the fictions, and even the downright lies. Then it began to get embarrassing. Interviewers would ask me about thrilling things I'd done that for some odd reason I couldn't remember.

Finally, I asked the press agents why they couldn't print just as many items and stick to the truth. Their answer was blunt, and disdainful of the question. "The public is not interested in Truth. It's neither provocative nor glamorous enough."

My mistake. If I hadn't asked the question, I wouldn't have had to wrestle with the answer. The glitter lost some of its brilliance. I began to feel like a processed cheese . . . cheap, highly-adulterated, but very marketable. And my wedding became the biggest Velveeta commercial in history.

Maggie Ettinger's supreme achievement was lining up Life Magazine to cover my marriage to Bill. The full import of such a picture story escaped me when I was told. I was spared the preparations, so my first rude awakening came the moment I appeared out of the bride's anteroom into the church.

Dressed in bridal gown, flowing veil, holding my bouquet, and shaking like a leaf, I walked right into a photographer on his knees yelling "Hold it!" The flash blinded me, and my instinctive reaction was to bolt and run for home. I vaguely remember being grabbed, soothing voices reassuring me, the organ music swelling, and being forcibly pointed in the direction of the center aisle.

I still have a complete set of photographs to "refresh my memory" of that afternoon . . . and no recollection whatever without them. As far as I knew, I'd married a camera.

The pictures make it look perfectly beautiful, and I suppose to the spectators it was. Bill and his ushers in their full-dress Marine uniforms, with shining swords . . . my bridesmaids, visions in silk and tulle. Selznick is there, grinning, surrounded by an entourage of notables I'd never met. Shirley Temple among them, attending her

16

first wedding in misty tears. (I wonder if we were introduced?) I must say I was pretty lovely myself, in my Mary Queen of Scots coif . . . looking too young to be confirmed, much less married. And we did the whole thing in one take.

Life Magazine was delighted. They upped it to a Feature Story . . . "A Marine Takes a Wife." They even followed us to our honeymoon cottage in Laguna Beach. The photographers gave us a two-day respite from the flash bulbs, and then descended on us like relatives. We spent a day frolicking on the beach for the benefit of their lenses, and then, at last, they were gone.

Newlyweds.

If Bill had any hidden hope that he'd married a master chef, he got over it fast. Among other rather splendid wedding presents was a simple copy of "The Joy of Cooking" from some astute friend. That helped a lot, but I could still get into trouble on my own.

Bill was a very gregarious man, and chums from his base were often brought home for pot luck. I should have been flattered, but knowing how *much* luck went into any pot of mine put me on the edge of panic every time.

But one night I was ready for him. I had a stand-by chicken in the fridge, and when Bill arrived with two extra fliers I blithely went right to work on a recipe I'd watched Mother prepare dozens of times. I knew it backwards. Broiled Chicken.

I arranged it all in the baking dish with onions and bay leaf, and with a confident flourish I slipped it under the broiler.

Well, pride goeth before an underdone, charred, thoroughly inedible chicken. I'd missed one little technicality. My mother, the queen of logic, called it Broiled Chicken because she bought broilers to make it with. What I forgot was that she didn't broil it. She baked it.

I did learn from my mistakes . . . sometimes. In this case I changed the name of the dish immediately. It's really a grand way to *bake* a broiler.

Baked Chicken with Onions   *289*

17

A pregnant moment from "Betrayed" with Robert Mitchum

Try making a feature film in ten days while you're pregnant. "When Strangers Marry" (later re-released as "Betrayed") was a quickie William Castle was directing for the King Brothers, and we shot the whole picture in 10 days because that was the budget.

I hadn't told anyone I was "with child" for fear Selznick would put me on suspension. That was the custom when an imminent addition to the family made you unemployable.

And this picture wasn't a drawing room comedy either. The script had me fighting off murder attempts and running for my life through miles of tunnel. When the shooting was completed, I told Bill Castle about my condition and he had to lie down.

By now my baby began to show, and Selznick, exercising the provisions of our contract, suspended my salary. Hedda Hopper, always ready to print anything mean about David, praised Sam Goldwyn for *not* suspending Teresa Wright during her pregnancy, and called Selznick a cheapskate for treating me this way.

What the Mad Hat didn't know was that David had stuck to a strict business policy, but had personally offered me any financial assistance I might need . . . any sum I wanted at the mere mention. I reminded him that I had a husband to look after me, but it was a generous gesture nevertheless.

My little independent production gave me a lot of time on my hands. Mother had bought a house in the San Fernando Valley, a nice sprawly ranch-type house on two and a half acres. There were roses climbing the fences, scattered fruit trees on the front and back lawns, and a grape arbor leading to a proper orchard in the rear.

Bill had been transferred to El Centro, and had no desire to spend more time than necessary at the base, so I stayed with Mother and he commuted. The carefree marriage had begun to strain a bit at the seams, but we were both looking forward to the baby. Our fun and games might have slowed down, but not our optimism. Yet.

The neighborhood in Encino was friendly and sociable, with Paul and Bella Muni on our block and Edward Everett Horton just up the street.

It was a lovely, pastoral period those months. We picked our own grapes and fruit, and kept a coop of chickens for fresh eggs. One lovely piece of serendipity was the artichoke patch we discovered out back of the orchard. Mother and I hadn't been acquainted with this vegetable in Michigan or Florida, so we experimented together and it became a joyous addition to my pint-sized repertoire.

Do all women feel a territorial imperative about their kitchens? Mother would never turn me really loose in hers. Here I was a grown-up married woman, and I still had to do everything her way, always inhibited by her hovering. Years later, my own daughter tells me she had the same trouble with me.

Naturally I was having off-beat cravings for certain foods, and I persuaded Mother to teach me two recipes that at six months pregnant I really needed. *Blueberry Muffins* and *Baking Powder Biscuits.* Damn the calories! I was *hungry!*

HOLLYWOOD VERSUS THE MOTHER COUNTRY

Bill was sent back into combat in the Pacific just a week or so before our baby arrived. My brother Gordon was in town, and did some proxy pacing for Bill while Kathryn Deirdre was born. A model of motherhood, I hired a nurse and was back at work in a month.

I made two more films under my Selznick contract, "You Came Along," with Robert Cummings at Paramount, and something for the Army called "Reconnaissance Pilot," with William Holden. And then I was summoned into Selznick's office for the last time.

It was the gentlest of boots. In a sense, he was kicking me out of the nest. Since he had both Jennifer Jones (later his wife) and Dorothy McGuire under contract as well, he felt I'd do better on my own. We could all three play the same sort of role and, naturally, the more established actresses were going to get first consideration from him. Stuck at his studio, I just might die on the vine. So after two years we said a friendly and affectionate farewell.

Hollywood is no place to be with nothing to do. I mean you can only get one suntan at a time. I was coming down with a mild case of panic in Paradise when the phone rang. Remember those back-of-the-head tests I'd made for "Spellbound" a year before? Well, you never know.

Michael Powell and Emeric Pressburger were in from England on a talent-search for an American girl to play the WAC in "Stairway to Heaven." They were having dinner with compatriot Alfred Hitchcock, when Hitch remembered my "sitting in" for Bergman and suggested that I might be a good bet. Gamble they did . . . on Hitch's word and Micky Powell's whim . . . and I arrived in London a month after VE-Day, June '45, ready for work.

(Incidentally, "Stairway to Heaven" was called "A Matter of Life and Death" everywhere in the world except in the United States. The American distributors were dead certain that the U. S. public would never buy tickets to something with "Death" in the title. The U.S.A. was also the only place in the world too sensitive to view one nude scene of a cherubic boy goatherd piping a tune to his flock. His "frontal nudity" was discreetly hidden from view, but the beautiful little sequence was still tagged "lewd" in America and edited out.)

Filming in England didn't start immediately. There were only three Technicolor cameras in all of Britain at the time, and our company had to wait its turn, an unexpected delay that meant five weeks for me in an expense-paid suite at the Savoy with nothing to do. Talk about Heaven on Earth.

My love affair with London began. I met so many people . . . some that remain friends today. I saw every show playing, I haunted the galleries and bookshops, and rubbernecked all over that enchanting town.

The English were in the depths of austerity, but boarding at the Savoy Grill couldn't be called a hardship even then. Rationing was a challenge those chefs met with absolute bravura. Their *Queen of Puddings* was almost enough to make me apply for citizenship. Somehow you don't ask a waiter at the Savoy for a recipe, but I did some research among the amateurs I knew, and came back with a reasonable facsimile.

As we started work on the film, I was almost fired immediately. Here they had gone to great expense to get an authentic American actress, and my speech had suddenly turned bastard-British. I hadn't heard American spoken for weeks, and I'd picked up a definite London lilt. They found me a camera grip who was Canadian, and he talked me down to normal, but throughout the film I had to work consciously to keep it Yank.

The work was grand . . . and I couldn't imagine working with more stimulating and delightful people than David Niven, Roger Livesey, and Marius Goring. Micky Powell's superb direction was a combination of Puck and de Sade, which kept everything lively, and drove us to excel, if only to get one up on him.

The most difficult sequence to shoot was a ping-pong game with Roger that went in and out of reality with freeze-frames. A long scene, it couldn't be broken up, and was shot with two cameras simultaneously. We had to keep up a running dialogue and make game points on cue. We'd been coached for weeks by the Australian table-tennis champ, but it was still a monstrous technical hurdle.

It was going very badly for me. On the twenty-fifth take of the match point, I leaned in for the kill, forgot my line, and missed the ball. Roger groaned, and Micky was ready to throttle me.

"Cut! . . . Really, my dear. A simple assignment. You *did* pass yourself off as an actress, y'know."

My paddle went flying at his head and he ducked, thank God. As I burst into tears, Micky burst out laughing. Exactly what he wanted. A release of tension. The next take was perfect.

On the last day of shooting I was in misery. I didn't want to leave. For six months I'd been living a life that was compatible and natural. Now I'd go back to all the pressures and bewilderments of Hollywood.

I tried to figure it out. Hollywood had been exciting at first. Cinderella had gone to the ball. I'd lived the fantasy, but I found myself constantly under siege to hold onto *me*.

In England the concept of *Image* never came up; it was the quality of work, and one's personal pride in it that mattered. Even

. . . going to London to see the king — "Stairway to Heaven" was chosen for the first Royal Command Film Performance, and I was presented to George VI and the royal family.

that garish world of publicity was more dignified over there. And outside of work, one's life-style was one's own prerogative, taken for granted . . . I couldn't imagine the Ford-Cadillac question ever arising.

How could I fit my reality into that Hollywood scene of the mid '40's?

Arriving home in December, I had a lot of thoughts to sort out. I also had to face a marriage that was falling apart. Our hopes for its chances had been fading before Bill went to the South Pacific. Back together again, they gradually went phfft. And divorce proceedings followed.

We girls stayed on with Mother. Kathy was fourteen months old now, but I still felt the need of a nurse so I'd be available for work.

23

Heaven sent us Lucille Marino. More than a nurse, Lucille was 200-plus pounds of Italian warmth and good nature. When Kathy began talking, among other things Lucille taught her to speak Italian. It did wonders for her English . . . complicated syllables simply rolled off her tongue.

Lucille brought Italian into our kitchen, too. On special occasions she'd bring out her old family recipe for *Lasagne*. Not too often . . . the preparations were formidable. And there was another deterrent. The Marinos only made *Lasagne* when there was a complete gathering of the clan. The recipe was gigantic, and Lucille didn't know how to cut it down. For us, even with friends in, it would be Lasagne Week.

I've tried to recreate Lucille's masterpiece in slightly more reasonable dimensions. And I've stolen a few adaptations from my friend Jimmy Coco. Jimmy's lasagne is an aria of abbondanza, filled with chunks of meat and sausage. I've followed his lead with no compunctions whatsoever.

. . . my friend Jimmy Coco . . .

24

"Top billing Monday, Tuesday you're touring in stock:" . . .
Stephen Sondheim.

And damned glad to be there, that summer of '47. I was back
on the stage in an Eastern stock tour playing "Claudia," when
another Selznick entered my life.

Irene Mayer Selznick. She and David were separated, or
divorced, and Irene had become a top-flight producer on her own in
New York. She sent an associate to see me, who suggested I read for
the part of Stella Kowalski in her production of Tennessee Williams'
new play, "A Streetcar Named Desire."

A Broadway play! Of course I was petrified. Here I was
approaching the Pearly Gates. Bill Leibling, one of the best theatrical
agents in New York agreed to handle me. On our way to the reading
he gave me three words of advice. "Loud and clear," said Bill. And
stepping out of the darkness into that cruel work-light of a dark
theatre, that's all my nerves would let me remember: "Loud and
clear." I got the part.

I have a theory. The more one knows, the harder it goes. And if
one is a rabbit by nature, the more terrifying it is. I was by no
standards green in my profession, but my accumulated experience
was no security blanket either. It only made me aware of how much
more there was to being an actor. And since Broadway for me had
always been synonymous with the very best in the world of theatre,
I went to the first day's rehearsal in a state of rigid panic. Was I up
to it?

I was living at the Algonquin Hotel, within blocks of the
rehearsal theatre. At the end of the third day's work, Elia Kazan,
our director, suggested he walk me home. On the way, he took me
into a bar, bought me a drink, and let me have it.

What the f--- did I think I was doing? If they hadn't thought I
could play the f------ part, they wouldn't have cast me! Now, would I
for Christ's sake cut the sh--, and come into f------ rehearsal next day
and do something outrageously bold . . . not necessarily as an
expression of "Stella," but just to break out of my f------ personal
bind?!!

Et fucking cetera.

I was told later that it was his last ditch attempt to shake up my
tensions and find out (1) if he could cut through the catatonia at *all*,
or (2) if he'd be forced to fire me. I must have responded positively.
I don't know whether it was the barrage of four-letter words, or my
grateful realization that he really cared, but on the fourth day I

began to see and hear and react, and Stella eventually began to breathe.

We opened at the Ethel Barrymore Theatre in New York on December 3, 1947, and the play was a smash hit. David Selznick attended our opening night party at "21," and in the early morning hours I found myself in the middle of a tug-of-war between Irene and David. Irene was claiming the greater faith in my talents, and David was justifying his dropping my contract, protesting it was no lack of faith. They weren't talking about me or my talents at all, bless their hearts. That was the last time I saw David.

"Streetcar" settled in for a long run. Kathy was brought East to join me, and we moved through a series of sublet apartments and other hotels.

The closest approximation of permanence was a tiny top floor of a beat-up little apartment hotel on West 49th between 6th and 7th Avenues, the block Damon Runyon called "Dream Street." I bought some simple furniture and really splurged on the best record player I could find.

Here I finally got back to cooking. I suppose I was acutely bored by restaurant eating or I'd never have tried it. Not that I had what anyone but a Hopi cave-dweller would call a kitchen. The fridge was an insulated box requiring bulk ice. (Shades of Detroit.) The "sink" was a choice between the tub and the bathroom sink, and the *stove* was a two-burner booby trap with an invaluable suicide feature, a hood that could convert one burner into an oven. The storage space was an artistic arrangement of orange crates. I was a regular Betty Crocker.

Needless to say, my best efforts were improvisational. I had my most consistent success with something we began calling *Goo du Jour*. The quantities of the "recipe" were determined by what was in the orange crates at the time, but basically: I sautéed sliced onions, green pepper, chopped garlic . . . added ground beef, canned or fresh tomatoes, sometimes mushrooms, and whatever seasoning I fancied . . . all simmered together for half an hour or more. Its character would vary from Italian to Mexican to a curry to the unidentifiable. Over rice or noodles, and accompanied by salad, it became a feast. And Kathy loved it.

What a kitchen! Even Stella Kowalski had a better one over on the Ethel Barrymore stage. At least, as Stella, I had a real refrigerator.

And I didn't really have to cook for Stanley. The food for Blanche's birthday party in Scene Eight was cooked for each performance by Moe Jacobs' wife. Moe was our property master.

One night, though, Moe must have gotten the fried chicken somewhere else, and it was badly undercooked. Marlon Brando still had to dive in and "make a pig of himself," devouring it with great savor and gusto. I don't know how he got through it.

26

Marlon's accusing eyes went directly to me — Marlon Brando, Jessica Tandy and me in Scene Eight from "Streetcar"

After the curtain calls he was furious, and didn't care who knew it. He cursed out the whole backstage crew.

"Stupid bastards! How'd you like to be stuck out there eating a God-damned raw chicken?! I'd rather eat dog-shit!"

Well, the next night in Scene Eight Marlon picked up his napkin and guess what was on his plate. That's right. One of those doodoos from the joke store. Given his infallible sense of truth, Marlon's accusing eyes went directly to me. I had prepared the meal, right? I thought I would die.

And Jessica Tandy's opening line was, "I don't know what's the matter, we're all so solemn." From there on we played the whole scene not daring to look at each other.

We never had trouble with the chicken again, but that rotten dog turd kept turning up for days . . . in Blanche's trunk, behind the radio, under a pillow . . . one never knew.

I was finding New York a very exciting city to live in, a much friendlier place as a resident than as a visitor. Its pace had bewildered me when I arrived, but now I was discovering one could take one's own tempo . . . go at half-time, quarter-time . . . fit it to a limp or a gallop. As a town it was much more tolerant than smaller communities. As in London, here the unorthodox was virtually ignored, giving one a sense of freedom and personal worth. I loved it . . . the delights, terribles, advantages, disadvantages . . . all of it. I still do.

I had joined the Actors' Studio, a workshop for professional actors that was formed just a week before we started rehearsing "Streetcar." It was founded by Kazan, Cheryl Crawford, and Robert Lewis. For the next five years it was a godsend . . . a place to learn, test, and grow as an actor. (Lee Strasberg eventually became Artistic Director.)

Kazan was always discovering the special joys of New York. One night he and John Steinbeck took a group of us to dinner at La Zambra, a cafe on West 52nd Street owned by Vicente Gomez, the Spanish guitarist. Though the food was excellent, it was Gomez' playing everyone came for. Whether he played the songs of Andalusia, or the classics of Bach and Mozart, he was a great artist.

I went back to La Zambra time after time. One unforgettable evening I was there with actor Warren Stevens. There were a few people in the bar, but Warren and I were the only patrons in the restaurant. We were finishing our favorite *Picadillo and Black Beans* when Gomez came to the table and apologized. He couldn't possibly play to an empty house.

He must have noted our deep disappointment, because when we'd finished coffee one of the waiters beckoned and led us behind the stage, up some stairs, into a storeroom for liquor crates. There were two chairs facing a third, and in a few minutes Gomez joined us and proceeded to play a thrilling concert of Bach, Flamenco, and classical Spanish music for almost an hour. Playing what he loved, I do believe he was as happy as he made us.

Don't you agree that nostalgia is a very important flavor in food? Whenever I make *Picadillo* I recreate La Zambra. The place is gone now. Gomez picked up stakes and moved to California where I lost track of him.

Vaya con Dios, Vicente!

Friedman-Engeler

Myself, Marlon Brando, Irene Selznick, and Jessica Tandy ... celebrating our 500th performance

29

. . . Saturday morning I flew to California to make "Deadline: U.S.A." with Humphrey Bogart.

In spite of an odd reluctance to look for a permanent apartment, I was planting my roots more and more firmly in New York.

The first job that took me back to the Coast was the film version of "Streetcar," early in the fall of '50. And though it was the grandest of work experiences, it awakened no longing to make Glamourland my home again. When the film was finished, Kathy and I headed straight for Manhattan and that kooky flat on 49th Street.

Sidney Kingsley's play "Darkness At Noon" followed, on Broadway . . . and the next summer I was in California again, to film "Anything Can Happen" with Jose Ferrer. This time I had a more tangible reason to scoot back to New York. The reason's name was Robert Emmett.

Bob and I first met in 1948, and for a couple of years enjoyed a casual, fellow-actor relationship, getting to know each other a bit better as we danced and warbled our way through "Razzle Dazzle," an Actors' Studio project of Anna Sokolow's. But it was Melvyn Douglas who unsuspectingly changed the whole picture. He cast us both in his touring company of "Two Blind Mice."

From the opening in Washington in May, 1950, we went on to a three-month stand in Chicago . . . the most beautiful and glorious summer that ol' Windy City has ever known. *And* the most romantic . . . and though Mel could hardly be mistaken for Cupid, he was no mean aider and abettor.

In the clear, colder light of New York, it proved to be more than a summer romance. And a year or so later, we joyfully made the ultimate commitment. We advertised in The New York Times for an apartment and found a dream on Grove Street in Greenwich Village. The movers picked up Bob's belongings from 46th Street, ours from 49th Street . . . and stuffed the whole jumble into our tiny new love nest.

That was on Friday. Saturday morning I flew to California to make "Deadline: U.S.A." with Humphrey Bogart.

Bob fought his way through the barrels, boxes, cartons, and sorted out the apartment; cooked and cleaned; played eight performances a week in Bert Lahr's "Two on the Aisle"; and grappled with the most formidable of the challenges . . . a six-year-old girl-child.

He survived it all, even the first taste of being a father. And I returned a few weeks later to launch nervously into the role of domestic partner for my second attempt at nesting.

The apartment was so small I could bluff my way through the housekeeping. Cooking was harder to fake. Oh, I'd improved enough to get by . . . but Bob was not indifferent to food, and had been a bachelor long enough to know a few tricks himself. My limited talents could bore him to death before we'd lived together a month. Heart in mouth, I barged ahead . . . blithely pretending I knew what I was doing.

And got my first surprise . . . of a long line of surprises he's still springing on me. Bob turned out to be the greatest ally a fledgling cook could have. He was curious, interested . . . above all, encouraging . . . and his sense of the ridiculous refused to allow any flop to become a disaster. He gave me my first truly valuable lesson in cooking . . . relax and enjoy it.

For all his encouragement, though, I did feel he was overdoing it slightly when he presented me with a pressure cooker for Valentine's Day. He's still hearing about *that* little gesture of romance.

Anyway, the search for new recipes was now for fun as well as survival. My *COLLECTION* was beginning to grow.

Meat Loaf was one of the first . . . isn't it everyone's? Like most, ours just sort of evolved until it gradually locked in the qualities we like best . . . moist, flavorsome, and loose, just barely holding together. Of course there are variations and optionals . . . no fun to make it exactly the same way each time . . . but with all or none of them, it's still a taste treat.

Another new recipe was stolen from a Barrow Street neighbor and friend, writer Cathleen Schurr. Our table was tiny, so serving any number over four automatically became a buffet. Kay Schurr's *Shrimp and Cheese Casserole* is a lifesaver, and adaptable (on a plate) to knees, floor, or even standing up.

Along with the pressure cooker and a new blender, I remember another kitchen aid we kept handy in those days: a jug of *Leland Hayward's Brew*. Strictly for cook's morale, it's guaranteed to improve any cuisine.

Bob worked with Leland a great deal from 1956 on, but at that time we didn't know him. Just how the formula came into our hands isn't at all clear. I think a friend stole it from Jo Mielziner, the scenic designer. When I told Leland about it years later, he gleamed demoniacally and wondered how many others in New York and elsewhere had bottles brewing away in some dark closet.

Most of our parties were small enough to fit comfortably in the apartment . . . but once in a while we'd throw caution to the wind and have a bash. We were in several plays during our Grove Street tenancy and cast gatherings were always a temptation. A lot of our cohorts were squeezed in from time to time . . . friends of mine from "The Children's Hour" and "The Chase," and Bob's from "Two on the Aisle," "Midsummer," and "The Knight of the Burning Pestle."

Leland Hayward

We knew they were coming, however. One bash we "gave" was naïvely, totally unexpected. In March, 1952 . . . Academy Award night . . .

It was the last year of the radio presentations, and I was up for my performance in "Streetcar." The press had wanted me to join the other New York nominees at a midtown bistro, but I chickened out. If I lost, or if I won, I didn't want to be "on." Better to listen quietly to the results on our own radio in the privacy of our own apartment.

Or so we thought!

The evening started off quietly enough, though fraught with heavy vibrations. I was nervous as a cat, but only Kathy and Bob had to deal with my overreacting. Kathy got it first when she ceremoniously presented me with her "Emmett Award" . . . for consolation in case I lost Oscar. I burst into wildly sentimental tears as I fondled that beautiful creation . . . an 8x10 treasure of cat drawings peeking out of flaps, extravagantly decorated with sequins and brilliants.

Bob tried his darndest to teach me pinochle after Kathy went to bed . . . patiently explaining and re-explaining the simplest of rules that went out of my head as soon as they went in. The East-West time difference was torture. Not till 10 or 11 P.M. would even the preliminaries start.

At last the hour arrived. We turned on the radio . . . and our "peace and quiet" was shattered by the first ring of the doorbell. A photographer from one of the dailies. Next, a reporter. In no time, the *WORLD* was entering our apartment. Since I hadn't gone to the bistro, they came to us . . . just "in case." They had their stories to get . . .

Soon every chair available was taken . . . and bodies were spreading out on the floor. Strangers were followed by friends . . . and more strangers, reporters, photographers . . . talking, shushing, yelling, "Turn up the radio for God's sake!" . . . By the time my category was announced there were 50 or 60 people in our tiny pad . . . and through the roar I heard Bette Davis accepting . . . for *me* . . . My God, I'd won!!

I was beside myself . . . delirious about our winners: Karl Malden, Vivien Leigh, me . . . furious about the losers: the film, Elia Kazan, Marlon Brando, Alex North's gorgeous music . . . Questions were flying, pencils waving, cameras flashing . . . phone ringing . . . chaos, trying to hear, talk through the pandemonium . . . stepping over bodies, onto bodies, oops . . . A regular orgy, it was.

We brought out what liquor we had, raided our neighbors' supplies . . . and scrounged for scraps of food to accompany the booze . . . All I remember is *Garlic Bread.* The aroma of garlic bread. Oscar and Garlic forever!

Oscar arrived two weeks later by parcel post in a little coffin-like box that we bored holes through and used as a planter.

34

My God, I'd won!!

Oh, yes, we got married, too. But we've never been absolutely sure of the date. We think it was December 20th . . . we know it was '51.

There was no time for technical wrap-ups before I flew off for "Deadline: U.S.A.," and it was almost muffed when we did get around to it. We learned a good rule. Don't plan your show without consulting the M.C.

The management of "Two on the Aisle" had promised Bob a weekend off for a "honeymoon," so we decided that Friday would be a good day for the formalities. We wanted the Reverend Carl Hermann Voss to tie the knot, but he'd been out of town on a lecture tour and wasn't due to return to N.Y. until the Wednesday just before. It didn't matter to us what time on Friday. We weren't planning a big to-do and could easily fit our schedule to his, so we went ahead with preparations.

Our friend Lester Coleman (M.D.) made us a wedding present of our Wasserman Tests. We found our way into the maze of downtown New York and got the license. And chose our wedding rings at Arthur King's shop on West 4th Street. They had to be made to order and would be ready early Friday morning. Sort of free-form bands of gold. (King has sinced moved to Madison Ave. . . . he's very posh these days.)

Carl didn't get back on Wednesday until evening, after Bob had gone to the theatre. The arrangements were left in my hands. When I got Carl on the phone, he threw the curve that changed the day that caused the confusion that . . . *Friday he was lecturing in Texas.*

Thursday was out. Carl was free in the afternoon, but we had tickets for a special actors' matinee of "Antony and Cleopatra" with the Oliviers (Vivien Leigh and Laurence). We could always get married, but how would there be another chance to catch that performance? It looked hopeless until Carl quietly suggested, "Tonight?"

Hooray!

I alerted Bob at the theatre, and he said, "What about our rings?" Of course he didn't have to have one, but wasn't there something in most ceremonies that called for sealing the bargain with *a* ring?

I called my best girl immediately. May Boehlert. Maybe she had a guard ring she could lend us. She didn't, but said, "Don't worry. I'm in the middle of making curtains and I think the rings are finger size. I'll be over in a flash, as soon as I can get dressed."

Then I called the rest of our "party." They all thought a midnight wedding was a super idea and excitement was riding high.

May arrived with the brass ring which almost fit. And we dashed to Sheridan Square to get a couple of bottles of champagne at Rossano's before they closed. Aphrodite, our flower shop, was still open, too, and we couldn't resist. We each picked out a modest corsage, and then flew home to figure out what I could wear with mine. I'd just remembered the dress planned for Friday was in the cleaners, and they were *not* still open.

The only dress in my closet May and I could agree on was a navy blue silk . . . not very gala but it would have to do. We were getting a bit giddy by now, but I managed to be dressed and ready when Bob got home after his show. He changed quickly. Kathy was awakened and dressed. And the four of us grabbed a cab for Carl's apartment where we converged with Henry and Tanya Jacobi (Henry was Bob's best man), and Lester and Felicia Coleman who'd introduced us to Carl in the first place. Felicia had performed a feat of magic on this night of nights. She'd routed out her baker at 9:30 P.M. and talked him into baking us a wedding cake. It was still warm under the icing.

Carl was ready, and Mrs. Voss lighted the candles on the mantel of their fireplace. And then she noticed the clock. She fiddled with the hands while reciting a bit of folklore that promised good luck if one got married when Time was moving up, not down, and the ceremony began.

It was simple, beautiful, and unforgettable. (I heard it this time.) And when it was over, we popped the bottles of champagne and cut into Felicia's cake and had a gay, short celebration before everyone split into the night.

The next day, of course, no one knew if we'd been married on Wednesday or Thursday. Mrs. Voss couldn't remember what time it was before she'd changed the time. No one else was paying attention. Carl must have written down some date on the certificate, but we've never seen that piece of paper. Anyway, he was in no better position than the rest of us for accuracy.

We assume it was legal, since Carl was a bonafide minister. For years he's been dedicated to getting peoples of all persuasions together . . . Protestants, Jews, Catholics, Buddhists, Agnostics. Whichever "day" it may have been, he got us together just fine.

And Friday, Bob and I exchanged our proper rings. May never got her brass ring back. I whimsically hung on to it for years. And would have it still if we hadn't been burglarized in '69. Among other things, every stitch of jewelry I owned was pinched, including that brass ring. I hope the chap got spat upon when he tried to sell it.

About May. We first met when she was Irene Selznick's production secretary. Hers was the shining, friendly face that led me through the bleak corridors of the Henry Miller Theatre to the stage when I read for "Stella." We went from the professional to the personal, and have been sisters ever since.

Bob met May during my Russian period, when I was rehearsing "Darkness At Noon." I was deep into Gorki, Chekhov, Dostoievski. I bought Soviet records at the Four Seasons Book Shop and played them continually on my new Fisher. And cooked *Beef Stroganoff* at the drop of a hat. (Borscht came later . . . it takes too long to cook Borscht and rehearse, too.) I was very Slavic those days. They may have taken to each other in self-defense. At any rate, May and Bob hit it off at once.

The early Stroganoff was a fine stew . . . but not very authentic. Our Russian friend, Nina Fonaroff, straightened me out in time, and now it's a super recipe. I cook it even when I'm not rehearsing Russian.

Although "Darkness At Noon" was very Russian, few in the cast were . . . Claude Rains, Jack Palance, Brian Keith, Lois Nettleton . . . We all had to create our own reality of time and place, but I may have been the only one who inflicted it on my friends. A habit of mine during rehearsals, whatever the play. Until the character seeps into my bones, I live with it day and night. Which can be rather trying for those around me . . particularly if it's an unsympathetic part. Luba was fine, she was a loving sort . . . but there've been others that have made Bob wish he'd married a trapeze artist. It would have been less harrowing. Hester, in "Hello and Goodbye" (a play by the South African, Atholl Fugard), was so hateful she threatened our nuptial bliss and came within a hair's breadth of sending me back to analysis.

Beef Stroganoff (Nina Fonaroff)   *261*

Arlene Spiller

Hester, in "Hello and Goodbye" was so hateful . . .

39

NOW WE ARE FOUR

Early in '53, plans were made for Bob to become Kathy's legal father. We were clearly one family without the legal folderol, but in this day of forms and numbers and technical fuss over identification, Shakespeare's "What's in a name?" was romantic but impractical.

The first step was changing Bob's last name in the courts. He was born McMenamin, a distinctive and charming name, but an impediment for an actor. Few people could spell or pronounce it. He'd been using his father's given name, and he now went about making Emmett our legal name.

Kathy's adoption was more complicated. New York State laws in such matters are intricate. First we contacted Bill Baldwin to get his permission. He was a bit reluctant, but generously consented. Then (are you ready for this?), as Kathy's natural mother, I had to give *my* consent to her being adopted by this other couple . . . Kim and Bob Emmett. (At one moment, in judge's chambers, she was actually a ward of the court.) The authorities probed into our lives until everyone was finally satisfied that we would make proper parents, and the date to meet the judge for the final decree was set.

We figured it was a day to celebrate, so brought our swim suits to the Court House, planning to go to the St. George pool in Brooklyn afterward for a splashy afternoon. We hadn't anticipated the awesomeness of judicial surroundings.

There we stood at attention before the judge who was solemn as Solomon, each of us clutching our towel-wrapped bathing suits behind our backs to avoid looking frivolous.

I was sure His Honor would see us as rakish "showfolks" instead of solid citizens to be trusted with this child, but either he didn't notice, or was human enough to refrain from comment. Kathy became *OURS*.

All three of us were now bonafide Emmetts. And in the spring of '53, a fourth Emmett was conceived.

We'd lived in the Grove Street apartment a little over a year and a half, and were extremely fond of the shipshape compactness of it. But try as we might, we couldn't figure out a way to stretch the space to accommodate our prospective new member.

The search for another apartment began. Our hope was to find one in the Village, but we had no luck. We ended up with an enormous eight-room flat on 68th Street, just west of Central Park, and moved September first.

The living room faced 68th Street . . . and the rooms retreated like a railroad flat, ending with the kitchen. The distance of half a

Govie's table in our dining area today.

city block to the living room might have been good for exercise, but only a running footman would have made it practical.

Bob did a beautiful job of scraping and finishing all the floors before we moved in. A good idea, because when the furniture of our tiny Village apartment was transferred to that gigantic place, we saw a *lot* of floor. Mother, bless her heart, came to the rescue. She sent us a vanload of furniture and other household necessaries from her overcrowded home in Encino.

It was a bonanza. Among other things was a dining table . . . a lovely, round, mahogany table that Govie had had made in the Philippines, one that we still use. The most I can seat around it is six, and there's no room to serve at the table, but it's such a convivial shape. It's become the scene of some grand meals.

Patricia Neal and I were playing in the revival of Lillian Hellman's "The Children's Hour" when I became pregnant. Patty was fascinated with numbers, and figured out that the baby conceivably could be born on her birthday. It became our private joke. When anyone asked me when the baby was due, I'd say January 20th.

Sean Robert Emmett was born January 20th, 1954.

With a huge apartment to keep clean and organized . . . two careers in the family . . . and two children, one brand new . . . some outside help was in order. We preferred seeing to Sean ourselves, so a cook-housekeeper was elected. It worked fine in the cleaning department, but I lost a bit of ground as a cook.

We never really adjusted to living "cook's hours." We follow a certain routine, generally, but none of us liked following someone else's whose mind is on getting home. As soon as Sean was old enough to trust with a sitter, we'd escape once in a while and have dinner out.

One of our favorite restaurants had always been The Blue Ribbon, on 44th Street. It was just off the heart of the Theatre District. Good food, informal, unhurried but expeditious service . . . perfect for lunch during rehearsals, dinner between matinee and evening performances, or a drink and bite to eat after the show. Or when one wasn't in a play at all and wanted to have dinner at a civilized hour.

One of our "hooky" nights inspired me to return to the kitchen on our tyrant's day off to concoct a recipe . . . for *Lentils*. Bob and I were continuing to make discoveries about each other . . . and one

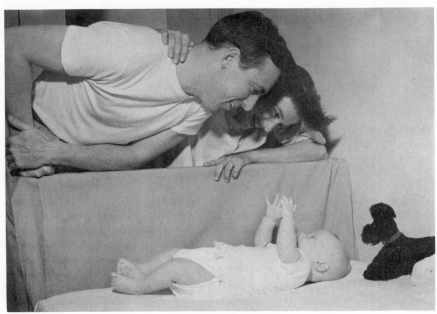

The way we were.

night The Blue Ribbon uncovered our mutual admiration for those murky but delicious legumes.

Usually we would order *Tartar Steak* ... something we loved and never had at home. Kathy wouldn't touch it. (She eats it now, but Sean is still holding out.)

The serve-wash-run maid was replaced before long by a part-time housekeeper and I went back to cooking. We were all relieved. I even stumbled onto a *Tartar Steak* solution. When Sean was four or so, it finally occurred to me to serve the kiddies hamburgers on buns, all of us a large salad, and Bob and I could indulge in our taste for raw beef to our heart's content.

Lentils	*238*
Tartar Steak	*265*

A fan, Hal Holtzman, snapped this picture of Patricia Neal and me as we were leaving the theatre in December, 1952, after a performance of "The Children's Hour."

Until Sean was three months old, it was as if he knew he'd been born into a theatrical family. I'd intended to nurse him, but that didn't work. I simply wasn't producing enough milk. So to keep the poor babe from starving I switched to a formula the day we left the hospital. The next few weeks were pretty hectic until we found the *right* formula, but once he was content with his diet he settled into the happiest of schedules. For us.

The first morning call for a bottle came not at dawn, but at 8 A.M., and the rest were as regular as clockwork, every four hours. He dropped the 4 A.M. feeding rather quickly, and we were patiently awaiting the midnight bottle to follow. But lo and behold! . . . he chose the 8 A.M. instead! He went sleepily off to dreamland at midnight, and awoke cheerily at noon . . . a baby made to order for actors.

Until April. We bundled up the kinder and flew to Miami Beach to play a week of stock with Jeffrey Lynn. The play was "The Moon Is Blue," one of the few times Bob and I have acted together.

We hired a nurse for the performance hours, and the four of us had a grand holiday-time around them . . . sunning on the sands, swimming in the ocean and the pool. We all got lovely tans. Even Sean . . . a mini tan, thanks to a large, floppy hat that made him look rather silly, but kept his debut in the sun from becoming a disaster.

We soon began to curse the sunshine, however. Sean was waking up earlier and earlier each morning, and we were certain all that Florida brilliance was the reason.

Sunshine indeed! One night Kathy had trouble going to sleep and discovered the real culprit. In spite of her instructions, the nurse had decided Sean was getting too long in the tooth for that midnight bottle and stopped giving it to him.

We could have killed that nurse. We even lost the grace of an 8 A.M. reveille. In the confusion, Sean's conversion to the norm was total. He began rising regularly at 6 A.M. Of course, he and we would have had to adjust eventually. The only night nursery schools I know of are in Las Vegas.

Sean took to the new schedule quite cheerily. Night light, day light, it was all the same to him. For us, it was tricky to live his hours *and* ours without going into coma periodically. Especially if we were working. So we grew somewhat circumspect about joining parties we knew would be late nights. We've never been very good about peeling off early.

One of the few times Bob and I had the chance to play opposite each other — onstage in "The Moon Is Blue" in Miami Beach, 1954

There was one invitation, however, that the new regime couldn't quash. Kirk and Trudy Alexander's great Sunday night suppers. If we fell apart the next day, sobeit.

There'd usually be four to eight people of varying interests . . . amiable gatherings that sparkled with lively conversation flowing deep into the night. Kirk was a TV director, a magnificent cook, and a highlight of the evening was his marvelously simple but elegant menu. It began with a great soup, accompanied by warm, homemade bread . . . a superb tossed salad, and a mouth-watering dessert. Wine, of course, and I seem to remember candlelight.

Eventually I had the *chutzpah* to steal his menu, and evening, and spread the good life around a bit. We've accumulated a large collection of soup recipes, but the three here are the most treasured. I cheat on the bread. Someday I hope to turn out a fitting loaf . . . in the meantime it's Zito's (of Bleecker Street) famed Italian, heated up.

The *Chicken and Chinese Cabbage Soup* was a creation of Bob's, and the *Lentil Soup* reminds us most of Kirk's evenings . . . one of his best.

Charles Zito waves good morning through the window, having been up since pre-dawn creating masterpieces in bread

The *Borscht* ... well. I've enjoyed many variations in my lifetime, but Nina Fonaroff's puts them all to shame. It's an experience. It's also a day's project, but definitely worth every minute, every beet stain, potato stain, and sore muscle.

(Nina, an alumna of Martha Graham's Dance Company, is teaching choreography at the London School of Contemporary Dance at this writing. London's gain is sadly our loss.)

We haven't seen Kirk for years, but I'm still happily wielding the same garlic press he put into my hand back in 1954.

Bob had been an actor, a dancer, and at 68th Street he launched into a third area of the arts . . . writing. It wasn't exactly out of the blue. He'd been an English major in college (U. of C. at Berkeley), had written revues for the Mask and Dagger Society, *liked* writing, and had always meant to get back to it. But as with most "mean to's" it took a crisis to do it.

Usually when one of us is unemployed the other isn't, or not for long . . . but we hit a prolonged period when jobs weren't coming in for either of us. We were feeling the old "I'll never work again" panic, a common nervous disorder of actors, and the dwindling bank account was another nudge. He locked himself into one of the eight rooms and wrote a comedy script for television. The U. S. Steel Hour bought it, produced it, and he was started on another career.

For a while he continued acting and split his time between the two. Then Flora Roberts, our old friend and his new literary agent, finally talked him into making a choice. Writing won . . . and although he has acted since, he's not really an actor anymore (except in the deep recesses of his heart).

There was a brief experiment in renting an office, but he usually works at home. It was an adjustment for all, particularly the children. His closed door now meant: keep the nattering down; it's no time to get the bicycle fixed; disputes have to be arbitrated later; etc. Unless, of course, the muse isn't communicating freely. At those times he's delighted with any distraction. The rules got rather fuzzy.

One of the most seductive diversions is the kitchen. He's become an inveterate snacker . . . and his cooking activities increased noticeably. He can be incommunicado for days when the work is going well. When it's not, well . . . pencils need sharpening . . . a little cole slaw might get chopped . . .

Gradually salad became his bailiwick. Shopping for the greens was a welcome escape to get outdoors for some fresh air. Washing them could take any amount of time, without too much concentration, and the physical activity was useful while he was sorting out ideas or script problems in his head. Tossing the salad at meal time followed, until eventually it became a ritual. I'll put it together under pressure . . . when he's out of town, or working a deadline . . . but his improvisations are so spectacular, I happily avoid competing.

His choice of ingredients is loose . . . he works mostly from inspiration and what's fresh and beautiful at the time. Fresh is vital.

He's ruthless about throwing out anything that's gone a moment past its prime.

His salad dressing also tends to follow impulse . . . but he has obliged me with the Herculean effort (for him) of recording a recipe. It's delicious . . . even when *I* make it.

Bob out of town — working on Julie Andrew's TV Special at Gower Champion's in Malibu

We had lived at 68th Street for six months before one by one we confessed we didn't like it very much. There were a few virtues . . . Central Park, elbow room, three bathrooms (unbelievable luxury), fairly convenient transportation. But the apartment was charmless, the space was monstrous for cleaning, the neighborhood was depressing, food shopping was a hassle, and, let's face it . . . we missed the Village! We spent the next six months looking for an apartment downtown.

Bob was the one who found it, the end of September. I was in Boston with the pre-B'way tryout of "The Tender Trap" . . . he sent me sketches of the street and the apartment . . . and he was moved in by the time I got home. It was a grisly experience, one he's expressed a hope never to repeat . . . to arrange for the movers, pack up 68th Street, arrive at a new apartment again surrounded by barrels, boxes, scrambled furniture, incredible chaos . . . with a nine-year-old daughter in one hand, an eight-month-old son in a sling over his shoulder . . . and no Kim!

Even when I returned I was of little practical value until the show opened at the Longacre. But I was properly sympathetic, and vociferous in my delight with his choice.

The building was originally a carriage house. The buggies were kept on the ground floor . . . the horses were stalled on our level, led up and down a ramp that predated the present staircase . . . and the two floors above stored the feed. Some 15 years before we moved in, after the removal of three truckloads of horse manure, it had been converted to apartments. They did it with a bit of spit and paste in a rather slip-shod way but it definitely had style. And panache. And fireplaces. And though our flat offered a string of disadvantages that 68th Street couldn't begin to match, it had everything the other didn't have . . . charm, homeyness, and aesthetic, if kooky, pleasure. We haven't moved since.

As the structure was built to house horses, not people, there's no basement. We're hooked up to a furnace and boiler three doors down the street. There are a number of other buildings hooked up to the same facilities. This tends to put considerable strain on the furnace's already limited capacity to function magnificently, which leaves all of us without heat or hot water from time to time. Usually when the occasional blizzard hits the city.

The lack of foundation also gives the building a rakish look. The roof suggests a giant's bowling ball dropped on it at one time. The dip in the middle is quite spectacular.

*Our apartment has its
irregularities, too . . .*

Our apartment has its irregularities, too, though not quite as dramatic. The living room slants six inches from one end to the other . . . doors must be rehung as the building continues to settle . . . of the ten basic walls, none are squared off (all of them have fascinating texture, however).

The kitchen? Well. There was a sink, a stove, a fridge, and one wall cabinet. Each item was of indeterminate vintage, and sized ideally for a family of midgets. Right away we bought a few cabinets to provide a modicum of storage and counter space, and I bit my tongue a lot. (It was better than 49th Street, wasn't it?)

We simply turned a blind eye to all the little idiosyncrasies. We were so relieved to be out of 68th Street, it was truly a new lease, and we loved it.

I think we sensed immediately that this was to be our home for a long time. At any rate, Bob began bringing home-like memories to the fore . . . and one of the gems of our collection was introduced to me at last. *Tamale Pie!*

Bob was born and grew up in Monterey, California. His mother's best friend, Marie Allaire, was delivered of a daughter in the same hospital at the same time Bob's mother brought him forth, and the two giddy women would often switch babies during the nursing period. As Marie's parents were Catalonian, Bob swears he has as much Spanish blood in him as Irish. It's certainly true he prefers Old California Spanish food to almost any other.

Tamale Pie was a true family recipe. They all could make it, but Bob, his mother, and the eldest brother George were the experts. Each had his own method, of course. The recipe here is Bob's, which I naturally consider the authentic one.

Part of the tradition in making it is to have a bottle of *vin ordinaire* open throughout the cooking. None of it goes into the *Pie*, but it adds a certain flavor to the conversation, and warmth to the spirit.

One note of caution. However many personal variations there are in the recipe, the entire family agrees on one point. The olives should not be pitted. The pits are supposed to add some mystical flavor. I suggest it's a friendly gesture to warn newcomers to the dish . . . to avoid broken teeth.

Tamale Pie (The McMenamins)   *248*

Bob with Dorothy Allaire — "The Spanish Twins"

A MOOT POINT

May Boehlert married Joel Katz, M.D., on December 3, 1955, in our apartment. Since the Emmetts had fallen in love with Joel, too, it was a particularly eventful day for all of us.

We four have been blessed with remarkably compatible chemistry. Even to the offspring. With our Kathy and Sean, and their David (who arrived in '57), and Natasha (in '60) . . . we've produced a small miracle of two families of eight bodies who enjoy and sustain each other.

There are even fringe benefits. For example . . . beans. Bob is a bean freak. I like them, too, but they don't like me, as the saying goes. That needn't stop Bob from cooking them and experimenting, since the Katzes share his pleasure and the pot. I include his favorite and most oft repeated version of *Frijoles*. (No pun intended.)

Friends are tested in many ways and we've been through the gamut. But our most stringent test came in '57 when David was six months old. We lived together . . . seven of us . . . for seven weeks. If two families can do that under trying conditions and still remain friends, they must be doing something right.

The occasion was Joel's vacation. Summer, naturally. Psychiatrists need rest from work like everyone else, but they try to skip town at the least traumatic time of the year for their patients. (Patients can debate the choice, but then most don't want their psychiatrists to take vacations ever.)

That year we could swing a holiday at the same time, so jointly, and bravely, we rented a house in Ocho Rios, Jamaica. The suggestion was ours. We'd had a glorious Christmas-New Year holiday there a year and a half earlier. Of course, we hadn't rented a house. We'd stayed at a superb inn, the Shaw Park Hotel.

Life in the Tropics in the summer in a house named *Moot Point* was something else. We rented it sight unseen with great confidence. The name of the rental agent, Lord Ronald Graham Associates, Ltd., sounded so . . . reliable. And the owner, Lady Pamela Bird . . . how could a Lady Bird own a house less than smashing?

We might have suspected the whole project was marked for doom before we left New York. Instead, we chose to interpret the fire in the taxi on the way to the airport and the four-hour delay taking off (due to propeller malfunction) as an unfortunate beginning to what would certainly be a happy ending.

The first of the distress signals to Lord Graham's office went out within an hour of our arrival at *Moot Point*. Hot and tired after the long drive from Montego Bay's airport, May popped gratefully into the shower. She was nicely soaped up when the water disappeared.

"Oh yes, that. Mmmm. Happened to the tenants just before you, matter'f fact . . . Arthur Miller and Marilyn Monroe? They were awf'lly stuffy about it. Left. Know what the problem is, though . . . fix it for you in a jiffy."

It was fixed a day or so later. It was "fixed" a lot during the seven weeks. The prolific roots of tropical vines surrounding the house would grow right through the pipes from time to time. At war with the invaders, man and his plumbing, they'd found the ultimate put-down.

There was a bathroom as well, however, and the tub pipes didn't always clog up at the same time as the shower pipes. But the bathroom was the favorite club-house of the local crabs. They were large crabs, about six inches in diameter, and moved in an upright position on two legs when in a hurry . . . or in a temper. Fearless creatures, with great speed at their command, they'd chase us about the house in a fury if we dared object to their squatters' rights.

The house came with a staff of five . . . cook, laundress, maid, yardman, and general assistant who washed and/or broke dishes (that we were billed for). Pauline, the laundress, seemed to know what she was doing. But the house didn't provide her with a water heater for the laundry, so her best efforts were frustrated. Our clothes gradually developed a musty old-world aroma.

Ivy, the cook, did very well with the marketing . . . no mean feat since we hit the worst drought the Island had known for ten years. But she was a dreadful cook. She did have antiquated equipment to work with, but even if it'd been a model, modern kitchen, I wonder. She insisted on the very best produce when we shopped, and then proceeded to annihilate it in the cooking.

Palmer, the yardman, was simply hostile. The raking of leaves, one of the few chores he didn't assiduously avoid, he'd perform at 6:30 A.M. . . . under the bedroom windows. His reply to objections would be a Socialist lecture. The brush that got dangerously dry because of the drought, and encouraged every form of insect breeding, was not cut back once during our seven weeks. His argument against it was "preservation of natural beauty." He was provided with a machete that could have accomplished our needs and his aim neatly, but we suspected he was saving the blade for us.

As for the house, it was unique. All the other houses in the area were designed in relation to the Trade Winds . . . which blow there from East to West. Lady Bird's architect was the only one who defied Nature and common sense by putting the living area to the West, and the kitchen to the East. The result was a continual wafting of garbage and kitchen aromas throughout the rest of the house. (There was one garbage container that was collected once a week. Its overflow problem was staggering.)

The combination of the underbrush, overgrowth, and garbage produced all sorts of excess vermin and insect life. Roaches in the refrigerator . . . rats in the yard and house, particularly unattractive dashing through the dining area at mealtime. The normal population of crawling and flying insects in the Tropics was to be expected, but we had them in supernatural quantities. It was unnerving for all, and lethal for May and Bob. They were more susceptible to bites than the rest of us, and though the local hospital at St. Ann's Bay tried to be helpful, Bob was finally bedridden, thoroughly poisoned.

David was spared, as May kept him surrounded with mosquito netting except when he ate. Of the rest, I was luckiest . . . my years in Florida must have set up some kind of immunity.

Sean got a bite of another sort that was cause for consternation. Dog bite. He and the dog had been playing happily . . . at Jamaica Inn, after one of our few good meals . . . and when the dog turned to go, Sean clutched at his rear. The dog responded spontaneously and naturally for dogs . . . he wheeled around, snapped, and broke the skin on Sean's forehead. Confusion followed and the dog disappeared immediately. He was a stray, an unknown, and with Sean bleeding, the incident was fraught with lousy possibilities. Doctor Joel took over, got no satisfaction from St. Ann's Bay Hospital, so finally contacted the head of the Island's Medical Department at the University in Kingston.

"But Dr. Katz. There is no rabies serum in Jamaica. You would have to go to Miami for that. You see, there has never been a case of rabies reported in the history of Jamaica. I would suggest you're unduly worried."

Of course. We didn't worry anymore. After all, though the dog couldn't be found we had a thread of reassurance. No one had seen him foam at the mouth. It was also nice that Joel was a psychiatrist. We helped him a lot the next two weeks . . . to get in shape for the return to his paying patients.

Other than the physical plague, the dire cuisine, the pitiful inexperience of most of the staff, the evil eye of Palmer, the feudal equipment of the house, the open garbage, the paralysis of plumbing, we really enjoyed ourselves.

The day finally came to leave. We piled us and our luggage into the little car, waved to the staff, and with our welts and memories freshly upon us, we took a long, last look at *Moot Point* . . .

It certainly was.

Frijoles (Bob Emmett)   *232*

Most of the early live TV anthology programs came out of New York, but by the mid-50's California had unceremoniously invaded the field. CBS's Television City in Hollywood fairly teemed with good shows and I commuted for them all . . . *Climax!*, *Studio One*, *Playhouse 90*. They were exhilarating years.

Playhouse 90 was particularly exciting. It introduced the advantage of extra time to develop a story, and provided a first-class production to mount it. Attractions that lured the very best of writers, directors, and actors. And the camera, technical crews were fantastic. I've done a great many television shows and they tend to get muddled in memory, but I recall vividly each of the six Playhouse 90's I was in, beginning with Rod Serling's classic "Requiem for a Heavyweight" in October, 1956. When the program died in the 60's, Television's Golden Era virtually died with it.

I'm referring, of course, to the days of *LIVE* television. There is Live and there is Tape, and the difference is greater than meets the eye. Tape may *seem* like Live, but one's life isn't really on the line. It's done ahead of air-time so mistakes are retractable. It can be edited, "blipped," or even stopped and repeated . . . like if all hell should break loose.

Not so with Live. Live is irretrievably now-or-never. You have only *one* chance with Live, and if all hell breaks loose during a live show, it simply hangs out there for all the world to see. It can be taped for posterity, but the only way it can be fiddled with at the time is to cut it off the air altogether. Go to black and cover with music.

We who grew up in television under the frantic demands of Live found Tape something of a let-down when it came on the scene. I remember my first taped show as a crushing experience.

The director had assured us that he was going to shoot it exactly as if it were live. The only difference would be longer breaks where the commercials normally came . . . extra time to prepare for the next section. I took him at his word, and my adrenalin was riding high.

The opening shot was a complicated swoop of the camera on a crane, zeroing into a tight closeup of me and the beginning of the first scene. I got the usual tap on my ankle from the floor manager to let me know I was "on," opened my mouth to speak, and over the P.A. system heard our director roar "Take five!" I couldn't believe my ears. (The crane hadn't swooped exactly right, and it was so close to the top of the show he'd decided to start over.)

Live-on-Tape indeed! My first reaction was *FOUL!* The wind was gone from my sails, and I felt positively violated.

Well, I managed to pull up my socks for the second take, but the outrage lingered on. We got through the rest of the show with no other surprise stops, but now I knew they were possible. And since this wasn't film, it was just all *wrong*.

I lost that first resistance naturally enough, and made the adjustment to Tape quite amenably. But *LIVE* . . . those were the days.

Some of the elements were the same for both, of course. There was the scheduled rehearsal time for the actors and director. And toward the end of that period, a run-through in rehearsal hall for the technical crews to make notes. Then we went to the sound stage for camera blocking . . . the tedious period (for actors) of working out camera moves, setting lights, positioning sound booms. All the values we'd found in the rehearsal hall seemed to disintegrate as the technical problems took precedence. The transition was hard, but gradually everything would come together after a "push" through, a run-through or two, and finally dress rehearsal. The first run-through was always a shambles, and sometimes dress rehearsal was too. No matter, you pulled yourself together to do the very best you could for the show.

And there the similarities between Live and Tape ended. In Live, it was also going into orbit.

That irreversible "moment of truth" . . . everyone in opening positions . . . the final countdown coming over the P.A. system . . . then deathly silence . . . and *blast-off*, YOU'RE ON THE AIR! It was breathtaking, sometimes it was to throw up, but dammit, it was electric. Everyone from director to technicians to performers . . . at a fever-pitch of nerves, concentration, excitement, and potential.

And mania?! Changing clothes between scenes *anyplace*, just so a working camera wasn't pointed at you. Dashing like an Olympic runner to the next set, desperately trying not to pant as you launch into a languid love scene. Or getting there first and hearing the camera racing behind you . . . praying it arrived in time. The futile efforts of the makeup department, waving a powder puff at your nose as you sped past. Grateful for the minute of commercial to catch your breath and get a dangling eyelash glued back on.

Something could always go wrong, and frequently did. Time was one of the worst villains. The famous story of the director who ran out of the control booth onto the set and got himself under a camera to catch the actors' eyes . . . and then frantically signalled: "The show is too *long*. Cut every other line!!"

Lines could also be forgotten, God knows. Eva Marie Saint had the unsettling experience of playing a scene in an airplane with an actor who blew his lines when they were supposedly flying high in the clouds. He panicked, said, "Well, this is where I get off" . . . and blithely walked out of the plane.

One actor, during a "Climax!" John Frankenheimer directed, couldn't escape. His eyes went blank and he started to walk off the set, but the camera operator who had him in focus scooted ahead and physically pinned him to the wall with his camera! They cut the sound, threw the dazed actor his line, and the show miraculously went on.

It was working on the brink of disaster . . . but at the same time, the possibility of greatness was always present, too. The burst of sheer inspiration when the chips are down . . . of thrilling performances soaring under the pressure of *"This is it!"*

It was exciting for the audiences, too. You never knew. You could tune in to catch cameras photographing wayward cameras, or be gripped by never-to-be-forgotten brilliance. Whatever you got, it wasn't canned. It was live . . . very alive.

During those dramatic days I bunked in with Mother as usual. The Encino house had been sold and she was living within a stone's throw of Television City . . . in the Parklabrea Towers. It couldn't have been more convenient.

Close to both Mother and CBS was the famed Farmers' Market. There was a wire fence separating the Market from the Studio, with a gate that gave us access during the lunch hour . . . and actors, directors, technicians, would swarm through to join the rest of the crowds. The fascinating complex of shops and stands sells nearly everything from general merchandise to specialties of cooked and uncooked delicacies, vegetables, fruits, meats, sweets . . . on and on.

I fell into the habit of grabbing a taco for lunch and wandering around to look for some goodie to bring home for dinner. The rehearsal halls at CBS were air-conditioned to within a degree of deep-freeze temps, so perishables could easily survive the afternoon. (We weren't always sure *we* would . . . my God, it was working cold.)

One of my finds developed into a number-one family favorite in New York. *Flank Steak* with a pocket . . . stuffed. When I first brought it to Mother, she prepared it with her own stuffing. Later we agreed it wasn't worth the bother. Pepperidge Farm did it faster and was nearly as good.

The one homemade touch that does make a difference is *Mother's Cranberries* on the side. They're magical. A heavenly accompaniment to anything, stuffed or no . . . turkey, chicken, flank steak, pork chops. Also roast beef, ham . . . or anything else you might think of. Try them on ice cream sometime.

In dramatic TV, Tape eventually replaced Live, and now of course, most shows are filmed. And Anthology series are so rare, they're almost archaic. Oh, we still have Live. On-the-spot coverage . . . Sports. World affairs. News. Senate Hearings. Press Conferences. I watch them all when I can. But I long for the good old days of Live comedy and drama. It was a thrill tuning in . . . taking a chance . . . the unexpected, the exciting, anything was possible.

In February, 1957, the Emmetts appeared on Edward R. Murrow's "Person-to-Person" . . . *LIVE* from *NEW YORK.*

A week or so before the show, preparation interviews with Murrow's assistants began, calmly and professionally. And our personal preparations began, with irrational frenzy.

Who can see details on a television screen? Have you ever seen dust? Except in a commercial? We weren't being logical, we were manic. We organized and cleaned and polished the entire apartment as if we were preparing for a Naval Inspection. Nothing was skipped . . . every prism of the chandelier, every corner of the woodwork, it all got it. The flurry of activity was breathtaking.

If only one of us had been working at the time, we would have said to hell with it, let them take us as we are . . . neat, but not scrubbed. But we were not working. We had time on our hands. Time to grow very nervous about the whole idea.

The show didn't relate to any of our previous experience on television, and *Tape* wouldn't have made it calmer. It wasn't a play. It wasn't an interview in a studio. It was us at *home*, pretending it was perfectly natural to invite Ed Murrow and millions of unseen, unknown Americans to "pop in" electronically, see the way we lived, and have a chat.

One of Murrow's assistants said it wasn't unusual for us to be nervous. Theatrical people were always more skittish on "P-to-P" than non-show-biz types like generals, executives, seed growers. He figured it was because they weren't aware of what could go wrong. We were. Somehow that explanation didn't give us much comfort.

The day came and the camera crew and other technicians arrived at 2 P.M. The entire neighborhood gathered around our front door downstairs to watch, fascinated. But our superintendent dashed upstairs in utter panic. "My God, the weight of all that equipment is going to collapse the building! You can't! Tell them to go away!"

We did our best to reassure him, but he very likely might have been right. It'd slipped our minds before, and now it seemed too late to bring up the point. How did you say, "Sorry, boys. Tell Ed we're awfully sorry, but he'd better make other arrangements for his show tonight." (A musical interlude over a stock shot of Central Park?)

So up they came, cursing our slanted staircase, with three pedestal cameras, sound equipment, lighting equipment, and cables and wires that made the phone company look like a two-bit operation.

. . . at three, he had an uninhibited vocabulary . . .

We left. With Sean. We whisked him to the Katzes' for the rest of the day and the night. He was just three years old, and had never been on his best behavior awake at 10 or 11 o'clock at night. And with all that activity there would have been no way possible to get him to go to bed "as usual." Also, at three, he had an uninhibited vocabulary that might have shocked the nation. Sean was banished.

We then met Mr. Murrow for the first time. At the Barbary Room for cocktails at 4. That meeting was our only hour of true pleasure until after the show was over. Ed's intelligence and charm were disarming, and we had a thoroughly delightful and relaxed visit. But that was the last we saw of him.

We went back to the Village. Home, it wasn't. The furniture had been shifted to make room for the cameras and tons of equipment, and to arrange better backgrounds for the "pictures." Absolutely nothing was familiar except Kathy, and she was in shock. The living room, bathed in blinding light, looked all set up for a police grilling.

The makeup man took us one by one into the bathroom to give our faces a color that would survive the lights. And eventually the rehearsals began.

The instructions were simple. We were absolutely free to say and do whatever we pleased, as long as we kept to the prescribed pattern of moves, order of topics, and "cue" lines for Ed (in the CBS Studio) to ask the next question.

Oh yes, we were asked if we could please find a moment to call the viewers' attention to the slanted floors so they wouldn't think the camera operators were drunk.

One of the cameramen had his own plea. It was February, and it was cold. And he was stationed outside on a terrace adjoining Kathy's bedroom. He needed the extra distance for focus when our "tour" of the apartment led us to her room. Would we please be kind enough to close her door to the living room when we left, so he could come indoors without the risk of being caught on screen by one of his mate's cameras?

Well, as with all things, we got through it somehow. We even remembered to close the door. And the cameras didn't fall through to the floor below. And I have never been so nervous in my life. Even my eyeballs shook.

Kathy came off the best. She and Ed had an unscheduled chat that was the delight of the show. He latched on to her interest in history and politics and dropped the "script." He was so enchanted by her refusing to be trapped into a "party" endorsement, or giving stereotyped answers to his questions about our social system, he promised to be her campaign manager if and when she ever decided to run for Senator from New York.

At last the show was over. We heaved a huge sigh of relief, pulled our frayed nerves together, and brought out a supply of drinks and food for the crew.

Kathy came off best.

They began packing up their equipment immediately. And as each department got its gear into the trucks downstairs, the men came back up for a cup or several of cheer and a midnight feast.

I'd prepared two casseroles the day before . . . *Jambalaya*, a great and good dish to stretch for a crowd . . . and *Mexican Stew*, an old Cole recipe.

"Mexican" is a misnomer. It's nature is closer to Italian, but it's been passed down blithely as Mexican Stew for at least four generations. I've added chili powder to the original recipe . . . not to make the name more legitimate, but because we like it. It's optional.

Incidentally, that CBS crew was marvelous. They not only put everything back as they found it, they swept up and left the apartment just as unnaturally immaculate as it was when they arrived.

Jambalaya	*306*
Mexican Stew (The Coles)	*245*

Two of the four generations of Mexican Stew makers.

Grandmother Cole   **Grandmother Cole's Mother**
Mary J. Williams Cole   **Jane Bird Neff Williams**

I have a writer friend, Coleman Dowell, who taught me a thing or two about dinner parties and such. He's a fantastic cook . . . turns out all sorts of gourmet marvels in his kitchen. I was getting along famously in mine these days, a far cry from my beginnings, but "gourmet" I wasn't. And Cole's magnificent spreads had me so intimidated I refused to invite him to our house for dinner. I told him so. Compete with his moussaka or pâté-in-shell? Not bloody likely.

Of course, I finally did have him over. Bob's teasing, Cole's teasing, and my own embarrassment ultimately pushed me into a corner. But I agonized over the preparations like a wet hen. I don't know what I thought I was in competition *for*. A Michelin rating, for God's sake? At any rate, when the evening came to an end, I felt pretty silly.

After all my frettings, Cole ate the dinner and enjoyed . . . just like normal people. We had a happy time with lots of good conversation. And if I'd turned out something miraculous in the food department it wouldn't have made one bit of difference to our enjoyment. The meal was a pleasant part of the sociability, but it wasn't the evening's *raison d'être*. My muddled brain finally got the point.

The point of Cole's evenings, too. He may have set a magnificent table, but he and his friends were the basic delight .

It was at one of Cole's dinner parties that we met Carl and Fania Van Vechten . . . the beginning of a friendship lasting until Carl's death several years later. And one evening at the Van Vechtens', I was given another boost to my confidence . . . a super dessert recipe.

Before their buffet was served, however, I got a "good to know" of a different sort. It'd been a hectic day, and I'd had no time to do anything with my bedraggled hair except throw on a stretch-wig to hide the disarray.

While we were enjoying a few blown-up slides of Carlo's famous photographs, one of his guests ruffled my "hair" in his enthusiasm . . . and the wig came off in his hands. He blanched and dropped it like a hot potato. I laughed and popped it back on, but the gentleman was traumatized. He kept a safe distance from me the rest of the evening, and in his memory I have *secured* my wigs ever since.

But to the recipe. Among the other delectable dishes served was a fabulous *Coffee Mousse*. I raved until Saul Mauriber, Carlo's assistant, promised to send me the recipe.

Two of Carl Van Vechten's "not so famous" photographs

From The Estate of Carl Van Vechten

He did. But the dessert was so very, very good, I was convinced it was going to be very, very difficult to get it to turn out as superbly as I'd had it at the Van Vechtens'. Well, I was wrong. It wasn't tricky at all, even for me.

In fact, it encouraged me to ask Coleman for a couple of *his* recipes. He not only responded immediately with two beauties, he complimented my derring-do by naming one after me! *Mousse Kim Hunter!* And at the risk of seeming unduly cocky, I've learned to do rather well by both of his creations. (The *Veal with Pasta* is actually an adaptation of an adaptation, but the Pesto and the Mousse are all his.)

"Good-to-Knows": First . . . a dinner party is not to get all uptight trying to cook more than you're good at; and secondly . . . all elegant, delicious dishes are not necessarily culinary Mount Everests.

Coffee Mousse	*359*
Veal with Pasta and Pesto	*270*
Mousse Kim Hunter	*360*

Photo by Tullius Frizzi, Courtesy of New Directions Publishing Corp.

Coleman Dowell

I've had many happy times and adventures in the country, but have always considered myself a city person at heart. For year-to-year living, that is. The third possibility, Suburbia, had never entered my mind.

Then, in 1961, I joined the American Shakespeare Festival in Stratford, Connecticut. I lived in the area for three months, while playing Rosalind in "As You Like It," the First Witch in "Macbeth," and Helen of Troy in "Troilus and Cressida."

It was an exciting and fulfilling summer of work . . . my first experience in true repertory. What a joy! To come to each of the plays with renewed enthusiasm, a fresh "go" as it were . . . no way to get stale or in a rut, the eternal bugaboo for actors in commercial long runs.

It wasn't quite *all* joy. There's an old theatrical super-stition . . . "If Macbeth is in the repertory, disaster is bound to strike." It did. The first mishap was a broken foot . . . one of the supers. Then the wigs were stolen. One of the actors fell off the stage, mightily bruised. Lois Kibbee tangled with a truckful of smart-ass kids while riding her bicycle to the theatre . . . concussion. Jessica Tandy slipped a disc. I fell off a section of the stage known as the "tray" and broke a rib. And so on. Every week seemed to herald another catastrophe . . . all during or related to Macbeth perform-ances. Even the poo-pooers of superstition . . . Pat Hingle, Carrie Nye, Will Geer, Donald Harron . . . all were very jumpy by the end of the season.

But to Suburbia. We rented a house in the nearby community of Lordship. Five of us moved in . . . the four Emmetts and Anne Waldman, a school friend of Kathy's.

None of us spent too much time at the house. Kathy got a job with the theatre press department; Anne worked backstage as an unofficial assistant to the stage manager; Bob was with us off and on . . . work kept yanking him away to New York or California; and I was mostly rehearsing or playing. Sean, though he usually chose to tag along to the theatre, was the only one who really got to know the neighbors. The area swarmed with children, and he made friends with most of the six- to nine-year-olds. But he also got on the stage . . . for three performances. One small cast member of Macbeth was unprofessionally whisked away by his parents . . . vacation week for Dad . . . and director Jack Landau was stranded without one of his apparitions.   Sean substituted with glee, trying desperately not to giggle at Mom when we met on stage.

The bit of time I did spend at our home-away-from-home was my debut in the suburban "Lady of the House" role. After the privacy of NYC apartment dwelling, it was an astonishing experience. Also, a little unnerving. I was not accustomed to opening the door to one after another of local ministers and priests, urging me to "join" the community (if not their church). Even more unsettling was the extraordinary feeling of living in a fishbowl, every movement marked, and, I assume, interpreted. We were surrounded by neighbors' eyes.

No superintendent to cope with plumbing, electrical problems, etc., added to the nonplus. And though the yard wasn't huge, it was large enough to intimidate souls used to gardening in window boxes. We were startled out of our wits one day when the owner's copy of The Last Supper (painted by-the-numbers and hung over the dining table) crashed to the floor during some sort of faster-than-sound maneuver from the nearby air base.

If I'd had any latent, unrecognized longing to become a Suburbanite, that summer scotched it. Oh, for the peace, privacy, and quiet of *the City!*

We did enjoy one aspect of that life, however. The outdoor barbecue. Bob and I are particularly fond of barbecued *Spareribs*, and though it's easy enough to prepare them in a city apartment, outdoors is much more gala. And the careful turning and basting of the ribs over low coals for four hours or so adds a special magic to the flavor. Whenever time allowed, we'd start up the grill and experiment with all sorts of sauce combinations.

Of course, back in New York we've narrowed the recipes down to a group that suffers little from the loss of open sky and four hours. One calls for damson plum preserves in the marinade . . . another, orange marmalade. They're quite different in flavor and texture and each is grand.

A third is rather unusual, also delicious . . . called *Pearl Buck's Spareribs.* Whether it was really that illustrious lady's recipe, who knows? My experience with Maggie Ettinger taught me never to believe what I read unless I get it from the horse's mouth. I picked up a clay-pot recipe for chicken once, purported to have come from the kitchen of Mrs. Vidal Sassoon. When we met in London, some time later, she denied ever having cooked it in her life!

Pearl Buck's Spareribs	*280*
Spareribs Number Two	*280*
Spareribs Number Three	*281*
Chinese Mustard	*281*

. . . playing . . . the First Witch in "Macbeth" . . .

With Ethel Griffies in "Write Me A Murder"

One thing leads to another. And the Bard led to an English part in an English play on Broadway . . . Frederick Knott's "Write Me A Murder." Leaving Stratford, I went straight into rehearsals and my British period.

The entire cast was English. Not that that helped me. No two accents were alike. James Donald's was clipped and brisk, Denholm Elliott's was veddy Mayfair, Torin Thatcher's had a Midlands lilt, and Ethel Griffies . . . well. First day of rehearsal she offered help with mine and I gratefully accepted.

"Of course y'know your flat A's are the first thing that will give you away, dear."

I listened . . . and Griff, unmistakably British, spoke entirely with flat A's.

So I went to Alice Hermes, top speech teacher in New York, and got my own accent. I added a fifth variation to the troupe and even managed to fool members of the audience who were English.

It was around this time that Mother moved to New York. I helped her settle into a cozy apartment during non-theatre hours, and she took over from there. She made friends, played bridge, went to the theatre, concerts . . . and adapted to New York life in general.

And for the first time was exposed to dinners in *my* home. I twittered like a debutante, but gradually pulled myself together and was able to give her fair samples of my fare. She was generous with her compliments. But they were delivered with such delight . . . even awe . . . I suspect her true reaction was relief.

Mother had clearly trusted to the maxim . . . "When in doubt, do as was done unto you." *Her* mother's philosophy had been "the girl will have plenty of time to learn the domestic arts *when the time comes.*" In the meantime, her mother encouraged her to follow her star . . . which happened to be music. Mother was an extremely gifted pianist.

When she left the family nest, Mother was as unprepared as I . . . to wield a vacuum cleaner or turn out an omelet. Until her marriage to Daddy, she didn't know a spatula from a slotted spoon.

She survived, learned, and developed into a superb homemaker. But there was a glaring difference between Mother's experience and mine.

She gave up any thought of a career and devoted full energy to the distaff world. She also had a mother-in-law who moved in the first year of her marriage. A dubious delight . . . but Grandmother

Cole was apparently a help as well. Little catastrophes like cayenne instead of cinnamon in her first apple pie, and mysteries like the swelling capacity of rice all got sorted out under Grandmother Cole's supervision.

I didn't give up my career. There wasn't an in-law in sight (thank God, I think). And it took a very long time before I had any continuity in a kitchen or home of my own.

Following *her* mother's theory turned out to be a long shot with me. And Mother had a long wait to find out if her filly had won or been scratched.

I wasn't Julia Child, but I wasn't bad. And could turn out rather splendid dishes on occasion. It was a load off Mother's mind. (She charitably turned a blind eye to my housekeeping deficiencies.)

Our kitchen relationship, at last, had reached something like peer level. She began asking for recipes of mine! And now that she was virtually a neighbor, I could catch up with some of her specialties . . . old favorites such as *Creamed Chicken*, and *Spanish Cream* . . . grateful I had the privacy of my own kitchen to test and perfect them. When the recipe was hers, she was as much the hoverer as she'd ever been.

She . . . adapted to New York life in general — **With Mother at film's-end party of "Anything Can Happen" in 1951.**

"Summer Vacation" has such a nice ring to it. Until I grew up and got into theatre it even had a yearly reality. Ah well.

Not that we don't have free time in the summer . . . and in the fall . . . and winter and spring. It's called unemployed.

It's the nature of free-lancing professions, but there are compensations. It means we do what we want to do when it's offered. And we don't have to accept whatever job offer comes along, unless the landlord is breathing down our necks.

We do, on occasion, take off . . . ignoring the inner certainty that the one job we'd give our eyeteeth to do will be offered the minute we're incommunicado on some island paradise. Something snaps and we split. Jamaica, Cozumel, Chichén Itzá, Banff and Lake Louise, Maine, Puerto Rico . . . we've done our share of playing hooky, consequences be damned. But a pre-planned summer vacation that our kids' friends would understand is rare.

Summers are mostly between-job weekend freeloading on friends who have establishments on Long Island. We leap at any and all invitations. Jane and Arnold Warwick, our upstairs neighbors, have a house in East Hampton. We've mooched on them a lot. May and Joel Katz built a house on a bluff overlooking Gardiners Bay. Some years they rent during the high summer months . . . but we can still visit during the mild surrounding weeks.

One recession year recently they didn't have a taker. They'd already made plans to go to France with their youngsters, David and Natasha . . . and to avoid vandalism, gave us the keys. Bob, Thor, and I moved in with glee. (Kathy and Sean were doing their own thing that summer.) And immediately my California agent called. I flew to Hollywood, did the job, and got back to East Hampton just in time to be called West for another show. Of the six weeks, I spent two on Long Island. Bob built a grand retaining wall of rocks for the Katzes while I cavorted before the TV cameras of Lotus Land. Our second-honeymoon windfall shot to hell.

Two summers only have we had true vacations. (Three, counting the *Moot Point* fiasco.) In '62 and '64 we took a chance and rented cottages on Fire Island for the whole season. Both times we were the last ones to the rental agents and drew what was left.

The first year our cottage was in a great location . . . just over a dune from the beach . . . but a shambles. A glorified leanto. We couldn't have cared less. We packed up, hired a car to get us to Bay Shore, ferried to Ocean Beach, and moved in . . . Bob, Kathy, Sean, Thor, and me.

The Katzes at their
home in East Hampton —
May, Joel, Natasha,
and David

Thor, incidentally, joined the family in November, '61, when he was a ten-week-old Norwegian Elkhound puppy. Our pride, joy, and love. Bob thought a boy should have a dog. Sean adored Thor, but guess whose dog he was.

The summer was heaven. Kathy got a job on the Island newspaper as a reporter to fill in the non-beach, non-social, non-reading hours. Bob and I enjoyed the sun and sea, books and friends, only slightly interrupted by work. Being so close to Manhattan it was a breeze to go either there or to L.A. at a moment's notice. Our luck held . . . only one of us ever had to go at a time, and never for long.

Sean joined Group (the Island day-camp), roamed freely (no cars, thank God), wallowed in the joys of the beach, and met the "Daddy Boat." Every household had a wagon for carting . . . groceries, laundry, luggage . . . and enterprising young men would meet the incoming ferries to pick up a quarter or two, helping passengers haul their belongings home. Sean restricted his enterprise to the Daddy Boat. It got its name from the working fathers who routinely caught that Friday evening ferry to join their families for the weekend. And since it was routine, families rarely "met" the Daddy Boat. Business for boys with wagons was brisk, carting tired daddies' briefcases and weekend cases from pier to cottage.

Sean also fished a lot . . . disgusted the locals by not bringing home the eels he caught (they consider them a delicacy . . . Sean didn't) . . . but showed up with baskets of blowfish.

Blowfish are nasty looking, miserable fish to handle. Fishermen out for blues or other splendid fish loathe them, and blowfish abound in those waters. Once cleaned and prepared for cooking, however, a metamorphosis takes place. They're a delicate and delicious white meat . . . fully deserving of their posh name, "Sea Squab."

Cooking was a picnic . . . literally. Only once did I get out of my depth. I brought lobsters home to cook. Never again. My God, what a trauma. No one told me they *yell* when they go into a pot of boiling water!

The second summer we had an honest-to-God cottage. Someone had finked out at the last minute and we got it. It was almost chic! And our living and my cooking mirrored the up-grade from the primitive. We could even bring Mother out for a week or so of sea air.

Flora Roberts had the cottage across the sandlot behind us, so we spent a lot of time together. By this time we were old hands at the casual drop-in, drop-out social life of the Island. And sailing and clam-digging were added to the activities.

It was the easy and the good life. And it's a good thing we enjoyed it while we had it. Work on the West Coast has changed so much in the past several years, another "summer vacation" is unlikely. What used to be an all-year-round business is virtually closed down from January to May. The heavy concentration of TV and film work is now from May through December.

But there's still the odd weekend freeloading. Guests, anyone? Bob will wash the hosts' car . . . I'll cook. I'll also steal the house recipes, so perhaps I'm a risk. Some choice additions to my *Collection* have come from East Hampton, Gardiners Bay, and Ocean Beach.

Grilled Chicken Breasts (Jane Warwick)	*298*
Vegetables in Foil (Jane W.)	*231*
Marinated Broiled Lamb (May Katz)	*273*
Fire Island Fish (Fire Island Fishermen)	*304*
Chicken Flora (Flora Roberts)	*284*
Lemon Soufflé (Jane W.)	*353*
Polish Cake (Jane W.)	*378*
Fruit Compote with	*358*
Mock Devonshire Cream (May K.)	*387*

Flora Roberts had the cottage across the sandlot behind us . . .

75

LIVING COAST TO COAST

Mother's moving to New York was a fine thing, but it played havoc with my living arrangements in Los Angeles. So I tried all the establishments New York actors usually went to . . . the Montecito, Chateau Marmont, The Beverly-Rodeo, The Sunset Marquis, etc.

The Sunset Marquis turned out to be the best. Ira Wallach, our friend the writer, first suggested the place to Bob. I'm sure there were non-theatrical guests, but the overwhelming majority seemed to be *of the business* . . . writers, actors, nightclub performers, Playboy bunnies from up the street on Sunset. Some, like Bob and me, were transients . . . there for a job and out again. Many others maintained permanent homes.

The Marquis offered apartments with kitchens and an easy atmosphere. The pool on weekends was like Fire Island. You could join the *group* or keep to your exclusivity . . . or enjoy a bit of both.

A gregarious, lovable chap named Jack Sachs had . . . still has as far as I know . . . a corner poolside apartment. He was known as the jolly Mayor of the Marquis. Without him, it might have been a desert. At that time, like Harry Brock in "Born Yesterday," he was in scrap metal. Now I understand he's become an actor. As the major-domo of so many theatrical lives I guess he finally longed to get into the action.

We all cooked, of course, for ourselves and for others . . . there was much sharing of hospitality. And it was at the Marquis that I really discovered the joys and beauties of L.A. *Supermarkets.* Wheeling your cart through their aisles is a mind-boggling adventure . . . day, night, and Sundays. With five items on my list, I'd spend hours just sight-seeing.

We don't have them like that in New York City. We have what are *called* Supermarkets, but whom are we kidding? Every N.Y. supermarket manager should be given a free tour through an L.A. supermarket . . . just once. God knows if ours would change, but at least the managers might start rumbling.

New York is not truly the stepchild of the country, however. Our supermarkets may be scruffy, but our specialty shops are fabulous and myriad . . . little miracles. It may take you two days to do two hours marketing, but you can eventually round up the finest of foods from any and every culture of the world.

Living in Greenwich Village might not be the best . . . but it's almost. We're blessed with the few remaining Bleecker Street pushcarts, Balducci's, and the Jefferson Market for fresh veg and

fruit; Cheese Village for homemade quiche as well as cheeses; fresh eggs and chickens on Sullivan Street; homemade pasta on Houston Street; Bosco's for Italian salami and Fontina; McNulty's for coffee beans and teas; Sutter's for French pastry; Zito's for the best Italian bread in the world; the Village Bake Shop for black Russian bread and other delicacies; Casa Moneo for Spanish and Mexican foods, fresh and canned; on and on. Some shops are so tiny you freeze your you-knows in the winter, waiting to get a turn inside.

One of our particular gems is the Prime Meat Market on Bleecker Street, owned and operated by the Ottomanelli dynasty. They carry almost any kind of meat or game you could ask for. If they don't have it, ask. They'll get it. They also have their specialties . . . milk-fed baby lamb at Easter; suckling pig at Christmas; homemade pork brasciole; wild game in season, such as hare, venison, boar, quail; sweetbreads and calves brains; fresh squab and fresh Long Island duckling; their old family recipe for superb sweet and hot Italian sausages; seasoned veal roasts; and just *VEAL!*

Their veal is not to be bested anywhere. They have customers who've moved miles away and still return for the veal. They have an infallible eye for the very finest quality when they buy it. And their practiced hands know exactly how to section and slice veal scaloppini to perfection . . . no membrane, no fat.

We could live on their veal if it weren't so expensive. Their sausages are also a favorite, and perhaps I do go a bit haywire there. I'll sneak them into every recipe I can. Aside from veal, Ottomanelli's is not as expensive as one might expect (and even their veal is not as dear as I've seen it on the West Coast). For the superior quality and lack of waste one really comes out ahead. Steaks and all prime cuts, for example, are extravagantly well-trimmed *before* they're weighed.

The fish markets are a joy, too . . . on Bleecker Street, and the Jefferson Market on 6th Avenue. Our favorite for years is gone. Well, the market isn't gone, and it's still fine, but Mr. Visco is gone and I miss him. I'd go in to chat, gossip, or get cooking lessons as much as to shop. Mr. Visco was a benevolent,. droll tyrant. On shrimp: "No salt! Salt if you have to after they're cooked . . . not in the water. You *want* tough shrimp? Put salt in the water."

Life in the Village is as friendly as the shopping. And as casual. Of course the neighborhood knows I'm an actress, one of the local "celebrities." But I'm also an old shoe . . . part of the scene, the family. They see me in false eyelashes, dressed to the nines on the way to a gala. And they see me in jeans with no makeup. It's all the same.

After a TV show I'll get "critiques" attached to the morning newspaper, or pinned to the cleaning when it's delivered. Agnes (the

A cook's best friend — John Ottomanelli

*The Marquis offered . . . an
easy atmosphere* with
Jack Sachs, "The Mayor of
the Marquis," David Opatoshu,
scene-stealing, and me.

checker) and Chuck (the greengrocer) at Gristedes tell me in no uncertain terms which shows they enjoyed, which they didn't. Joe of the corner Mobil Gas Station will stop his work to discuss the philosophy of a program. Mike, our recently retired cop, would slow his patrol car to natter and compare notes about our respective kids (when Sean was younger, he retrieved him from several near J. D. escapades).   Our Sanitation Department crew yell at me, "What's your next TV show?" And connoisseurs that they are, they've even yelled, "When the hell are you doing another *play?*"

I can also stroll about the Village and get lost in the crowds. Sometimes the tourists will stop to point and whisper, never the natives. Other tourists can be too intent on a quest . . . the middle-aged Lotharios on weekends who tap you on the shoulder to ask, "Hey! Where's the *action* in this here Village, sister?"

It's all in a day's living.

Veal Parmigiana	*268*
Veal Piccata	*268*
Veal Chops Sautéed with Garlic	*267*
Chicken and Sausage Casserole	*288*
Nutty Sole and Brown Rice	*303*
Sautéed Shrimp	*308*
Broiled Scampi	*308*

. . . on TW3 . . . I read a blistering speech that Marya Mannes had written and delivered at the Women's Press Club in Washington to an audience of Senators . . .

NECESSITY, THE MOTHER OF A PURCHASE

The American version of England's satirical "That Was The Week That Was" had its gala premiere on NBC-TV in November, 1963. It was then launched as a regularly scheduled live program in January, '64, and our lives went berserk.

Leland Hayward produced "TW3" and Bob was chief writer for the spin-off and the first six months. It was a grueling schedule. The week started Saturday morning with the planning, and writing feature sketches . . . studio conferences began Monday . . . Tuesday, rehearsals . . . and the writing of last minute news sketches continued until air-time Friday night at 10. Bob's "moment" of relaxation came after the show . . . until bedtime. And Saturday A.M. the rat race began all over again.

It was very exciting. But our home life went to pot. Some of the writing was done at home . . . most of it at NBC . . . sometimes we'd have him for meals . . . a lot of the time not.

Life really got complicated when I was working, too. Fortunately the kinder were no longer babes. Kathy was 19 and in college. Sean was 10 . . . at home, but not helpless.

My first job that year was on TW3, too. I read a blistering speech that Marya Mannes had written and delivered at the Women's Press Club in Washington to an audience of Senators . . . giving them humorous (?) holy hell for their standards of morality and ethics in politics.

I did one other show in New York . . . "Russians: Self-Impressions" for CBS . . . but the rest of my work during the siege was in Washington, Salt Lake City, and Los Angeles. Obviously something had to be done to keep Emmett bodies and souls together.

A new fridge would help.

The original antique of the apartment was still with us. The landlord insisted it was adequate, but one cubic foot of freezer (and forget ice cream)? So I went on a shopping spree, bought a gorgeous Frigidaire with bottom-door freezer, and returned the "adequate" box to the landlord for scrap.

A fridge with room, and a proper freezer that kept its zero temperature steady!! We were in heaven.

It meant a re-education process in shopping, but we took to it like penguins to ice. The freezer filled up in a flash. And I could organize the food supplies so Bob and Sean wouldn't have to scrounge when I was sent out of town.

I also found I was paying more attention to cuts of meat I hadn't tried before. With freezing facilities at hand, I could buy on impulse and if the immediate time-schedule was too tight for experimentation, the food could just sit there until the moment was ripe.

Both John and Frank Ottomanelli (as well as the half dozen other O's in the market) bombarded me with fresh ideas . . . and one of our all-time favorites entered *the Collection. Lamb Shanks* . . . braised . . . succulent, moist, delicious, and as much as we like lamb, they're the *best.*

We haven't given up the rest of the animal, of course. In fact, I found buying a whole leg was a great way to stock the freezer for the boys during their bachelor weeks. The Ottomanellis would slice off four to six steaks, and then cut up the rest . . . one pile earmarked for *Shashlik*, and with the other I'd make a stew or a curry. At least half a dozen meals frozen and ready.

The *Shashlik* chunks usually waited till I got home, though. It came to be a party dish when Kathy gave me a handsome set of skewers for an anniversary present. (If she was hinting for kabobs, she certainly got them!)

About Shashlik. There was a kitchen sequence in "Anything Can Happen" (the film based on George Papashvily's delightful book of the same name, recalling his early experiences in this country). Jose Ferrer played Giorgi (a Russian) and I played Helen (an American journalist, later his wife), and in the scene he chided me about the insane way "foreigners" cook Shashlik. He indignantly pointed out that each ingredient has its own quality and cooking time . . . the meat, the onions, the tomatoes, etc. What could be more stupid than to put them all together on the same skewer and expect them to be done at the same time?

I'm sure Giorgi Papashvily was right. It *would* be more sensible to string each ingredient on its own skewer and broil accordingly. But would it have that festive look? Or the Slavic panache of each to his own sword, as it were?

We all survived TW3 . . . even Bob (barely) . . . and genuflect slightly when it's recalled. Anno Frigidaire Gratias.

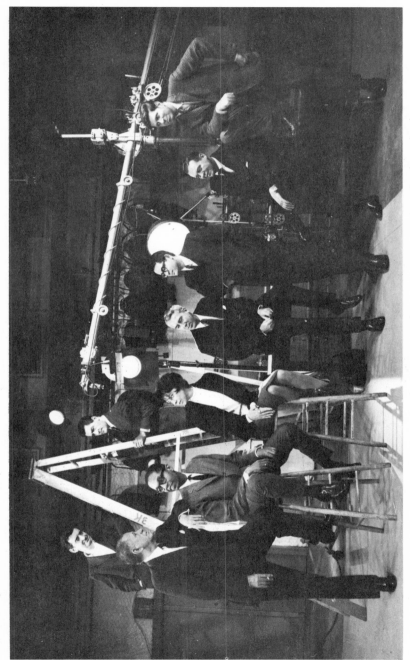

The original American TW3 gang: left to right, Leland Hayward, Billy Taylor, Patricia Englund, Bob Emmett, Gerald Gardner, Marshall Jamison, Hal Gurney. On the ladder, George Hall and Charlie Manna.

Kathy went to college . . . Radcliffe

As noted, Kathy went to college . . . Radcliffe. And set off a chain reaction of sustaining magnitude.

Like all enterprising Harvard sophomores, a chap named David Rosen checked out the roster of incoming Cliffie freshmen . . . and recognized a girl he'd met at a summer camp in the Berkshires when he was a "Forester" and she was a lowly "Primitive." The photo showed her to be pretty, and if she were permitted to enter that hallowed enclave, she had to be bright, didn't she? He'd have another look.

Dissolve. Three years later . . . David had graduated, magna cum laude, and went to England for a year of graduate study. And Kathy wrapped up her last year in Cambridge in one term, magna cum laude, and flew over to join him.

Three months later there was an historic phone call from London to New York. The news was two-fold. "We've both been accepted at Yale Law School next fall!" We cheered! "And we want to be married in New York in June!" We cheered again, with protestations . . .

"Why don't you get married *there*, for God's sake? You'd have a built-in European honeymoon!"

No, no, we didn't understand. They wanted a *wedding*. In New York, so all their friends could be present. There were other stipulations. Kathy wanted to be a "bride" bride . . . long white dress and all . . . but they both wanted the day, the ceremony, and everyone else to be informal. They also wanted to be married by a rabbi.

Good God, a wedding? Our modern, anti-establishment young couple? I'd only been to one "wedding" wedding in my life, my first own, and I couldn't remember tuppence about it! What did I know about giving a *wedding!?!*

The call came in early May, so even an old hand at this sort of thing might have had a tremor or two. Kathy was our beautiful pride and joy, and David was the White Knight of the Eastern seaboard. Our usual "wing it" response to bolts from the blue simply wouldn't do. Hal Prince had never faced such pressure to produce a hit . . . and Steve Sondheim was nowhere in sight.

With my ignorance manifestly apparent, I flew to Amy Vanderbilt. (Research is also a good stalling maneuver, I discovered.)

I was deep into Ms. V's tome, underlining every pointer I could find except items that didn't seem to apply to an informal rabbi presiding over a long white dress, when an airletter from London arrived with the first installment of the guest list. It cheerily stated there were more names to come . . . a *lot* more.

Kathy had mentioned she thought our home would be the happiest place to have the festivities. Home? We've squeezed in 50 people on occasion, but it was a subway-rush-hour crunch! And there was no indication this pair was going to settle for 50 or anything like it. "Hello, London? We have this problem here . . . "

May and Joel came iffily to a possible rescue. If the wedding could be held on a weekend they could offer their huge West End Avenue apartment. (Joel's office was on the premises, and as a psychiatrist he tried to avoid one *patient* bumping into another. Wedding parties in evidence would be a strict no-no.)

Since Kathy and David weren't returning from London until after David's school let out . . . June 7 or thereabouts . . . and a "weekend" for a rabbi meant sundown Saturday through Sunday . . . that gave us about three 12-hour options. In June . . . the swinging month for brides, when most chaps who marry people are booked solid and have been since March. Add to that the normal response of rabbis to marrying a Jew to a non-Jew and you have the picture.

I simply blanked out on that little problem. I was having struggles of my own with Amy V. "Let George do it."

George didn't lift a finger. Bob and Herbert Rosen did. And the miracle happened. A benignly chauvinistic committee of three . . . the two fathers and Rabbi Goldman of the Free Synagogue . . . met and ironed everything out. The date was set . . . Sunday, June 19, 1966. *Whew!*

We had a place, a rabbi, a date, and a time . . . 4 P.M. I could avoid it no longer. The ball was in my yard.

The guest list had reached and seemed to be settling in at 120. Invitations! Should they be printed, engraved? Do we have time for invitations at *all*? I whizzed around the corner to our printers on Hudson Street and went back and forth through all the possibilities until the proprietor slapped my wrist and said, "That's it. *Now* . . . or your list won't know you're giving a wedding until the bride is enceinte."

From that point on, I ignored London. Kathy would simply have to have faith. For better or worse, I plunged ahead . . . with considerable aid, comfort, and "help from my friends," yea Beatles!

Joel was our leader when we decided champagne would be the basic liquid refreshment. The Katzes and the Emmetts had several riproaring evenings testing brands and vintages, until one label was agreed upon.

. . . several riproaring evenings testing brands and vintages . . . Joel and May Katz, Bob and me, Bram and Lila Pais

Bob took care of the ordering, plus the side liquor, ice, et al. And held my hand a lot.

Sean's contribution was a copy of "How To Be A Jewish Mother."

And May. Ah yes, May. With her help, all those incredible details somehow got covered, like Hertz Rent-a-Wedding (the bar, glasses, chairs, plates, silver, trays, coatracks, etc.) . . . flowers, for the rooms and the principals . . . wedding cake, photographer, etc., etc. May had never given a wedding either, but she had been a whale of a theatrical production assistant. A wedding wasn't too far afield.

We had one brief contretemps. With the wedding at 4 P.M., we'd decided against serving a meal, but we did want canapés. Lots of them. My love of cooking be damned, I was all set to track down a caterer when May looked aghast and said, *"WHAT!"*

"What do you mean *WHAT?*"

"Good God, girl! None of those prefabricated soggies are going to be served in *my* home!"

And so we did it ourselves. In two weeks, we pre-prepared the lot and stacked May's over-sized freezer with everything from hand-picked-over fresh crabmeat to ground chicken to finely chopped fresh parsley and paper-thin cucumber slices . . . minced shrimp, grated cheese, toasted rounds from thinly sliced bread . . . on and on and on. Nina Fonaroff prepared a huge batch of her chopped chicken livers . . . and David's grandmother, Ida, baked a beauteous wedding challah. The only edible masterpiece not prepared lovingly and frantically by non-commercial hands was the wedding cake from Leonard's Baking Company, Inc.

In the meantime, of course, there were Mother-of-the-Bride and Grandmother-of-the-Bride dresses to get. Kathy had bought her dress in London, but there were still all the accessories. And a suit for

Sean, the ring-bearer. He hadn't had a new suit for two years. The last one came up to his knees.

I was rolling now, like a snowball down-hill . . . I wasn't sure what I was doing but I was doing it with a vengeance.

And inevitably, like opening night, *THE* Sunday arrived.

Josephine and Pierre Le Gall and helper came to the Katzes' in the morning to create incredibly beautiful canapés from our defrosted "makings." The Emmett entourage arrived shortly after noon. We girls put up our hair, dressed, and were generally hysterical and giddy in the Katz bedroom. And gradually the 120 families and friends dribbled in.

Someone must have had an eye on the time, because in the vicinity of four a signal was given. Nina was at the piano, and she burst forth with gorgeously improvised Russian gaiety. It all began.

Dr. Goldman took his place at the far end of the living room . . . David and his best man, Bob Abrams, marched in . . . Sean followed, grinning like a Cheshire cat (I was told) . . . then Emily Levine, Kathy's best girl. And finally . . . Kathy, looking beautiful and serene . . . flanked by Bob and me, looking God knows how, trying *not* to grin like Cheshire cats . . . the three of us steadying each other as we tried to walk a straight line to David and Dr. Goldman.

The informality, which also meant no rehearsal, had Bob and me doing something like a buck-and-wing to get out of the way . . . and the ceremony began. I found myself facing Kathy and David, off to the left of the rabbi. An appalling place to be. David had made me solemnly promise not to do a dumb thing like cry. And there I was, face hanging out, no way to hide it if I did. With superhuman effort I didn't fail him. My God, a wedding does call up the most extraordinary sentiments, doesn't it?

The ceremony was short, thoughtful, warm, and just right . . . topped off with David and Kathy falling into each other's arms and the room bursting into a party, on cue.

And such a party! It carried on for two hours of uninterrupted laughter and merriment, with David emceeing the whole shebang. It was his party . . . from the ceremony of the challah to guiding the cutting of the cake . . . seeing that strangers met and enjoyed . . . gleefully calling "Time, Gentlemen" when he was ready to whisk his bride away.

After all the flurry and exhaustion and panic and conviction that nothing would arrive when it should and nothing would go right . . . it was perfect. By golly, we did it!

There were even bonuses. Old friends from both the Emmett and Rosen camps hailed each other on arrival with hoots of surprise and delight.

Natasha Katz, Sean, Kathy, David, Shirley Rosen (David's mother), Ida Rosen (David's grandmother), Joel Katz, Grace Stebbins (my mother), myself, and May Katz

And Bill Baldwin! Kathy had finally "met" him in 1962, and thought it would be very nice if he came. But Bill had never met Bob, and hadn't seen me since 1947, and none of us had any conviction that a formal, impersonal invitation would be very persuasive. So Kathy wrote an encouraging letter as well, and it did the trick. He came, beamed with pride, stayed to the end, and had a grand natter with that woman who'd fallen in love with him back in 1943 . . . the jolly originator of the Stebbins Stinger!

It's unlikely I shall ever be on the giving end of another wedding, but I came away from that one with a "good to know" for large parties in general.

For instance, Bob and I gave a "Greenwich Village" party in '69 or '70. An "after nine" . . . for some 40 people, old friends and neighbors. Instead of trying to do a hot buffet at midnight for such a large gang, I took a tip from the wedding and prepared nothing but hors d'oeuvres. Masses of them. (Including a huge platter of tartar steak with bread and chopped onions on the side.) There were a few before-party disadvantages . . . they took a lot of time to prepare, and it was a strain on the fridge. But once everything was out it was pure joy. People ate when they were hungry, there was no "pleasing the hostess" dance if they weren't, and I was as free-wheeling as my guests. A most pleasant way to enjoy one's own party.

In mid-winter, 1967, my agent, Tom Korman, sent me a film script. I read it, found the script in general quite good, and the part enchanting. So I called him, "Fine. Just one question. How do they plan to solve the technical problem? I mean, these characters seem to be real *APES.*"

Tom replied cursorily, "Oh, I suppose they'll attach bits of fur here and there. Don't worry, for God's sake. 20th Century-Fox is a reputable company. If you like the script, I'll pursue it."

His description sounded rather scruffy to me and I forgot the whole thing. Who knew if I'd hear any more about the film anyway?

A few weeks later I got a long distance call from someone in the casting office at 20th. "How tall are you, Miss Hunter?"

For a moment I felt like the child actor who's trained by Mama always to say he's as old as the part in question. But this mysterious chap wasn't giving me a clue. So I gave him the facts . . . 5'3½". He said, "Thank you," and hung up. It was the damndest, weirdest call.

Eventually, I did hear from Tom again. He'd made a deal for me to play Dr. Zira in "Planet of the Apes." Shooting would begin sometime in April or May. From now on I'd be hearing directly from producer Arthur P. Jacobs' office.

That was as much as I knew in March. They were smart.

The first call from Jacobs' office was to come to Hollywood for a fitting. Three days. Two for travel, one for the fitting.

I gaily reported to Mr. J.'s office the morning after my arrival, and was led to a rather clinical-looking laboratory. For a fitting? A fitting for *what?*

I was introduced to John Chambers and his assistant, Werner Kempler . . . and was seated in a barber's chair. They showed me photographs of the results of nine months of research, design, lab work, experiment, testing . . . and there they were. Orangutans, chimpanzees, gorillas . . . not bits of fur here and there at all, not in the least scruffy. They looked real. How right Tom was to trust 20th.

I was still detached, an objective on-looker . . . fascinated and impressed.

And then it began.

John and Werner put a small block of wood between my teeth, slapped some thick, white, globby stuff all over my face, and set a timer. I sat there . . . dutifully immobile on the outside. Inside, hysteria was unmistakably rising. John, intoning dulcetly, talked me through it until he sensed I, not the masque, was going to crack.

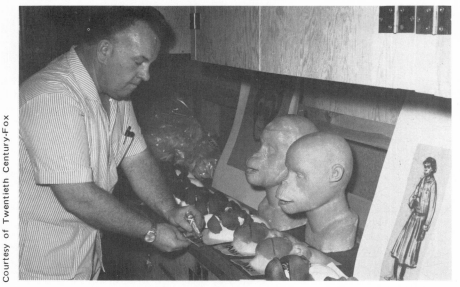

Courtesy of Twentieth Century-Fox

I was introduced to John Chambers . . .

They whipped it off in the nick . . .for *me* . . . they weren't too sure about the mold. But after a quick test, they let me go. It was possible they'd have to call me back to L.A. for another go at the glob, but if all went well, my next "call" would be in a week or so for the first makeup test.

If they'd called for the glob, I wonder who would have played Dr. Zira? (I wouldn't have been the first to say "No, thanks." Edward G. Robinson, Mickey Rooney . . .)

When I went out for the makeup test, I wasn't quite as bouncy walking into Jacobs' office. Not that I had any tangible reason for apprehension . . . yet. I only had to be submerged in the glob *once*. The makeup would be different. Wouldn't it?

It was. Quite different. I could watch. Werner applied the "makeup" for that first test. It took four and a half hours.

It began with sponge rubber "appliances" that covered everything except my eyes, from mid-forehead to the bottom of my chin. The two sections were glued on firmly with spirit gum. Except just above and below my lips where anatomical glue was substituted, for elasticity. The edges of the appliances were tissue-thin and ground into my skin with a metal instrument, so the demarcation line between flesh and appliance was virtually undetectable. Next, surgical adhesive was stippled all around the edges, and on top of the

92

adhesive they painted another glue called "seal." The brown castor-oil-based makeup followed . . . over the appliances and all remaining visible skin, to the hairline and including eyes and neck. The "face" was then given the artistic treatment . . . shading and all that.

Dr. Zira was a chimpanzee, so I got an extra the orangutans and gorillas missed. Large ears, enclosing my own. They were glued on with spirit gum.

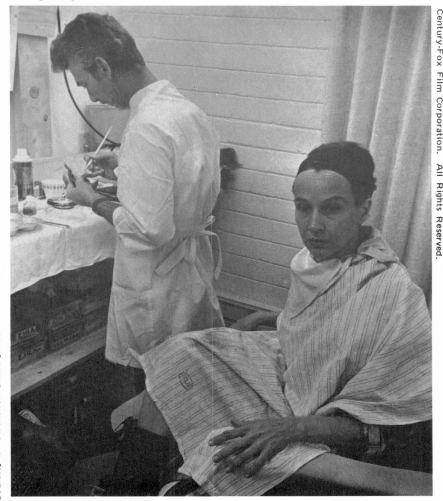

We met in the special makeup trailer . . . at 4 or 5 every morning – **Leo Lotito beginning operations**

Off to the hairdresser for the wig . . . a gorgeous black wig. And back to the torture chamber. More spirit gum. This time for the lace hair-pieces that were shaped to go around the outside edges of the appliances and lay back over the wig and ears. The top and side hair-pieces were combed deftly into the wig. Those in front of the ears were cut short enough for some of the ear to show. Then individual crepe hairs were laid on top of the lace with something they called "avocado" . . . spirit gum mixed with Fuller's earth, to keep down the shine.

On to the hands and half-way up the arms. Brown nail polish first. Then brown makeup. More spirit gum for hair-pieces . . . and finally, crepe hair between each knuckle.

The costume covered everything else. The only untouched, uncovered smidgeon of my body were my eyeballs. Even my *teeth* were painted black . . . so the camera wouldn't accidentally pick up two sets of teeth. The chimp's teeth were glued onto the appliances.

Breathing? Oh yes, they'd made arrangements for that. You could breathe through your mouth. Or if you weren't needing too much air for a moment, you could close your mouth and breathe through a slit in front of the chimp's teeth that made a narrow passage to your nostrils. The chimp's nose, part of the appliance, was aesthetic, not functional.

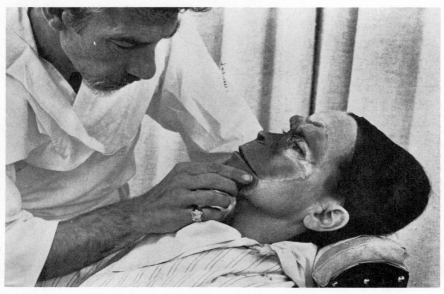

It began with sponge rubber "appliances" . . .

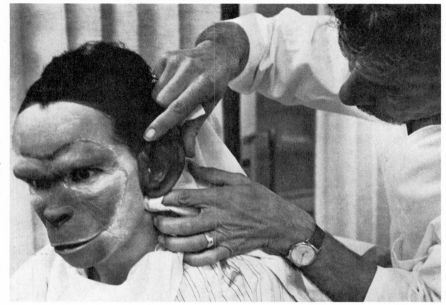

Courtesy of Twentieth Century-Fox

. . . I got an extra the orangutans and gorillas missed.

The costume was in layers, too. Lady chimps don't have much in the way of breasts, so I was given a special bra to flatten me. A padded muslin harness covered my back . . . to give it a more ape-like shape. Over that went the dress . . . high neck, long sleeves, and straight . . . down to the ankles. The effect was a hobble skirt. Over the dress was the jacket . . . hanging straight and loose from a very thick leather yoke that went high up the neck . . . to eliminate the human neck indentation.

On the feet were long "gloves." The base was espadrilles-to-fit, to which they sculpted "hands" . . . extending some three inches beyond the espadrilles themselves. The thumbs, of course, went off to the inboard sides. The total was then gloved with fabric extending up to the knee, zippered down the back for entry. A sole (concession to "people" actors) was attached to the bottom, and completed the boot.

Well, there I was. A chimpanzee. Embalmed, mummified, hobbled, tripping over my lower thumbs . . . and dangerously claustrophobic. *Act?* Were they kidding?

There was a dense air of anxiety on the test set. Everyone was there . . . Art Jacobs, director Franklin Schaffner, cameraman Leon Shamroy . . . and we apes. Roddy McDowall, Maurice Evans, a few gorillas, and me. Some "humans" . . . Linda Harrison and others.

95

Charlton Heston and the other astronauts didn't have to attend this session. This was the nitty gritty. In John Chambers' words, "We'll either be believable, or we'll be Mickey Mouse."

The production people were worried about how their creations photographed, sounded . . . how much expression could come through the appliances . . . whether we really embodied the "evolved ape" concept . . . were there still flaws to be detected in the makeup . . . all that.

Roddy, Maurice and I were infinitely more concerned about simple survival. My God . . . would we live through this day?

We did, somehow . . . sheer grit. And the day was longer than scheduled. It seemed our voices came out muffled. So we were shepherded off to the recording theatre to make further tests with just a mike. We read selections from Dickens, Vonnegut, Pogo, anything around . . . to figure a way to speak, be understood, and have the voice come out free of nasality. In "speech" vernacular, we finally agreed it was possible if we consciously placed the vowels and consonants very far forward, into the teeth. (Our human teeth, that is.)

The problem hopefully solved, we were released. Back to the torture chamber to get it all off. Inch by inch, the hair-pieces, wig, ears, and appliances were removed. The quickest way would have

Courtesy of Twentieth Century-Fox

. . . the artistic treatment . . .

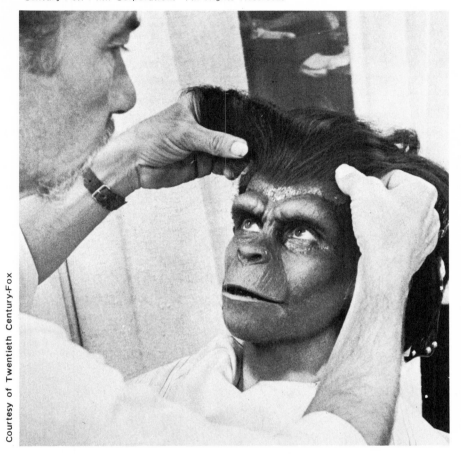

. . . What's a little pain for one's Art?

been with acetone. Acetone cuts into glue in a flash. But our skin would have dissolved with it, and skin was needed to attach the appliances. So alcohol was used. A long, slow, but sure process. Painful . . . but gee, what's a little pain for one's Art?

One and one-half hours later I saw my own face again . . . free of foam rubber, glue, fur, and brown makeup. I couldn't believe it was still there . . . alive and breathing. Raw, mottled . . . looking a bit like a case of measles . . . but *there*.

I went back to the hotel and, like Scarlett O'Hara, would think about it "tomorrow." I got plastered.

97

In the sobering light of New York, I was traumatized. What hath God, 20th, and Tom wrought?! The predicament ahead of me was inhuman . . . literally.

That early phone call, incidentally, had been explained. Apes are shorter than men, right? And so no one was approached to play an ape who was over 5'10". To emphasize the contrast, no astronaut was under 6'2". Girl apes, of course, should be shorter than boy apes. First time my height (or lack of it) was a factor in getting a part.

Willy nilly I was committed. I took a few days to recover and then went to my doctor. He's a purist . . . the sort who refuses to prescribe antibiotics except for serious illnesses, and has no patience with people who think they need upper-downer assistance to cope with life. When I graphically described my recent experience, he turned green and immediately wrote a prescription for tranquilizers. For the makeup process, that is . . . I needed to be clear-headed on the set, whatever the cost.

Next step was a haircut. Like boys used to look . . . to help my head survive a wig during summer heat, and for nightly shampoos. The castor oil makeup might have been just dandy for the appliances, but it played havoc with the hair.

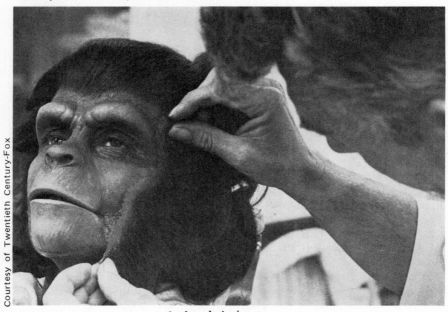

. . . the lace hairpieces . . .

98

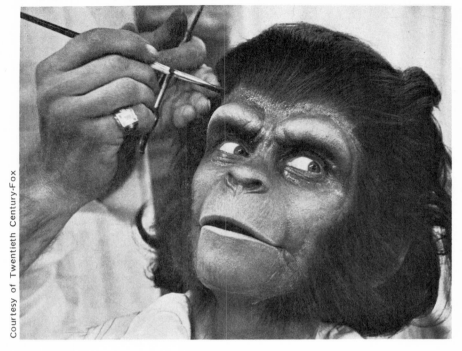

. . . with something called "avocado" . . .

The only other thing I could think of was cinching an apartment at the Sunset Marquis. If ever I needed a home away from home, and *friends* . . . this was it.

The call-to-arms finally came in May. "Fly to Phoenix where you will be met by a small plane to take you to the Company . . . in Page, Arizona."

Page is a town near the border between Utah and Arizona. Not too long ago, it had been little more than a camp site. Now, because of the development of Lake Powell as a "resort," it had grown to a main street and a motel. The surrounding country was absolutely perfect for the film. Unearthly. I doubt if the terrain of the Moon or Mars is any more strange.

We shot in Page for a week, and the rest was in California. At the Studio, at 20th's ranch in Thousand Oaks, and at Point Dume, north of Malibu. Three months, slimming down my lifespan by three years.

We learned to live with it . . . just.

At first we compulsively shared revelations of the agonies, until we found it was easier to bear if we didn't talk about it so much.

99

Roddy and I were the first two apes to work, and, together with Frank Schaffner, set the pace for "evolved" ape movement and behavior. Also, as the veterans, and finally convinced silence was the better part of valor, we would initiate the new members of our simian family as they arrived on the set. To their frantic questioning, "Do you ever get *used* to it?" ... we'd reassure them as best we could, "Sure. Takes a little time, but you will." And change the subject. *No* one ever got "used" to it.

From the producer on down, the Company was gentle and considerate. They couldn't experience our problems, but they could imagine them. When 20th executives started bringing visiting firemen to the set in droves to "see the monkeys" ... I yelped!

(Two reasons: A lot of bodies around increased the claustrophobia difficulties ... and the civilians were unconsciously rude and insensitive. Poor, dear animals in the Zoo, I feel for you. But at least your visitors can't get close enough to tug at your ears and ask if they're really yours ... or poke at your face to see what it *feels* like.)

I only had to yelp once. The NO VISITORS rule was so strictly enforced, I had a fighting time to get back on the set once after an early day. Makeup off, the guard wouldn't believe I was a member of the cast.

Our "muzzles" projected out from our true lips in varying degrees. The gorillas' were the fullest, but we all had our problems. Surgeon General be damned, it was no time to give up smoking. Art Jacobs might not have done much for our health, but he was an angel to our psyches. He ordered long cigarette holders by the gross and passed them out to all apes who indulged. Straws, too, were standard equipment near every water cooler and coffee urn. It was impossible to drink without them.

As for eating ... oh my. We were confined to quarters at mealtime. (I suspect they were afraid of a drastic drop in the gross at the Commissary. Our physical appearance wasn't a real appetite booster.) But again, Jacobs did what he could. Meals were brought in at his expense, to eat in front of mirrors ... long makeup tables set up for the purpose. It was tricky ... getting a fork or spoon through to your mouth without damaging the appliances. I gave up. Looking in the mirror, I wasn't appetizing to me, either. I holed up in my dressing room with a can of Sego and a straw ... and slept the rest of the lunch hour away.

My weight didn't vary, though. Lack of calories was balanced by lack of movement. Holding quiet helped keep the psychic seams from bursting. Also, the weight of the boots and the inhibiting factor of the hobble skirt took more energy than I was willing to waste. I needed every ounce I could muster for the camera.

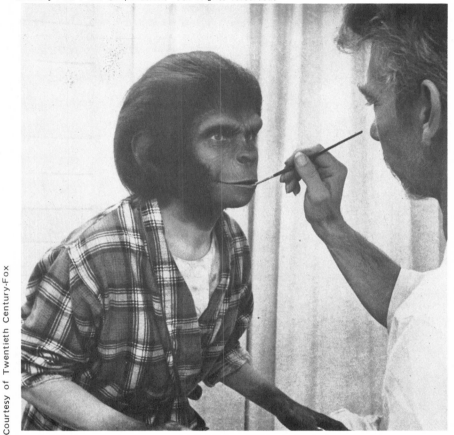

. . . shading and all that.

Werner remained in the Lab with John Chambers, turning out daily supplies of appliances. The alcohol cut through the glue, but also broke down the rubber, so we had to have a new set for each day's shooting.

Each of the principal actors had his own makeup artist. Mine was Leo Lotito . . . combination of leprechaun and benign Satan. We met in the special makeup trailer they'd built for the film at 4 or 5 every morning. I'd pop my tranquilizer, fall into the makeup chair, and the day began. After 3 weeks of this I decided to drop the pill. The process was now whittled down to only 3½ or 4 hours . . . I certainly should be able to sit through it without a crutch anymore.

Ummhmm. When we got to the set Leo gave me an ultimatum. "If you ever sit in that chair again without taking that goddam pill you can get yourself another makeup artist! I'm a wreck!"

We had another crisis. The camera was setting up for a big head shot of me, and Leon Shamroy noticed a bump on my "face," near the nose. Leo examined it, and sure enough, there was an air bubble between the appliance and me. The ape's and makeup department's nightmare! It was early for lunch, but the hour was called and Leo and I repaired to the trailer. Slowly but surely, he pried the appliance loose to the offending bubble while I gripped the chair for dear life. No friendly alcohol this time. And then slowly but surely he closed the gap with fresh glue. It took nearly two hours. But we were back on the set and the day was saved.

There were other makeup problems. Excessive perspiration was a hazard on the very hot days at the ranch. And saliva would break away the glue around the mouth. But generally, John Chambers had done a brilliant job and the appliances held up remarkably well. Our skin was the major problem. They brought in dermatologists to try to solve it with creams, etc. But I found the best solution was drowning my face in plain old vaseline every night when I went to bed. By the end of the week, however, the only help was Saturday . . . and two days respite from glue.

The other skin destroyer was sun . . . around the eyes. The castor oil makeup was a gorgeous booster for sunburn, and at the end of the first day at the ranch my eyes looked like two fried eggs. So

**Zira and Leo Lotito,
my beauty expert**

sunglasses became part of the off-camera costume. I'd keep them on until just before "Action!" . . . toss them to Leo . . . and at "Cut!" he'd toss them back.

There was a lot of praying . . . against a possible cold (no *way* to blow a nose) . . . against a pimple, or a cut . . . any kind of skin eruption. Guys with sensitive beards were in agony.

Everyone who didn't have naturally brown eyes was fitted with colored contact lenses. The nurse assigned to the Company was kept very busy . . . putting in and taking out for those whose eyes never adjusted. I was spared, thank God. Because I was the only lady ape, it was decided I could be "different" and keep my hazel eyes.

There was a lot of horseback riding. Side-saddle for me. And the "thumbs" on our boots made stirrups either useless or death traps. Since the sculpted part of the boot was flexible and went three inches beyond one's foot, it provided no leverage at all. But if one got one's true foot into the stirrup, it meant the "thumb" was pushed in as well. And good luck getting it out if thrown from the horse!

But in spite of all the hazards, strain, stress, and agonies . . . the extraordinary thing was the fun in the performance. It was a crazy, marvelous holiday for an actor. We had an absolute ball in front of the camera while melting into a mass of psychoses off-stage. Roddy McDowall, for instance . . . He missed the second of the five "Ape" films, but went on voluntarily to do all the rest, plus the TV series. And yet it was Roddy to whom the assistant director *never* said lightly, or in jest, "You're through for the day." Not unless he meant it. In desperate relief, Roddy would grab his chimpanzee nose immediately and pull the appliance loose in shreds!

Our relationship to our makeup artists, and artists they were, was by nature intimate. We practically lived together. Short days did happen . . . even the occasional day off . . . but a "short" day was 5½ hours minimum, without doing a lick of work. Normal days ran at least 14 hours, beginning to end. Some were longer.

Leo and I became fast friends. We learned a lot about each other before we were through . . . and one of the revelations was a mutual interest in cooking. It was alluded to, not explored. Neither of us had much stomach for food those three months. And only two recipes exchanged hands. Leo to me. His own formula for *Stuffed Mushrooms*, a very tasty hors d'oeuvre, and an eggplant dish that's truly special.

A large drink at the end of the day was better suited to our needs. Leo's wife, Pat, donated a portable bar to the cause . . . and we kept it well-supplied. He'd sip his Chivas Regal, and I'd sip my Beefeater martini (through my trusty straw) while he went through the tedious process of returning me to the world of the humankind.

At the end of the hour and a half he'd lock up the bar for the next night . . . and we'd wend our weary, separate ways into the darkness.

Looking back, it's a little appalling what tortures actors will endure for the sake of their work. Of course, before the first "Planet of the Apes" none of us knew what we were getting into. But there wasn't that excuse when it came to the second, or the third . . . for me, at any rate.

Actually, my arm was twisted for the second ("Beneath the Planet of the Apes"). Dr. Zira figured only briefly in it . . . there mostly for "continuity" . . . and it did seem poor sportsmanship not to accommodate them. Accepting the third, however, was sheer ego-trip. (And veiled masochism?) In "Escape from the Planet of the Apes," Roddy and I were the stars. It was our story from beginning to end . . . and the parts were gorgeous. Even knowing the exact agonies I would be facing, I simply couldn't resist it. Also, could I possibly sit back and let someone *else* play my beloved Dr. Zira? Not on your life!

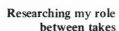
Researching my role between takes

Taylor (Charlton Heston): "Dr. Zira, I'd like to kiss you good-bye." Zira: "All right. But you're so damned ugly."

HOLLYWOOD IMPROVES A LOT

After I left California in 1947, my return trips for work settled into a predictable pattern. I would arrive at the last possible moment . . . do the job . . . and escape to New York on the first plane out. For years, I caught what Gothamites shudderingly call the "Red-Eye Special."

Gradually I gave up that mad evening dash to the airport. The security blanket of being on my way home was nice, but it became harder and harder to face the cramped catnaps of the night, and the numb oblivion of the next day. I now wait until the early morning flight. Sometimes I even take the late morning flight.

In fact, even if my agent says "stay over a few days in case this marvelous part comes through," I don't flail like a trapped animal anymore.

Not that I still don't want to go home pronto. But I don't have to. It's a difference.

It wasn't that I actually hated Hollywood. It just took a long time to lay the ghosts of '42 - '47 to rest. They'd meet me as the plane landed, and stay on my back until I left . . . ominous threats to my peace of mind and sense of self. Inside, I couldn't seem to avoid reverting to that old, naive child of the '40's, filled with anxiety, as insecure as if the interim time and growth had never taken place.

All confidence ashambles, I'd try "positive thinking," anything . . . "Good God, they paid to bring you out here, and with all the actors in L.A. they didn't have to do that unless they wanted you" . . . but it rarely worked. The old sense of being a commodity crept through the bluff. Only back on the plane to N.Y. could I breathe easily again, and it had nothing to do with smog.

Well, even ghosts get tired of the same activity year after year. Time was on my side. And Hollywood's. But the real and final exorcism didn't come until 1969.

Of course, it helped to have a warlock around. Bob was mine. He had dear, old friends from his Berkeley college days living in Westwood . . . Bellevernon and Barney Shapiro. I'd met them once, briefly, in New York . . . but I was shy about ringing their doorbell in L.A., even if we did have a lover in common.

Finally in the summer of '67, the first year of the Ape, with Bob's persistent prodding and Dr. Zira's off-camera need to communicate with people, I made a tentative phone call.

Well, to make a long story short, they virtually became my West Coast family. And in '69, I moved in.

106

Bellevernon and Barney Shapiro . . .
my West Coast "family"

I was due to come out for the second of the Ape series, and Belle suggested a try at operating from their house instead of a hotel. Brave of her. An actor working on a role . . . especially *that* role . . . is not the most convivial creature to have around.

"Give it a whirl," she said. "If it doesn't work for either of us, out you go."

It worked. Still works. For one thing, we don't make demands on each other . . . And when we spend time together, there's a lot of love and soul in the air. I have my own house key now . . . and use it even when they're off gallivanting in San Francisco or Rome. It's not as gemütlich on such occasions, but at least I rattle around in a friendly wagon.

Barney is a lawyer, and Belle was a Political Science major before she threw herself into raising three strapping boys. They're something of mavericks in their world, too . . . breaking or ignoring most of the rules laid out for "successful lawyer and wife" living in L.A. society.

They provided me with a patch of solid ground in that fad-ridden, image-conscious, jockeying-for-position community. Under their gentle patronage, my personal self-esteem found itself again. I can be the outsider at last without the pain of it . . . and accept, reject, be amused, disdainful, or embrace . . . on my own terms.

Interests at the Shapiros' are broad, and of course Bellevernon and I find time for food and recipes. I've passed on favorites to her, and she's given me beauties in return. The exchange began with desserts . . . what else?

107

She insisted on my investing in a Bundt pan, and gave me a list of cake recipes to fill it. They're blatant cheats, all . . . half from scratch, half from mixes . . . but so good I serve them with a flourish and no shame whatever. The *Caramel Supreme* is just one heavenly example.

The *Peach Soufflé* is not Belle's, but a bit of ambrosia from a Shapiro niece. Marilyn served it to us when Belle and I were on a diet. She substituted Dream Whip for the heavy cream, and conned us into thinking we were devouring "low-calorie" bliss.

Belle's *Apple Pudding* just may be my favorite of all time, but then I'm a pushover for puddings.

I had never baked a ham. Bob and I both like it, but neither of the children would eat it. I experiment a lot on guests, but a whole ham intimidated me. Until Belle taught me her variation. (I still haven't baked a ham from scratch.)

Belle's *Swingers* are glorified hamburgers . . . a jazzy change for the family, and great for an informal party . . . indoors or out. Since the cook is chained to the frying pan, outdoors is probably better. Unless you can chat with your guests from the kitchen. I can't.

Caramel Supreme Bundt Cake	*372*
Peach Soufflé	*351*
Apple Pudding	*363*
Ham-in-Pastry	*278*
Swingers	*247*

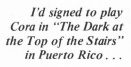

I'd signed to play Cora in "The Dark at the Top of the Stairs" in Puerto Rico . . .

108

There's only one business like show business or words to that effect. Since we never know what's coming next, we play it by ear. Fine for Bob and me. We chose the life, and though each of us has had moments of "What am I doing?" the doubts have never lasted long enough to propel us out.

With Kathy and Sean it was different. They didn't choose. They were born into it. And they had to learn to roll with the punch.

They had a certain continuity of schools and chums, but any other similarity between their peers' lives and their own has been purely coincidental.

I could be securely resident Mother when they left for school in the morning, and by afternoon a bag would be packed to fly West . . . for three days, a week, a month. Who knew?

Bob's typewriter might be clacking away in his office one day, and the next he'd have it in Philadelphia, doctoring a play . . . or in Las Vegas, organizing "talk" segments for Streisand . . . or in L.A. for a TV Special.

Rarely would we both be away from home at the same time, but if it happened we'd usually pack up the kids, too. The one time we left them behind, both came down with Chicken Pox.

I'd signed to play Cora in "The Dark at the Top of the Stairs" in Puerto Rico, and since we'd never been there before it seemed a jolly idea for Bob to join me, a sort of first honeymoon . . . (without children, that is). We got our friend Grace Davidson to move into the apartment, took off for San Juan, and they burst into the spots as we were over the Atlantic. Grace sprung the news on the first call home. She'd had their doctor in, had them rolled in sheets with cornstarch, and said, "Stay and don't worry!" So Bob stayed on, and they were back to normal when we returned, but the "honeymoon" was not quite as carefree as planned.

Carting them along was less worrisome for us, and often fun for them. When we toured in "They Knew What They Wanted" the summer after we were married, Kathy joined the cast as one of the wedding guests in the second act. She adored it . . . staying up late, all that. She learned to sleep our hours, didn't have to adjust to strange sitters, and became so much a part of the Company it was one of the two times in her life that she considered acting as a career. A large part of the lure seemed to be that paycheck she noticed we got at the end of the week. (Her allowance was pretty meager at age 7.) The second occasion, a brief moment during her first year at

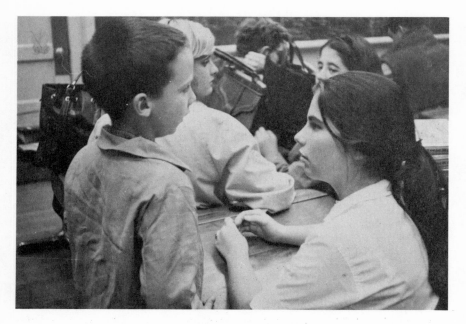

Kathy discussing a problem with Sean at Friend's Seminary

college, had to have been a pure artistic hankering. By then she was well aware it was no profession to choose for economic security.

The first summer of the Apes, Sean travelled up and down the Eastern Seaboard with Bob during the tryout of his musical, "Peg," starring Eartha Kitt. The 13-year-old spent the weeks helping with props backstage, falling in love with Eartha's soul-food cooking, and positively flipping over one of the costume accessories. He wore it constantly, and brought it home at the end of the season . . . a Derby Hat. That year, he, too, was perilously on the verge of becoming a performer . . . à la George M. Cohan. (Bob contributed to his "act" by teaching him a few soft-shoe steps.)

Eyebrows were raised on both occasions . . . small children joining troupes of actors in bars after the show. It was different when they were with me during "Linda Stone Is Brutal" at Olney, Md. The atmosphere was more wholesome . . . lovely country all around, no dens of iniquity within miles. But Sean could still raise an eyebrow or two. Kathy helped out with the ushering those three weeks, and at one performance she escorted our then First Lady, Mrs. Lyndon B. Johnson, to her seat. Sean wangled an introduction during intermission and gave Lady Bird quite a turn by showing off *that* summer's prized possession . . . a large snake he'd caught in the woods.

As small ones, they usually had free run backstage . . . thanks to having learned early that it was verboten to talk during the performance. They also had their own theatre equipment . . . sneakers. Shoes were changed at "half hour," and the clattering of feet wasn't a problem either.

There have been advantages and disadvantages to the life. I'm sure both Kathy and Sean can spin many a tale of woe, being forced to make instantaneous adjustments to the unexpected. On the other hand, they've grown up to take nothing for granted. And in a world that changes with breathtaking speed from day to day, adaptability isn't a bad trait to have. Also, having been jostled so much themselves, they've developed an acute awareness of the jostlings of their fellow men. Insensitive they're not. And the stimulation of frequent exposure to interesting people, places, ideas, and situations . . . just may have had much to do with making them rather interesting people in their own right. Or so I tell myself.

In spite of the gypsy life, though, we've had a permanent home as well. *We* may be on wheels, but it isn't. And it's like any other home. In its fashion. It's just that we never know who's going to be in it. Or for how long. The routine is somewhat variable, too.

Doris Shaw, our part-time housekeeper, works miracles to keep the apartment presentable when we're home, and prevents it from falling apart when we're not. Her "leaders" live together quite amiably when everyone is in residence. But when one or more is out of town, each has different ideas about priorities and organization. Mrs. Shaw manages by keeping loose.

We either adjust or reorganize on our return. I'm rather good about everything except the kitchen. I think of the kitchen as my domain when I'm home. I know exactly where everything is . . . each item has its own nook. When I leave, Emmett gremlins get in there and it's all up for grabs. They seem to be able to find things, but nothing is ever where I can find it. So I do it over after each homecoming . . . "Mum's frustration."

But I muffle all complaints. There have been compensations. It's meant they've all been in there . . . cooking. Which they rarely did when I was home. I was as much the hoverer as my own mother, which didn't inhibit Bob but managed to put a damper on the children's natural inclinations to explore the culinary arts.

Of course, Bob always did most of the daily cooking when I was away . . . they weren't *that* eager to take over the inner sanctum. But my absence made it easier to test their wings when the urge arose, and with no help from me both have turned out to be quite at home in the kitchen.

Doris Shaw . . . works miracles

Kathy has gone on to become a very good cook. Her proficiency started when I was out of town, improved when she had her own digs at college, and since her marriage she's grown positively expert.

Sean started with desserts and then went on to bread, of all things. And when he was much older, left in charge of apartment and dog when both Bob and I had to be away, he got into the other areas . . . roasts, the works.

It was Bob who initiated the exploration of breads. Being from northern California, he's always been fond of *Sourdough French Bread*. When he first came to New York, this town, with all its cosmopolitan air, knew nothing at all about that great legacy from the '49ers. "Whaddya mean *sour*dough, all our bread is fresh, what kinda nut are *you*?"

So Bob set about to make his own. Off and on for years, we've had a culture in a corner of the fridge, and bowls of dough rising in the warm spots of the apartment. He has yet to make it to his satisfaction, but then he's a perfectionist. (And possibly hung up on confused memories of just how sour sourdough should be.) The rest of us non-experts have enjoyed it without reservation.

The whole process intrigued Sean. His first attempt was a recipe he found in the New York Times Cookbook . . . Tea Scones. He made a batch for a party the neighborhood children threw in nearby Bedford Mews. They were so good he went on to bake a car-trunkful for the 1969 Moratorium Peace March . . . and passed them out all over Washington.

After that he graduated to proper bread. Since I know absolutely nothing about baking bread, and am in awe of anyone who does, it was tackled quite freely even when I was home. I dutifully kept my mouth shut and my hands out of the dough. The larder was soon overflowing with an incredible variety of flours, yeast, cornmeal, etc. Some of the loaves were fine, some were like rocks. No matter . . . the good ones were enjoyed . . . and the rocks were chalked up to experience.

One recipe he pilfered from his grandmother's recipe collection . . . a *Banana Bread* that turned out magnificently every time. Since it was so good, and didn't call for yeast, I started making it, too. Another cake-like recipe that became a favorite is from my sister-in-law . . . Tillie Cole's *Rhubarb Coffee Cake*. Tillie's *Spoon Rolls* are the only yeasty items I've dared in the men's realm. They, too, are scrumptious, and the success I've had is tempting me to try the "big time." I'll want Bob or Sean around, though. I'm really quite amenable to having someone else's fingers in my dough when I know I haven't the foggiest what I'm doing!

In Norman Rosten's beautiful portrait of Emily Dickinson, "Come Slowly, Eden."

Most of my out-of-town work is so far away I can't get home until the job is completed. But occasionally it's close enough to Manhattan to commute. Once was to Atlantic Beach, for Williams' "Orpheus Descending" . . . Summer Stock, a week of rehearsal, a week of playing, and hours on the Long Island Railroad.

A longer engagement was the beautiful portrait of Emily Dickinson called "Come Slowly, Eden." For that we rehearsed in the City, and then played three weeks at the Nassau Community College in Garden City. Norman Rosten had been commissioned to write the play for a Dickinson Festival, and did it with love . . . one poet's homage to another. It was a very happy experience. Even the commuting was a joy. We were taken back and forth in style . . . in a limousine.

In the Spring of '68, I was reduced to the Long Island Railroad again . . . for an ambitious 12-week project called "The Long Island Repertory Festival," in Mineola. It wasn't true repertory, like Stratford, but it was an exciting plan and all who joined it had high hopes. It even held the promise of developing into a permanent theatre . . . to service Long Island residents who dreaded the long drive to Manhattan to enjoy a first-rate production. The actors and plays would commute to them instead.

The producers started out very grandly. They chose four plays, to run two weeks each. And to give each production the benefit of four weeks rehearsal, they hired four directors and two complete companies. Arthur Hill and Barbara Bel Geddes headed the first company and opened the season with "Come Back, Little Sheba." I and mine followed with "Eccentricities of a Nightingale." Then Arthur and Barbara, along with Beatrice Straight, in "Light Up The Sky," and we were to close the Festival with "Phèdre."

The first clue that all might not go as rosily as expected came the first day of rehearsal for "Eccentricities." The producers drew me aside and said "Phèdre" would be a slight problem. The production had been geared to the director's personal interpretation, and the director, in their words, had just "flipped out." Would I mind doing Chekhov's "The Three Sisters" instead? They thought they could get Arvin Brown of New Haven's Long Wharf Theatre to direct it.

I allowed as how that would be fine with me if the rest of the Company agreed. It's the most beautiful play, Arvin is a fine director, and did we have a choice?

That settled, we dove into "Eccentricities" with director Edwin Sherin, of "Great White Hope" fame. Arthur and Barbara had been rehearsing two weeks as we started our first . . . and all went quietly for the next two weeks.

Then "Sheba" opened, and rumblings of things to come filtered through their company to ours. The reviews were mixed (not astonishing . . . a new theatre always has an uphill time proving itself and gaining acceptance) . . . the theatre itself was ghastly to play in (that was more alarming) . . . and there weren't exactly lines at the box office. (Our "potential" audience hadn't got our message and was still commuting to the city, apparently.)

We were too busy to worry about all that yet. Problems of our own were developing. "Eccentricities" was Tennessee Williams' rewrite of his own "Summer and Smoke." The characters and locale were somewhat the same, but there were substantial changes from the original play. Many of the differences were exciting and good, but we were finding certain sections very difficult to motivate. We pushed through without changing a syllable, because to a man we deeply respected our playwright . . . but it was rough going.

At last it was our turn in Mineola, and at our first dress rehearsal we understood the first company's rumblings about the theatre.

It obviously had been built for movies, not plays. There were some 15 or 20 feet between the apron and the first row in the orchestra . . . and the rest of the auditorium went back forever. A long, narrow house. Ed Sherin immediately changed as much of the staging as he could, to bring scenes closer to the apron . . . but we still felt miles away from the endless rows of seats.

With all our misgivings, we still weren't prepared for opening night. The audience could hear us, but they got the words in delayed waves of sound. Visually, we must have looked like a movie out of "sync."

From the stage, the audience sounded as if it were under a giant blanket . . . and there were laughs in the play. The sounds that came through were delayed for us as well, so we'd hear muffled laughs long after the joke was uttered and gone. It was an absolutely horrendous evening.

And who was out front but Tennessee himself. Apparently he'd sat close enough to make out most of his play, because he was very pleased. (In spite of the theatre, which he castigated!) It was the second production of the play ever, and the first time he'd seen it. His comment explained a lot. "If I'd known it would be that good, I wouldn't have stopped at the first draft."

Good God . . . our reverence had convinced us that each word had been written in blood, and here we were playing his first draft!

As Alma Winemiller in "The Eccentricities of a Nightingale"

(No offense, Tenn. A first draft of yours is still a lot better than most playwrights' tenth.)

We adjusted to the theatre as best we could during the two weeks. But Arthur and Barbara were right . . . it was ghastly.

And it rather explained the lack of droves at the box office. If it were a question of "long-distance" reception, TV did it better. Still, a play of Williams' had its draw. Business picked up a little.

Not enough, however. Our next bombshell came during "Three Sisters" rehearsal. The producers had run out of money. But they were stuck with the theatre contract. Would we please be darlings and do the final two weeks with no sets or costumes? Just black velvet drapes and rehearsal clothes?

This time I refused to comment. If I said no, I was putting the Company out of work. If I said yes, those who felt the need to rebel would be in contractual hot water. They all finally voted whatthehell. We'd been rehearsing just long enough to suspect we had a performance we'd be loath to see go down the drain. Anyway, who had another job?

They did provide the girls with long black rehearsal skirts . . . and under threat of mayhem, a wig for me. Masha, in my still-short-Ape-haircut? We played the bejesus out of it, and we were right. Arvin had pulled together a fine production that even that impossible theatre couldn't destroy. But it was a depressing finale to what had promised to be so splendid.

Arthur and Barbara and Co. departed the scene with dispatch . . . but those from "Eccentricities" who weren't in "Three Sisters" were still around. So I gave a large party closing night for my entire gang. (And what a gang . . . among others, Patricia Elliott, Ed Flanders, James Broderick, William Hansen, Carol Teitel, Colin Fox . . .)

It was a late party. Most of us had to pack up our makeup kits and get from Mineola to the Village, no short distance. But it was a fine party. I'd made an enormous pot of *Chili* . . . the one great dish for a cast party when I'm a member of the cast. It's even better when cooked ahead and reheated, to allow the flavors time to blend.

It was a night of much-needed good cheer, a bit of raucous hell-raising, and a lot of comfort in each other's embrace. And the *Chili* was hot enough to get the taste of that miserable theatre out of our mouths!

It occurred to me later . . . The director who'd flipped out? Perhaps he was just cannier than the rest of us?

Chili with Beans   *250*

118

When Kim was the only parent around, Kathy saw a lot more of both my worlds. She wasn't the proverbial backstage child, but she'd visit . . . sometimes by choice, sometimes because I couldn't make other arrangements.

The movie set of "Streetcar" may have been one of the most gemütlich of her behind-the-scene adventures. She'd known most of the actors from the N.Y. run of the play, and the film crew embraced her as one of their own, too. She even helped the special effects department make waves for Vivien and Karl's scene on the pier. They allowed her to push the board up and down that rippled the water in the "moonlight." That was pretty exciting, but perhaps not as jazzy as whizzing around the Warner Bros. lot on the handlebars of Marlon's bicycle.

For quieter moments, she had a favorite toy those days . . . Jack Starlight. Jack was a white plastic horse that stood about a foot high. It was an odd toy to "cuddle," and the crew teased her unmercifully. They called the horse an elephant, a kangaroo, a monkey, anything but a horse. "What a handsome squirrel you've got there!"

Kathy took the ribbing as long as she could, and finally exploded, "You're so stupid, you wouldn't know the difference between an actor and a human being!"

I died . . . on the spot. What did she *mean*? Every latent guilt I had re Career vs. Motherhood positively *bloomed*.

She didn't explain what she meant, and I was afraid to ask. Maybe she hadn't meant anything more than there's a difference between acting a part and living a life. She also could have been thoroughly fed up with the way our human lives were always adjusting to the needs of the acting life, instead of the other way round. (I neatly sidestepped any deeper ramifications.)

It's true, of course. The work does call most of the shots. Even to the hours one keeps. It can be as unsettling to the actor-human-beings as to their small-charge-human-beings.

The "hours" bit is particularly jolting to the system. You hear people declaring themselves "Day" people or "Night" people? If an actor jockeys back and forth between the screen and the stage, he has to be either . . . on demand.

If you're making a film, it better not take you long to think "day person." Except for the occasional night shooting, you're required to be bright-eyed and bushy-tailed between 6:30 A.M. and 6:30 P.M. So you darn well go to bed early, or you're not going to make it through the next day.

In fact, Hollywood is so associated in my body with early rising and early retiring, I'm a day person there whether I'm working or not. I've pooped out on many a very good and stimulating party of Bellevernon's before midnight, mad as hell that I simply couldn't keep my eyes open any longer.

Back home in New York, my system does a complete flip-flop. Again, it's association. In a play, you're a night person whether you like it or not. Even the rehearsal period starts later in the day, not till 10 or 11. I live differently in New York, working or no, rarely getting to bed before 1 or 2 A.M.

Actually, I find the theatre schedule much friendlier, so maybe I'm a night person by nature: There's only one sticky disadvantage when I'm in a play. I eat dinner at an hour that suits no other civilized being, so it's usually a solitary affair . . . around 4 or 4:30. But after the show, that's a whole different kettle.

At six, Kathy fell in love backstage with Alan Rich, one of the "prisoners" in "Darkness at Noon."

One of the nicest traditions I know is the after-theatre get-together with friends. A late-night snack, of course, is part of the ritual, and whether you've been on the stage or in the audience, it's a very happy finish to the evening. A restaurant can be the meeting spot, or somebody's home. I really prefer the latter . . . it's less noisy (sometimes), and more relaxed . . . better for kicking off the shoes while mulling and discussing the evening's happening.

Our apartment is a frequent gathering place. If I know in advance, I'll have a supper planned. But usually it's spur-of-the-moment, so I've learned to keep certain basics on hand.

Our standard midnight short-order item is *Chili and Eggs.* Bob introduced me to the combo so I think of it as Californian. Some claim it came from Texas. Whatever the origin, it's quick, easy, and tasty. If I don't have homemade chili ready, a can or two of Gebhardt's Chili with Beans does all right for "store-boughten." Another quick item, somewhat heartier, is spaghetti.

Of course, spaghetti has got me out of many a hole, day *or* night. The times when Sean has come home unexpectedly with a troupe of hungry fellow-musicians (yes, he's gone into that) . . . or when Kathy and David have popped in without warning from New Haven . . . or I've been absent-minded and forgot to defrost the roast. Or once, oh, dear . . . our epicurean dog, Thor, purloined twelve gorgeous Ottomanelli veal cutlets put out to defrost. That was a shocker . . .

The "emergency" pasta can take any of several forms, but our favorite is a simple combination of drained, hot linguine tossed with oodles of melted butter and finely chopped, sautéed garlic. Served with freshly grated Parmesan cheese and a green salad, it's an easy winner.

I have a great recipe for a meat and sausage spaghetti sauce, too, and if I'm lucky there will be a jar in the fridge. But I'm not always clairvoyant. (Damn it, Kathy Emmett, I'm really very human!)

"The People Next Door" . . . later a film . . . was first a CBS Playhouse TV show. And quite a good one. Produced by Herbert Brodkin, written by J. P. Miller, directed by David Greene . . . it had me, Lloyd Bridges, Fritz Weaver, Phyllis Newman, Deborah Winter, Nehemiah Persoff and others in the cast. We rehearsed in New York, and then flew to Hollywood for the taping.

The story concerned the hallucinogenic drug scene . . . the pusher, the user, and the respective families affected by the results. It centered on the "bad trip." A really bad trip . . . the sort that hovers between life and death, and finally ends in the victim being confined to a "controlled environment" for years, possibly for life.

It was a heavy show to rehearse. Our few weeks together verged on group therapy sessions . . . stories of the drug scene, individual brushes with it. As it happened, nearly everyone had been related to some sort of experience . . . personally, or through family or friends . . . except Debbie. And Debbie played the freaked-out girl in the script. Fourteen-year-old Debbie had kicked the cigarette habit at twelve, and was interestingly precocious in other ways, but she was uncompromisingly Puritan in her attitude toward any kind of drug, even liquor or grass. That she was able to play the role so well was a tribute to her considerable talent, and the superb direction she got from David Greene.

The cast was a mixture of Californians and New Yorkers, and among the West Coast contingent were Lloyd and his wife Dorothy . . . old friends I hadn't seen in ages. Bud and I caught up a bit during rehearsals, but there was hardly time to really relax and chat. So after work one day I went with him to his hotel suite for a drink. Dottie was waiting, and we got so immersed in our nattering the dinner hour almost passed us by.

I called Bob to join us uptown for a bite . . . but he had a better idea and we grabbed a cab for the Village.

Bob had found a recipe of Julia Child's . . . Ramequin Forestière . . . and had the ingredients all set out when we arrived.

Starved by this time, the four of us squeezed into the kitchen and set to work. Bud chopped the shallots, Dottie grated the cheese, I chopped the mushrooms, and Bob did the assembling. And though we ran the risk of "too many cooks," the Ramequin turned out just fine.

The drug scene was forgotten for a few hours . . . and we had ourselves a light-hearted evening. Even gained an extra delight. Dottie "laid" a Bridges' recipe on us . . .*Créole Pancakes*.

Passing thought: Good friends getting together is a "turning on" unto itself.

Créole Pancakes   *340*
Ramequin Forestière can be found in the French Chef Cookbook. Julia calls it a cross between a soufflé and a quiche.

With Lloyd Bridges in one of the few gentle moments in "The People Next Door"

"BREAK A LEG"

When I was studying acting as a youngster, Mrs. Camine told me a story about Alice Brady. Before she said her first line on stage . . . opening nights in particular . . . one could hear the stage manager piping a note to give her a low vocal pitch. If he didn't, her voice could rise to a comic falsetto and stay up in the rafters the rest of the performance.   Nerves.

At the time I thought she must have been some kind of nut. She was an established star. Stage fright is for beginners. Right? Ummhmm. At this writing I have had 35 years of stage and film experiences . . . and am as tyrannized now by butterflies-in-the-stomach as on my debut. I've given up hoping it will be any other way.

My voice doesn't go berserk. It may shake, but I can control the pitch. My idiosyncrasies are all my own, and vary from show to show. I'm sometimes alarmingly calm during the day . . . and go into shock as I walk through the stage door. The very worst is when the nerves hide out until the moment I hit the stage. Some warning is easier to handle. The best is when I wake up in the morning in a cold sweat. The odds are that the terrors will run down by curtain-time, enough to avoid the uncontrollable shakes. Like when cigarettes are to be lighted, or papers handled, or tea cups held . . . it is very disconcerting to have hummingbird's wings for hands.

There is one predictable affliction I can, and do, prepare for . . . *every* night, not just opening night. I stash Kleenexes all over . . . on-stage and off, in the wings, everywhere. In films, I keep the makeup department hopping. I sniffle when I'm nervous . . . a lot. A runny nose can be very distracting . . . for the audience as well as for me.

Film-fright has another manifestation. I wake up every hour on the hour the night before "first day," and arrive on the set a bundle of nerves inside, comatose outside.

I'm hardly unique. The only actors I know who aren't plagued by opening night jitters are those who'd rather not be actors at all. Or else they're lying.

Something similar happens in other areas of life as well. Every time I travel, I go with butterfly-fever the first hour. I've forgotten something vitally important . . . I'm on the wrong train . . . the car is going to blow up. I've been flying since I was ten years old. I'm still convinced on take-off that the plane either is not going to get off the ground at all, or it's simply going to *drop* when it does.

And parties. I want them all to be smash hits, naturally. But I work myself into such a lather it's almost as harrowing as a Broadway opening night.

Once the first few guests have arrived, I'm fine. It's before that. Thank God I have Bob. Together we've developed a sort of routine to calm the nerves, and get everything done. It's a sharing of the labor, which tends to equalize the hysteria.   Mine, that is.

Bob copes with four of the basics . . . . the liquor, the flowers, the chandelier, and the salad. I do, or oversee, the rest. And with luck, we're both bathed, dressed, and ready at the appointed hour.

One problem. The cooperative spirit is beautiful and to be cherished. But what happens to joint preparations when the other half isn't there? And you've grown to depend on them for dear life?

It had to happen, of course. We'd promised Nina Fonaroff a large and gala dinner party to celebrate one of those "round figure" birthdays, and at the last minute Gower Champion called Bob to California to write the words for the Julie Andrews-Harry Belafonte TV Special.

I was settling into a nice rigid state of panic as Bob edged out the door bound for the airport. "Just call May and Nina," he said. "Try the word *Help!*"

I was on the phone in five minutes and they both answered, "Right on!"

Just knowing I wouldn't be alone gave me such a leg up, I got through the preliminaries in record time, including the liquor. And the day of the party was a ball. Nina took over the flower arrangements and the salad department . . . May brought the ingredients for the dessert and put it together here . . . I tucked in the loose ends of the apartment (had already said to hell with the chandelier), diddled with the finishing touches to the hors d'oeuvres . . . and had my face on before the first guest arrived.

Joel was one of the earliest and took over the bartending. The evening went smashingly. We all missed Bob, but not for organizational reasons.

My ego might have got a fine boost if I'd managed to bring Nina's bash off alone. I also might have been ready for the loony bin. But parties are to share as well as to give, and if one has understanding and adventurous friends, hallelujah!

I also copped another dessert for our *Collection*. May's fabulous, rich, elegant, *Chocolate Roll*. She taught me to make it . . . later . . . under calmer conditions.

Chocolate Roll   *374*

Like most people, we've had carpenters in to work on the apartment off and on . . . shelves in Bob's office, a cabinet in the bathroom, that sort of thing. The jobs were simple and took no time at all.

Even two semi-structural jobs were finished quickly and painlessly. We've learned to live with all our slanted floors except Sean's bedroom. That one proved to be hazardous. If you opened more than one drawer in his bureau at a time, the whole thing would topple over. So we had a false floor installed, the only level floor in the apartment. It took a day and a half.

The other was a false wall designed to cover one side of the living room. It gives a unity to the totally unrelated front door, window, and double glass doors, hides a bunch of crazy pipes, and the rest of the space provides us with ceiling-to-floor bookshelves. Our local cabinetmaker, Jaime Mora, constructed it in sections in his shop, and bolted everything to the wall in one day. It took us another day to paint it.

We'd gradually improved the comfort and attractiveness of the apartment, and were troubled practically not at all in the process. We shook in our boots every three years when it was repainting time . . . but remodeling? A cinch.

Our innocence was about to be shattered. It occurred to us to do something about the kitchen.

The fridge was great, but the rest was driving me up a wall. The stove, particularly. I'd got used to it, sort of, and had learned how to fiddle with the oven flame to get an approximate temperature. But one year the oven exploded, and even though it was pushed back together, the guessing game wasn't fun anymore. And I longed for a dishwasher. And the walls were so uneven, we all kept losing things behind the cabinets. And . . . oh hell, it was a dreadful kitchen.

A new stove was the most important, but it seemed a shame to put one in next to such a conglomeration of tackiness. So in January, 1970, when the time, money, circumstances, and permission from the landlord miraculously came together at once, we made the big decision to throw everything out except the fridge and start from scratch. Remodel . . . completely.

We were blissfully ignorant of the enormity of the chaos ahead of us.

Actually, the planning stage was fun at first. I joyously started making lists and trial sketches. Since we were going whole hog, I

. . . it was a dreadful kitchen —

at breakfast
with Sean in
the old one

wanted the kitchen to be as close to my "ideal" as this apartment
would allow. And that meant a two-oven stove, dishwasher, washing
machine, dryer, plenty of storage space, plenty of counter space,
stainless steel sink, butcher block for chopping, and so forth. (I also
made a list of smaller items to complete the dream . . . KitchenAid
mixer, Hobart coffee mill, ample spice shelves, apothecary jars, knife
rack, etc.)

It also meant figuring out where everything went so the kitchen
would be a pleasure to work in. The fridge, stove, and sink forming
points of a triangle . . . dishwasher to the left of the sink (for
me) . . . pot storage near the stove . . .

As I got past the what's and deeper into the where's and how's,
I began to wish the "money" had included an architect or decorator.
I wheeled all over town checking out model kitchens, appliance
showrooms, picking up brochures and catalogues, talking to friends
and strangers, getting pointers, recommendations, plowing through
all the ideas and material. And spent hours at the drawing
board . . . drafting, measuring, rearranging.

Dozens of sketches were discarded, until finally I had a working
plan I was happy with. It meant knocking out part of a wall and
losing our cozy breakfast table, but the extra nine feet of wall were
necessary to get everything in where I wanted it.

At last it was time to interview contractors. Our first big jolt.
Half of them wanted an arm and a leg before we even started. The
other half were livid that I had the temerity to figure out what I

wanted before they got there. It was a battle of wits and purses until we finally managed to join the plan with a contractor and set a date.

The appliances, cabinets, and equipment I'd selected were ordered, and everything was gradually delivered and stacked in the living room. The logistical problem of temporary storage was impossible to solve, and we didn't. We lived with an obstacle course that baffled even Thor.

Finally the date (March something) arrived, and the contractor arrived. The TW3 fridge was squeezed into the living room stockpile, and everything else in the kitchen was scrapped. The work began.

And three days later the contractor disappeared. His workmen as well. Cheerily at work one day. The next, vanished. Never heard of again. (He left behind a stepladder, and a cancelled check for initial expenses.   A $200 stepladder.)

And two days later, Bob skipped town. The "right" circumstances of January had disappeared by March, of course. He'd been writing the script for "Carol Channing with Her Ten Stout-Hearted Men" . . . the show to be Carol's London debut. And he and the entire company went on the road for the six-week pre-London tryout . . . Rochester, Toronto, and Baltimore.

There we were . . . Sean, Thor, and I. Hemmed in by a gigantic pile of boxes, appliances, and God-knows-what in the living room, facing a great gaping hole at the other end of the apartment, and no working kitchen facilities. I stared in wonder and was immobilized. My ship was sinking and I couldn't think of a thing to do about it.

The next day the phone rang. It was comedienne Evelyn Russell, wife of Joe Layton who was directing Carol's show. All I could think was — how nice, I'll go down laughing. And instead . . . dear Bob had reported my woes, and Evie was calling to set me onto a chap who'd done some great work for her . . . Bill Casey.

I laughed, cried, and got Casey on the phone that night. A week later he arrived to assess my disaster area.

As he looked it over he groaned. I *thought* some of the things the first chap had done looked a little peculiar. But what did I know? According to Casey, throwing away the old kitchen was the only thing he'd done right.

Casey ripped everything out and got the place down to an absolute shell. He checked my plan and approved it, with a few minor alterations, suggestions, and additions. And went to work with his crew.

The fridge was plugged in, I cooked on a one-burner hotplate, washed dishes in the bathtub, and with the toaster, electric coffee pot, and a sense of humor, Sean and I managed to survive.

It also helped to have a Village landmark, The Blue Mill Tavern, practically next door. We escaped to that haven for cheer and good food a lot.

With Casey at the helm, it was clear sailing from then on. For him. It was thoroughly confusing for me . . . his time-table was in his head, and all I saw was the never-ending mess. It took weeks (and then more weeks to get the plaster dust out of the apartment). But the kitchen was finally finished, and was gorgeous. And now it's such a joy to work in that, as with babies, the pangs of the birthing are almost forgotten.

Almost. Bob has long had an eye to remodeling the bathroom . . . completely. Please, God, let me be the one out of town for that?

Oh, yes, besides being my guardian angel and lifesaver, Casey gave me a recipe. *Shrimp Omelets*, a favorite hors d'oeuvre of his. In his words, "It's a gas!" (He meant "great," which it is, not gaseous, which it isn't.)

Shrimp Omelets   *210*

Hélène Stewart

The new kitchen. Oh joy!

Bob was not only the writer on Carol's show, he ended up performing in it as well. They lost one of their ten stout-hearted chaps in Toronto, and Joe Layton talked Bob into dusting off his dancing shoes and taking over until a replacement could be found. While the "swing man" (general understudy) substituted, Bob learned the routines. He played his first performance in Baltimore, opened in London, and stayed with the show four weeks before the replacement went in.

Well, my plan to see them in Baltimore was scrapped pronto. Naturally I chose to fly to London instead! It was a gala, exciting, gorgeously successful opening at the Drury Lane Theatre, and we had a *smashin' fortnit* together.

It was a dream fulfilled for both of us, to be back in London. Much of Bob's Naval duty during WWII had been based in England. As Communications Officer on an LST he was mightily occupied with D-Day and the invasion of France, but there was liberty, too. And every chance he had, he got up to London. He, too, had fallen in love with that marvel of a city.

We had a wondrously exciting time rediscovering it together . . . retracing old haunts, exploring new places, doing all the tourist things we'd missed the first time, traveling bus and tube routes in all directions . . . For two weeks it was OUR CITY, and we savored every moment.

The middle weekend we made a pilgrimage to Ireland. We flew to Dublin after the Saturday night performance, and next morning rented a car to drive around the Emerald Isle, South and West, as far as the tip of the Dingle Peninsula, and caught a flight out of Shannon just in time to get Bob back to London for the Monday night performance.

We spent Sunday night in Cork, at the Victoria Hotel. That dinner was our one leisurely meal, and we asked the waitress to suggest something truly Irish. She gave us a blank stare, checked the menu, and finally pointed to . . . would you believe? Maryland Fried Chicken. The rest of Ireland was very Irish . . . and beautiful.

(We didn't attempt to get up to County Mayo to drop in on the McMenamins. Bob's brother George had done that some years before, and his tales of being showered with nonstop conviviality and liquid refreshment made the prospect a dangerous side-trip for one with a "show" deadline.)

130

I came home at the end of two weeks, and yanked Sean out of school to fly over and spend the last two weeks with his father. Our son saw and explored London for the first time . . . and flipped. What is it about that city?

Before I left I looked up Elizabeth David's shop off King's Road. I knew her fine cookbooks, and the visit was a must, but it was also an exercise in frustration. All that divine cooking equipment, and I wanted everything I saw. It was enough to consider expatriation.

I did bring one thing back . . . a French steamer for fish. The clerk packed it tidily, but I wasn't about to trust the airline baggage personnel with the precious cargo. The box sat on my lap the entire flight home.

It was one of the happiest purchases I've ever made. Bob loves seafood, but he's never gone into ecstasies over ordinary fish. Until the steamer. Whatever effect it has on a fish, it's been responsible for his becoming positively a fishophile. Good show!

The fish steamer, at home on the range.

BACK TO NATURE

Sean had a great summer in '70. He drove to Vancouver, B.C., with a couple of friends, and then by various means of transportation, including foot, found his way out to the very northwesterly tip of Vancouver Island. It was a communal six weeks in absolute isolation . . . a "family" of ten adults and teenagers, and one baby (called Baby) . . . living the Call of the Wild.

They built shelter and fires with driftwood . . . protected themselves from the weather with plastic tarps . . . ignored clothing when the temperature allowed . . . and, except for a salmon contributed by some friendly passing fishermen, ate an all-natural, all-vegetarian diet.

The freedom and closeness to Nature got into Sean's city-bred bones, and he's never been quite the same since. His room changed first. Down came the scavenged street memorabilia and up went posters of woods and country, sea and animals.

Vegetarianism followed. He returned from the summer convinced his body felt much better without meat. Finally, in December, he decided to give it another try. And for the year and a half following, was a moderate vegetarian. He would eat fish, eggs, and milk, but no meat or fowl.

It was a whopping challenge for me . . . setting the table for two cuisines . . . but I got used to it and learned a lot about amino acids and all sorts of things in the bargain. With the help of Frances Moore Lappé's "Diet for a Small Planet" and a neighbor, Lois Seibel, I gradually accumulated a backlog of recipes high in protein and vitamins. Our shelves began to take on the look of a health food store . . . bags and boxes of all kinds of beans, grains, sprouts, cereals, nuts, seeds . . . ad infinitum.

I also found it was wise to cook in quantity. Surprising how many young vegetarians showed up around dinner-time those days.

Sean finally dropped it all out of self-preservation. In the Spring of '72, he had a job with a country-rock band in Tampa, Florida. Tampa hadn't got "the word," or Sean couldn't find the source. He went back to a conventional diet to survive.

But while it was still very much a part of his life, Bob and I would frequently go "vegetarian," too . . . with some of the new concoctions, and a lot of old favorites. Like lentils, and eggplant dishes. And the habit has continued. It's even increasing, as meat prices continue to soar. We're getting fonder and fonder of meatless days these days.

The Seibels: Lois, Ben, Jeff, and Eric (later Lois' Vegetarian)

On the set of "Escape from the Planet of the Apes" — Director Don Taylor, myself the chimp, and Bob.

With two children of my own, and a long parade of theatrical children of all sexes, ages, shapes, and sizes . . . Motherhood has become a familiar role. But I hardly dreamed I'd ever be playing Mother to a chimpanzee. A real live chimpanzee . . . in "Escape from the Planet of the Apes." No John Chambers creation, this baby.

In the story, Milo was a newborn infant. In life he was six months old, just off the boat from the wilds of Africa . . . with very large teeth he was well-prepared to use.

A "stand-in" Dr. Zira, complete in my makeup and costume, spent days with the chimp and his trainer, Jerry Campanilli, to get the babe used to the smells and strange look of "evolved" apedom. Their first contact was not too satisfactory. Milo bit her. In a very vulnerable area. The wardrobe department hastily constructed a large plastic breastplate to wear under the costume for future protection. Jerry also draped Milo in Pampers to eliminate possible mishaps from the other end. And finally we were introduced.

Our first meeting was fraught with trepidation. It took about an hour (and a great deal of sweet-talk) to get him to leave Jerry's arms for mine without his baring great menacing teeth. That step accomplished, we were on our own. Flung into our first scene together. No time for palsy-walsies on Company time.

In the shot, I was to carry Milo in my arms and run frantically through a derelict ship (moored in San Pedro Harbour) searching for Cornelius. "Action!"

I dutifully ran, promptly tripped over a mess of lighting cables, and went sprawling onto the deck. A sixth sense told me this was no way to begin a meaningful relationship with my "child." Instead of trying to brace my fall, my arms automatically went up to keep Milo from hitting the deck, too . . . a saving gesture he didn't immediately appreciate. I not only got a close and ominous view of every tooth in his mouth, he voiced his displeasure and terror in unmistakably rude tones.

Jerry dashed to the rescue, quite sure he was going to tear me to shreds. And with a bravado born of ignorance, I pushed her aside. I didn't know much about chimpanzees, but I knew if we didn't make friends again fast, we were in deep trouble. I hung on and played comforting "Mum" for dear life until his lips finally relaxed and those lethal ivories retreated. *Then* I gave Milo to Jerry.

It took me a great deal longer to stop shaking. And I discovered all sorts of interesting bruises . . . later. But as soon as I could stand without my knees buckling under, we had another go at the scene (the offending cables cleared away) and all went well, thank God. "Print!"

We had one more tense moment the same day. Again, a complicated running sequence through the ship, under huge, low pipes and over jagged, rusty debris . . . and, though cables weren't in the way, my sense of balance in that hobble skirt was sorely tried. I tripped again, this time over my out-sized ape feet, but caught myself in the nick and didn't sprawl. Milo was jolted considerably, gave me a startled look, and then relaxed. He didn't even bare one tooth. Trust, and the beginning of our love affair was underway. I was obviously some sort of nut come into his life, but harmless.

Except for the latent threat of those teeth, he was just like any human baby . . . affectionate, curious, playful. He'd get testy when overly tired or bored. Or fly into a tantrum when denied something he desperately wanted. But generally he was amenable and charming. And a natural-born actor. However bored he might be off-camera, he was immediately alert and "into it" when the camera was rolling. Only once did he hold up the shooting.

There was a sequence with a lot of circus animals . . . big cats, bears, smaller cats, and a baby elephant. Everyone was caged except the elephant. And Milo was terrified of the elephant. Every time it crossed his vision he'd cry out in panic, frantically free his arms from his blanket and cling to my neck for dear life. Don Taylor, our director, finally had to settle for positioning the elephant so Milo couldn't possibly see it, even if it meant the camera couldn't either.

The making of that third (and for me, last) Ape film was fascinating, but in one respect, very disconcerting. And for insight into human behavior, quite as enlightening as the first, for a slightly different reason.

In the first two of the series, the apes were in the majority. We may have seemed strange to the outside world, but we were familiar and friendly beings among each other.

In the third . . . except for the brief opening sequences when Sal Mineo was with us . . . Roddy McDowall and I were the only simians. All the rest of the cast was human. We were unmistakably the outsiders . . . the odd couple.

Oh, we were treated politely and gently, and there was much of the easy banter and humor that permeates a happy company, and ours was that, but the strain people feel in trying consciously to communicate "unselfconsciously" with the peculiar was always present. We were *different* . . . and vaguely repulsive to human sensibilities.

John Randolph (Chairman of the President's Commission in the film) finally verbalized it. Johnny and I have been friends for 20 years and I had to know if I was being paranoid. He tried to explain, the uneasy look in his eyes belying his jolly laughter: "Kim, I know

in my *mind* that behind all that foam rubber it's you, but the makeup is so damn realistic I feel as if I'm talking to a creature from outer space. It's downright uncomfortable . . . and dammit, *disturbing.*"

The only people who ever saw us out of makeup were the makeup artists. This time I had Jack Barron, who probably is one of my oldest friends in the business. Jack was an apprentice in the makeup department at RKO when I made my first film, "The Seventh Victim." He's made me up innumerable times since as a person, but he was also an old hand at apes, very involved in the important lab work for the first of the series.

Jack was there to keep my psyche in working order, thank God. When the feeling of social outcast grew too devastating, he would hold my hand and give Kim as well as Zira a renewed sense of self.

He gave me a recipe, too, of course. It came out of the blue as he was gluing on an ear . . . a rather jazzy sandwich he called a *Stuffed French Roll.* His words were simply, "Try it, it's good." I did and it is. Thank you, Jack Barron, for all manner of kind sustenance.

Incidentally, Milo and I met again some six months after the film was completed. 20th Century-Fox Publicity arranged for Roddy, Milo, and me to be on the Tonight Show . . . our little family, without makeup . . . a promotional stint prior to the movie's release.

Jerry brought Milo to New York and I spent an hour or two in their hotel room to get reacquainted before taping the show. No longer a cuddly infant, he'd grown into a very large bundle of chimp, as heavy as a human three-year-old.

Would he remember me? Particularly without the distinctive smells of the ape makeup?

The first moments of our reunion were very disappointing, and saddening. No question about it . . . he was unfriendly and suspicious. I kept talking to him anyway, through the bars of his cage, wondering how I was going to manage during the show. Through some incredible oversight, the breastplate had been left behind. But slowly he calmed down enough for Jerry to risk letting him out . . . tentatively, on leash. The moment was tense, and my hopes had slimmed to zero. He looked at me curiously. I said a few words. He slowly walked toward me. I said a few more words. And then suddenly he leaped onto the bed, squeezed his little rump close to mine, and gently leaned his head on my arm. I melted and damn near cried.

I carried him onto the stage that night to meet Johnny Carson, sagging under the weight, but grinning from ear to ear . . . the proudest Mother in captivity.

Stuffed French Rolls 348

Bob introduced me to Beef Jerky in '52, the summer after we were married.

"Two on the Aisle" had closed in New York, and we had a ten-week tour of "They Knew What They Wanted" coming up. Squashed in-between were three weeks of free time for our new family. We flew to Bob's California.

The welcome holiday ended with our camping out in Yosemite National Park, but first we went to Monterey . . . to visit the old homestead. For Kathy and me it was meeting Bob's family for the first time . . . all those McMenamins. My God, there were a lot of them, and if I was trepidacious, which I was, I needn't have been. With one large enveloping embrace, they brought the two of us into the clan as if we'd always been there.

We met them all . . . from father and mother, Emmet and Agnes, and Bob's brothers, George and Emmet, Jr. . . . to the raft of uncles, aunts, cousins, nieces, nephews. The name of McMenamin was pretty well known in Monterey. With that many around they'd be hard to miss, but they were also fairly involved in the life of the community.

The most prominent was Emmet, Sr., hailed wherever he went as "Mr. Mac." He had been Mayor of Monterey for years, and for many more years, County Clerk and Recorder in Salinas. (He finally retired . . . at 86!) He thoroughly enjoyed public life and had all the qualifications . . . gregariousness, humor, conviviality . . . and one quality not always found in politicians. He was unimpeachably honest. An able public servant, incorruptible, and beloved . . . a combination hard to beat. The few souls who dared to challenge his tenure from time to time were unceremoniously left at the post.

Besides getting acquainted with a bevy of new relatives, it was also the first look we'd had at that section of the California coast between Monterey Bay and Big Sur. I continue to be overwhelmed by its spectacular beauties each time I go out, but that first visit was awe-inspiring. Of course, Bob, being on a nostalgia binge, gave us the grandest of all Grand Tours.

We also ate . . . a lot. All the delights Bob had grown up with . . . the chiles rellenos, empanadas, Marge McMenamin's enchiladas, and chicken cacciatore at the great Italian restaurant, Cademartori's. We feasted our way through all the Mexican, Spanish and Italian specialties of the area, till I began to think of the Irish as Latins.

Beef Jerky was a new experience. The McMenamin brothers had doted on it as children, and it was one of the first things Bob had Kathy and me try. We quickly joined the long line of addicts. I'm told we have the American Indians to thank for this treat. Some resourceful tribesman on K.P. invented it as a way of preserving deer and buffalo meat.

For years the sale of Jerky was confined to the West, but I believe it can be bought almost anyplace now. No matter. In the spring of '71 the wardrobe man on "Gunsmoke," Jack Stone gave me a recipe for making it at home. Now I periodically relinquish the top oven of my new stove for three days to keep the supply of *Beef Jerky* coming in.

It's recommended as a snack when you're on a protein diet. It's a lightweight and nourishing CARE package to mail off to any of your tribesmen away at camp or college. It's also heaven just for the hell of it.

Beef Jerky   *350*

Golden Wedding Day for Emmet and Agnes McMenamin (between them, Agnes' sister Anne)

My mother died three weeks short of her 87th birthday, in 1971. She'd been incredibly healthy most of her life, and the last illness was brief. A blessing for her, but I was far from prepared. In spite of her ripe age, it never penetrated my mind that there would ever be a time when she wouldn't be here. Logic is not one of my fortes. But independence was one of hers. I think she just decided it was time, and let it happen.

Independence was characteristic of her cooking, too. She had a small collection of cookbooks . . . The Joy of Cooking (early edition), Fanny Farmer's Boston Cooking School Cookbook (1929 edition), one or two others, and her own 3½- by 5½-inch black leather looseleaf notebook. (The latter housed hundreds of recipes she'd copied from family and friends.) I rarely saw her refer to *any* of the books.

She'd learned and perfected all the basics, developed a few unbeatable specialties, and that was it. Her cooking was superb, and her table was always set with great style and care. Our meals were never dull or lacking in variety, but the exotic, the flamboyant, was not her thing. They were old-fashioned *good* . . . pleasurable to the eye and to the palate.

Her secret was simple. She used only the very best ingredients, she treated all foods with great respect, and she paid strict attention to their natural qualities. Her meats were tender, moist, pure in flavor. Vegetables were *au naturel* and crisp tender . . . (she had a horror of serving mushy vegetables). She rarely fried anything, and nothing was ever greasy. In fact, there was a glowing aura of health to every meal she served . . . in spite of a wicked leaning toward delectable desserts.

She wasn't against trying a new recipe now and then, but she seemed much more interested in perfecting to the *nth* what she already knew. And for that she didn't need recipes, it was all in her head.

I'm interested in improving old favorites, too, but our similarity ends there. I'm positively addicted to trying new dishes, and desperately need recipes. Oh, I improvise a lot, and know enough about most of the basics to survive. But for me to prepare almost any recipe in this book, for instance, I need the formula in front of me to do it. And it's my book!

Some of that dependence is due to the catch-as-catch-can life I lead in the kitchen. A lot of time can go by between repeating

**Mother at Grand
Lake, Michigan**

recipes. And the number I want to repeat keeps growing. I'm so spread out, I simply forget.

Of course, when Mother's little black notebook entered my life, I was quite willing to compound my faults and spread out even further. I eagerly set about to test each and every recipe.

Well. I was able to add a handful of gems to my own collection. But for the rest, she'd obviously copied recipes the way she cooked. One after another was either in a personal code I couldn't decipher, or in fragments, just the few notes she needed to complete what was in her head.

I gave up on most, but one continues to tantalize me. Mrs. Barry's Horn Rolls. She was Govie's pastry chef at Grand Lake Hotel, and her rolls were fantastic. Mother's copy of her recipe reads: "Heaping tablespoon lard to a cup of water, ½ cup sugar, 1 t. salt, 1 egg, then 2 yeast cakes dissolved in this mixture." Period.

Not one word about flour. Perhaps someone with an intimate knowledge of bread-making could figure out how much, a method for putting it all together, baking temperature and time, etc. . . . but with my dependence on a recipe, I can only flap about in pure frustration. Those rolls were so good I can taste them.

Mother's little black book yielded few decipherable recipes, but it was responsible for improving our lives in the kitchen nonetheless. Her collection wasn't exactly neat . . . it positively bulged with pages straining against several rubber bands . . . but by golly, it was all together.

The same could hardly be said for my chaotic collection. Loose recipes were floating about in drawers, boxes, folders, cookbooks, any odd place they happened to be stuffed. And unlike Mother, we *cooked* by them . . . not just me, but Bob and Sean as well.

Mother's little book sparked an overdue determination to correct this muddled state of confusion. It was no easy job rounding up all the bits and pieces, the file cards, scraps of paper, pages from letters, backs of envelopes, tattered sheets of foolscap, etc., etc. Sorting them was worse. And the typing-up was positively formidable, since I set about clarifying directions along the way, and also adding published recipes we repeated often enough to warrant inclusion. All this between acting jobs and the normal household routine. It took months.

But at last everything was together in one very *large* looseleaf notebook. For a moment, anyway. Since the *Collection* keeps growing, and the original impetus eventually flagged, I have a hard time keeping it up-to-date. But I do manage to stash the new recipes in one place now . . . an appreciated improvement.

Of course, when we were able to take a good look at what we had, we saw what was missing. Marge's recipe for *Enchiladas*, Mabel's *Chiles Rellenos*, Belle's *Cold Poached Salmon*, etc. So letters went off to the appropriate sources.

All that typing didn't do much for my cooking. But the lapse was temporary, and worth the results. The banshee yells of frustration in the face of mislaid recipes are a thing of the past.

I was also rather pleased with the way I put the notebook together, and recommend it highly. I have a plastic cookbook holder which I find invaluable . . . *except* when a recipe isn't complete on the opened pages of the book. If one is up to one's elbows in chopped parsley it's messy and inconvenient to have to pull the book out to turn a page. At the risk of paper profligacy, I made sure none of my recipes require page-turning. Can't tell you how many expletives it saves.

MY COLLECTION in its basic form

One of my request letters brought a bonanza of brand new recipes from my sister-in-law, Tillie Cole. It also got me away from the typewriter and back to the kitchen. I went on a grand cooking spree, trying them all, and some of our favorites are included here. Tillie is a whiz at baking, but she's a super cook in other areas as well. We seldom have an opportunity to eat at her table, though. She and my brother Gordon live in Wisconsin, not exactly commuting distance.

In fact, Gordon and I haven't lived anywhere near each other since childhood. My childhood, that is. He's 8½ years older than I, so the family's physical togetherness began to dissipate when I was ten. He had his own life to lead.

He'd learned to fly when he was 15, and aviation became his career. He went from Air Shows, racing and stunting, to testing bombers at Willow Run during WWII, and eventually "settled down" as an airline's captain. He's been based in many cities in the country, but never Miami, Los Angeles, or New York.

For years I'd say we lived a sort of loving antagonism. The age difference meant that in childhood I'd never been much of an asset to him, and Daddy's death when I was three meant Gordon was saddled with the old cliché . . . "You're the man of the family now" . . . a role he played to the hilt without much applause from me.

We managed to outgrow all that. But, after Gordon left home, it was primarily through Mother's letter-writing that we knew what the other was up to. Even our occasional visits centered around her. However, we sneaked into a relationship of our own eventually, independent of Mother, and near the time of her death it finally flowered.

We now correspond with astonishing regularity, and even arrange visits from time to time. If not in Green Bay or New York . . . in Atlanta, Detroit, wherever I might turn up "on the road." Growing up has its advantages.

As the bibulous Catherine in "And Miss Reardon Drinks A Little"

Dame Sybil Thorndike once admonished the membership of an Actors' Equity meeting with: "Get out into the provinces, dears! *That's* where Theatre is going to be kept alive . . . not on Broadway!"

I took her advice in 1971. I hope it contributed in some small way to the life of the Theatre. It shot my personal life to hell.

The offer was very seductive. A marvelous role, "Catherine"; in a fascinating play, Paul Zindel's "And Miss Reardon Drinks a Little"; Julie Harris playing her original "Anna"; the original director, Mel Bernhardt; major cities only and no "split weeks"; at most 5 months out, a shortie as such tours go. All elements seemed ideal.

But I'd never been on a *National Tour* before. I'd been on Summer Package Tours, with my family in tow. And there'd been pre-Broadway tryouts, without the family . . . short tours, five weeks at the outside, with the days busy in rehearsal. Our longest separations had been for films, and with the 12-hour work days of movie-making, one's too tired to be bugged by homesickness.

A National Tour turned out to be eight performances a week, a little over three hours in the theatre for each. That's a total of 24 hours. Add time for publicity appearances and sleeping, and you're "on the loose" approximately 85 hours a week, or 1600 hours in five months. In the "provinces." Miles away from your home and your family.

Naturally, we snatched what moments together we could. Bob and Sean came to Baltimore to see the show, I flew home from Detroit one Sunday, Bob flew to Pittsburgh, and the management gave us a week home at Christmas. But for the rest of the tour I was a displaced person and homesick as an old cat.

Fortunately, there *were* compensations. I'd been right about the part, the play, and the production. All first rate . . . a dream. And we did smashing business. Full houses, SRO, all that. It was also one of the most compatible companies I've ever played with . . . onstage and off. We enjoyed each other a lot. Thank God. (There's a rumor it's never otherwise when Julie is in a cast.)

That easy camaraderie is precious, even on a short tour. A long tour must be hell without it. A theatrical troupe spends a great deal of time together. There's the work, of course. But being outsiders wherever we go is a rather natural binding factor.

We get to know the cities we play in, to a certain extent . . . we find the art galleries, the museums, the best restaurants (the best for inexpensive meals), the zoos and parks, and almost all the special attractions any city has to offer . . . and we go in our own groups. Everyone is uprooted from home and *The Company* becomes a substitute family.

Not that the residents aren't often generous with their time, attention, and efforts to make us feel "at home." And it's warmly appreciated. But we're never in one place long enough to get to know anyone very well.

(Of course, there are the others who invite us to gatherings for "window dressing" . . . this week's social diversion. It's not as friendly being a "prop", but it helps keep interest in the theatre alive . . . so we accept it, live with it, sometimes enjoy it, and call it the nature of the beast. And find our relaxed moments with each other.)

Hotel living month after month can be very depressing, so several of us took advantage of our two longest stands, Detroit and Hollywood, to rent apartments. (I was luckier than the rest in Hollywood, I had the Shapiros, a welcome touch of home.)

Courtesy of Producing Managers Company, Inc.

The touring "Reardon" sisters — me, Julie Harris and DeAnn Mears

148

An apartment also meant being able to do our own cooking, which opened the door to one of the jolliest of our tour activities.

We were particularly active in the kitchen in Detroit, perhaps because the theatre management had thoroughly intimidated us about exploring the town.

"Never go out after 4 P.M. except in groups of three or more."

"At night, stay on well-lighted, main streets only."

"Don't ever wander alone, even at high noon."

Very nervous people, the Detroiters. It proved to be an oppressive five weeks . . . and except for an afternoon at the Detroit Symphony, and a number of visits to their superb Arts Institute, there wasn't much to lure us outside our own apartments.

I started the "cook-ins" our first night off, and prepared dinner for the 16 of us . . . cast, crew, and managers. A glorified picnic. Chili, fried chicken, sliced tomatoes, garlic bread, rice, and a salad of beautiful greens from Detroit's famed Broadway Market. The Broadway was also the source for the dessert, May Katz's rather special fruit compote. There was lots of good, friendly wine, and though it wasn't "21", it was cheering.

Cooking on the road is a challenge. I had a good stove, small but functional, a fridge that worked, and a delightful extra . . . a garbage disposal in the sink. But equipment? My first call for help was simply a coffee pot. For the rest, I had to buy what I couldn't cajole the porter into stealing from the vacant apartments in the building. (Mine had neither a sharp knife nor a pot with a lid when I arrived.) To cook for 16 seemed hopeless until I talked to the manager and discovered he had an inoperative restaurant on the ground floor. He turned me loose in the huge kitchen, and I came up with enough equipment to cope. (Most everything was geared to serving 50 people. Ever try to fit a professional pot on an efficiency stove?)

Anyway, that evening launched a series of parties that went the rounds of the company . . . each one outdoing the next with personal specialties.

My second was "commissioned." Julie and I had appeared together on a local television program, and one of the producers was an amateur organic farmer. As a gag, we were presented with three giant zucchini in a bouquet. Each must have been more than 16 inches long and 4 inches in diameter. (The gift was an "in" joke related to Julie's character in the play . . . a vegetarian kook.) We brought them to the theatre . . . everyone had his laugh . . . and I was left holding the zucchini.

Suggestions were abundant, such as "Better stuff them. You're apt to find a lot of pith in the middle." And Heinz Howenwald, our stage manager, promised to provide hors d'oeuvres and salad for the

A get-together with
the ushers of the
Mechanic Theatre,
Baltimore

occasion. There was no question who'd been elected to wrestle with the outsized zucchini.

I accepted the assignment with misgivings. It was a freewheeling improvisation, but miraculously they turned out rather well. In fact back in New York, I refined the original guesswork and added the recipes to our collection. For normal zucchini, needless to say. One stuffed for meat-eaters, one for vegetarians, and a really good tomato sauce.

When we got to Hollywood, we were treated to a professional feast, thanks to Heinz and our company manager, Bob Hulter. It was Thanksgiving week, and they threw the jazziest party of the tour in a private suite of the Hollywood Brown Derby across the street from our theatre, the Huntington Hartford. A roaring fire in the fireplace, cheering drinks, and a superb dinner. The restaurant staff brought the food to a buffet table and Heinz and Bob took over the serving. It was a warm and pleasant celebration for us homeless folk.

And shortly before we left for Christmas week at home, our property master Al Tins gave a Glögg party. His wife Lillie was with him most of the tour, a lovely lady of Swedish descent, and her *Glögg* was potable heaven.

Al Tins was my alter-ego backstage. The play opened with a bare dining table and closed with a bare dining table, and during the three acts a complete meal was served and consumed. "Catherine" was the cooking as well as the drinking sister. My hands were full, and so were Al's. He lined up most of the dinner for me to carry on stage, but the dessert, a mixed fruit "frappé", was prepared and popped into a blender in full view of the audience. Al worked hard

150

to buy fruit easy to handle, but Nature wasn't always with us. The script called for kiwis, and the kiwi season didn't last the run, apples and pears were frequently like rocks, and the bananas . . . ah yes, the bananas. Many a banana got laughs Zindel hadn't intended. One's skin was so tough I finally had to extricate the fruit through the side. Like a letter from an envelope. I didn't have a fingernail left at the end of the run.

After Christmas we went to the Royal Alexandra Theatre in Toronto, for three weeks. It was January and freezing and I didn't look forward to food shopping on foot, so settled into a hotel again and spent the offstage hours knitting an Icelandic poncho. Julie, an expert knitter, had finally seduced me into trying my hand. It helped . . . to keep the mind numbed until the glorious day arrived to fly HOME. Julie and I, that is. The rest of the company went on to Chicago with our replacements.

"Reardon" was my first National Tour, and was probably my last, unless Bob should ever see his way clear to write in odd hotel rooms across the country.

Sorry about that, Dame Sybil. I'm all for keeping Theatre alive and kicking, but you're obviously more of a gypsy than I.

Stuffed Zucchini	*254*
Stuffed Zucchini — Vegetarian Style	*255*
Tomato Sauce	*327*
Swedish Glögg	*199*

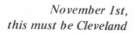

November 1st,
this must be Cleveland

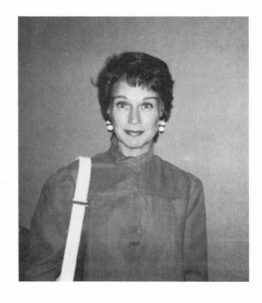

151

It was most curious, returning to Detroit after so many years' absence.

Our Company's being greeted with such stern "safety regulations" wasn't too surprising. As it turned out, almost every city we played "welcomed" us with its own brand of hysteria. New York must be the only city that doesn't. Of course, our visitors arrive already convinced that death and mugging stalk the streets day and night. (It's not true, but try to convince a non-New Yorker.)

Detroit certainly showed its tensions the most. I never got used to the sense of strain . . . walking in the downtown area near my apartment, never meeting a smiling face. If eyes met at all, they said, "Mind your own business, man." Everyone seemed uptight, unhappy, and walled-off. New York is "Fun City" for true, in comparison.

With neither family nor friends left in the area, I really had no feeling of "coming home." No ghosts showed up to haunt me. In fact, I could find very little at all to remind me of those first ten years. A few names . . . of streets, places, buildings, that sort of thing, but the look of them was utterly different. Except the Fisher Building. Our theatre was in the Fisher Building. In spite of extensive remodeling, it still looked familiar. But the one feature that enchanted me as a child was gone. The lights in the tower used to change from one glorious color to another, and now it's a pedestrian monotone. No more magic show.

I made only one pilgrimage. The columnist, Shirley Eder, an old friend from New York who now lives in Detroit, took me to the street of my birth. If I'd hoped to find some sort of physical link to the past, I was disappointed. I couldn't recognize a thing. The trees had grown enormous, making the houses look positively tiny, and our house wasn't even there. The one landmark that might have produced a rush of nostalgia had been torn down. In its place was a children's playground, which rather pleased me. If the old house had to be gone, I was glad it had made way for fun and games. There seemed to be all too little of that in my old home town.

It wasn't all fun and games for me when I lived there, but I have many happy memories, too. And even though today's Detroit stimulated few of either sort, they lie in wait . . . ready to be triggered off.

It's interesting how food will do it . . . simply carry me right back to age 5, or 8, or whatever.

I have many
happy memories
of Detroit

— from then
(first on ground
at right)

One of the most pleasurable of those memories continues to pop into my consciousness every time I eat rice. I simply adored it as a child, in any form, but my particular delight was Mother's rice and gravy. It never seemed to come to the table often enough, but, when it did, I felt especially loved. It was my "treat" night.

I may have collected more recipes for rice than for any other food. Some are included here . . . a sort of cross-section.

— and now

Benton Prather

Max Showalter

Marge Champion

Don Heath

154

EASY DOES IT . . .

During the preparations for his musical, "Sugar," Gower Champion rented a house in Beekman Place. The kitchen was well-equipped, and spacious, and Gower decided to add cooking to his long list of other talents. Result: A series of week-end cooking jags.

The party would gather in the kitchen and the director would assign such roles as onion chopper, salad chef, bread warmer, wine steward, etc., while he himself experimented with the main dish, which he'd never cooked before. I don't think he'd ever cooked *anything* before. But, with beginner's luck and a little help from his friends, the meals were terrific.

Bob was in on a couple of these cook-ins while I was on the road with "Reardon," and I joined them twice, on the precious hop home from Detroit, and on Christmas week home from L.A.

One evening I remember well for the frozen salad plates and forks. Gower wanted to make certain his salad would be chilled. It was. And so were we. The forks were so cold you could hardly hold them. The salad was fine anyway, as was the rest of the dinner . . . lasagne, hot bread, superb wine. Marge was in town, and actor-composer Max Showalter made five.

Of course we talked about food a lot. Bob at one point brought up the virtues of Chicken Flora, a way of cooking chicken we'd learned on Fire Island . . . and Marge and Max each came up with their own "easy" chicken dish. All three offer the advantage of minimum preparation, and the freedom of ignoring the pot after it reaches the oven.

I took notes, of course. *Max's Chicken* is the least complicated to put together and cook, and the most exotic in flavor. *Marge's Chicken* requires a little more initial work, but it's more truly a one-pot dinner.

For out-and-out lazy days, though, when you want to eat well, *Chicken Flora* is still the *laziest* best.

Marge's Chicken	*285*
Max's Chicken	*285*

Cris Alexander

Evelyn and Joe Layton

156

We ignored all the odds, all common sense, and made reservations for a trip to Europe the fall of '71. And of course "the best laid plans, etc. . . . ." A commission for Bob came up, and then the "Reardon" Tour. Bob's project never got off the ground, but I'd already signed my contract. The reservations were cancelled.

Then in mid-April of '72, when all the "Reardon" Company was back in New York, we threw a reunion party. It was a very happy evening, but it was also a reminder of the lost trip. The next morning Bob fairly exploded: *"Now!* Is there anything to stop us?!"

Well, with one thing and another, it was at least 36 hours before we got on a plane. To Zurich.

We left with a few loose plans, and two dates in our heads. The first date was May 3rd, the opening of Joe Layton's "Gone With The Wind" in London. The second was a departure-for-home date from Oslo, June 1st. We'd fill in the rest as we came to it.

The first of the loose plans got looser as the plane flew from Geneva to Zurich. We were rubbernecking out the window . . . "Can you see an Alp?" "No, can you?" We had a car reserved to drive through the Alps to Annecy, and the clouds in Switzerland were hovering at about the height of *Claire's Knee.* We never saw Zurich or the Alps. The car was cancelled at the airport and we flew to Rome.

Neither of us knew any Italian, but we managed to have an absolutely marvelous time . . . with the help of sign language, chutzpah, maps, instinct, and Jimmy Coco. Jimmy was there making the film, "Man of La Mancha," and first thing he got us out of our hotel into his *pensione* on Via Due Macelli.

We spent the days thrilling to as many of the glories of Rome as time allowed . . . and the nights socializing with Jimmy and another actor friend, Jack Betz. Jack had a car, was fluent in Italian, and the four of us explored the glories of Roman restaurants. We ate so well my clothes were getting very snug after the fourth day. With five and a half weeks to go, something had to give. But I couldn't think about dieting yet, not with the *Fettucini* that stared me in the face the fifth night. One taste and I was a goner. It had a name I couldn't pronounce or spell, but it was so delicious I dared to reproduce it when we got home. I won't swear the details are exact, but I came up with "something like" and it's heaven.

We made our May 3rd date in London . . . barely . . . after a stopover in Florence. It was very hard to leave Italy, and we almost wished we hadn't cabled Joe and Evie to save us seats for GWTW. We were even learning a bit of Italian. Ah well, someday . . .

As it turned out, that opening night in London was an historic occasion it would have been a shame to miss. The show received an enthusiastic reception from a glittering audience of all Britain's theatrical greats. And it was also the night that Sam, the live horse, made his entrance with Scarlett and Rhett and disgraced himself Stage Right while Atlanta burned. A Star was born.

This time we stayed in London just long enough to see a few other shows and get the laundry done.

We rented a car and took to the road. The first stop was Surrey, and lunch with Maurice Evans and Allan Foster in Maurice's beautiful country house. And then down to Devon and Cornwall . . . revisiting Bob's old Navy stomping grounds . . . Plymouth, Polperro, Falmouth. And a bit of nostalgia for me, too, near Barnstaple. We walked the beach and dunes at Saunton Sands, where some of "Stairway to Heaven" was shot. Erosion seemed to have passed it by . . . after 25 years the sands looked the same, as wide and beautiful as ever.

We diddled our way to Bath, through Wales, north into the Lake Country, Scotland, and around to Newcastle-on-Tyne. Two happy weeks, at the most beautiful time of the year . . . the legendary English Springtime. The flowers and foliage were in full bloom all the way, so colorful and luscious it was breathtaking. Rain or shine, we tramped through every ruin, every restoration . . . we saw a local Opera Society's "Hello, Dolly" in Falmouth . . . we climbed a true mountain in Wales . . . went on boat rides, up the Falmouth River, across Lake Windermere . . . ate a medieval banquet in a medieval castle (no forks or knives, we were regular Henrys-the-Eighth, we were) . . . had a thrilling evening of music in a pub in Llangernyw, Welsh choristers, angels' voices singing old Welsh songs. A trip to remember . . .

At Newcastle we turned in the car and boarded the S.S. Lena for Bergen, Norway.

Other than our Norwegian dog, and Bob's wartime glimpse of Oslo (his LST was briefly in its harbour), our only preparation for that magical land was a phone call to Patty Neal and her husband Roald Dahl before we left England. Norway is Roald's territory, and he gave us a general plan for the ten days ahead, the phone number of friends in Oslo, and his blessing.

The plan was simple. It was restricted to the south, unhurried, and suited us better than trying to "do" the entire country in so short a time. We took a small boat from Bergen up the coast to Sognefjord, and through the fjord to Balestrand . . . and when we were ready, another boat to Flåm, to the little train that climbs its way up to Myrdal. There we connected with the Bergen-Oslo express and had a fantastic ride through brilliant, eye-blinding glaciers.

Besides the incredible beauty of the fjords (and the photographs simulate but can't possibly capture the experience of it), we were again blessed by the time of the year . . . the exquisite blossoms of peach and apple trees blooming amidst all that grandeur.

We feasted. Our pleasures in the scenery and the people were insatiable, and sometimes in the food as well. There were spectacular smorgasbord spreads for breakfast wherever we went, but being a fruit-toast-coffee girl, the salads, fish, cheeses, etc., etc., were too much for my early morning capacities. But oh, the coffee . . . my God, they make superb coffee!

The lunches were more to my taste . . . great varieties of open-faced sandwiches, lovely to look at and delicious to eat. The shrimp was a favorite. I brought a recipe home, and also was inspired to make tiny versions as canapés that never fail to elicit cries of pleasure.

As for the rest of the cuisine, perhaps we were unlucky. We ate in first class restaurants as well as in ordinary cafes, and the food was good but not especially unusual or memorable. Except for one meatball casserole that was, and I promptly tracked down the recipe.

We called the Paul Jensens (Roald's friends) in Oslo, and Gunvor (Mrs. J.) picked us up to take us to their home. We had protested, suggesting a cab, but she said "No, no, not now. When you return to your hotel, yes, you will take a cab. Because I intend to have a drink while you are here." (The drinking-driving laws in Norway are fierce. Cars are stopped for spot-checks, and if the driver has had one swallow or ten, no matter. It's three months in jail.)

Gunvor and Paul were the delight of our last few days in Norway. We spent many happy hours with those warm, charming people. They were English-speaking, thank God, or it couldn't have been. Italian was one thing, but my tongue simply refused to fit around the Norwegian sounds.

We came home tired, but not exhausted . . . filled with enriching memories, but not satiated . . . And not nearly as poor as we'd expected. Off-season is a smashing time to go to Europe . . . especially if you're adventurous enough to tackle the B and B (bed and breakfast) routine, which we did all through England, Wales, and part of Norway. Our only disappointment was in Edinburgh . . . and wouldn't you know, it was a proper hotel, the County?

Fisherman's Fettucini	*328*
Open-faced Shrimp Sandwich	*348*
Shrimp Canapés	*206*
Norwegian Meat Balls	*253*

Kathy and David

When Kathy and David were still in law school we saw them quite often. They'd escape from New Haven at the drop of a hat, whenever the rigors of the curriculum allowed. In New York they could either stay with us, or with David's parents, Herbert and Shirley, or with David's sister Jane and her husband Elliott Barowitz. The visits were the impulse of the moment . . . when they would come, and who would get them for meals and/or bedding down, was highly unpredictable. We all learned to play it by ear.

I don't know how the others coped, but I was grateful I'd made a habit of keeping something in the larder for emergencies. It's a bit difficult to stretch three chops to feed five mouths if the stores are closed. But a curious phenomenon repeated itself so often, I rarely had to resort to the spaghetti pot.

Shortly after the wedding, May Katz had got me onto boneless sirloin for *London Broil.* It wasn't prohibitively expensive then, and we loved it. I'd buy the first cut if possible, and have the Ottomanellis slice off a huge hunk, at least three to four inches thick. It was much too much for three people, of course, but I'd section it, freeze part, and broil the rest to provide a meal, and sandwich fare for later. It was in the meat-tender about two to four times a month before freezing.

And who would invariably show up but the Rosens! It became a joke. As if my buying the cut had sent an ESP signal to the New Haven branch to pick up and head South.

It was pretty jazzy "pot luck," I must say, but I think David began to suspect I didn't know how to cook anything else.

The monotony of *London Broil* at the Emmetts' is no longer a risk. They have to plan their New York trips these days, which means I can plan, too. But now the visits are rare, and we miss them.

After graduation, they decided to stay on in Connecticut. David has his law office in New Haven, in partnership with another chap, Ed Dolan, and Kathy has joined the Koskoff firm in Bridgeport, some twenty minutes away. Nicholas was born in 1969, they bought a house, and Adam arrived in '73.

Their lives are too full and complicated to pop in as they used to, and we can't always visit *them* with ease. We keep in touch mostly by phone. But once in a while the timing is compatible for all, and we'll make a weekend trek to New Haven to catch up on news and thoughts, and enjoy each other in person again.

One such visit followed our return from Europe, and I came home with a delicious new fish recipe of Kathy's. I also came home with a few old thoughts to ponder.

In many ways our life styles are similar. With two careers (and children) in the families, we all appreciate the special joys of relaxed living . . . it offsets the outside work pressures, and minimizes housekeeping problems. Of course, neither family could function without a healthy respect for improvisation and cooperation. Whoever has the most free time and is the least exhausted is the one who does what has to be done . . . be it shopping, cooking, or calling the electrician, fixing the john. As to the raising of children, Mom and Pop are interchangeable.

But there are interesting differences, too, rather basic. I may be giving Kathy more points than she'd claim, but it seems to me she's made some happy improvements over her mum. And looking back to *my* mother's life, the contrast is startling.

All three of us women had our "thing" . . . but we each handled it differently.

My mother, at nineteen, was looking forward to a very promising career in music. She'd studied the piano with Edward MacDowall in New York, and was already a *"star"* in Canton, Ohio, her home town. She'd had an offer to tour Europe accompanying a fairly well-known diva, and Grandfather was going to back a program of study along the way . . . Then Daddy prevailed upon her to marry him instead. She dutifully gave up her career to become his wife, the mother of his children, and the keeper of his home.

An unusual musical gift went down the drain. But they were the children of their time . . . it would have required a good deal more rebellion of spirit than either of them had, to buck the rules of the period. "A Woman's Place" and all that.

I (with a beady eye on Mother's unfulfilled talent), was stubbornly determined *not* to give up my career for marriage. And the rigidity of that determination was probably one of the snags in my first marriage. Bill never suggested I should stop acting, but at the same time he never fully adjusted to the time it took away from my role as wife. And I wasn't secure or malleable enough to find a way to please him and me, too.

My life with Bob has been splendid . . . but I have his understanding to thank, and his ability to give me the space to explore my various selves. With the children, I've been blessed with luck more than sense, but at least I've tried . . . sometimes successfully, sometimes not. I'm sure both Kathy and Sean look back with some regret to the times I wasn't there to support their needs. So do I, but we got through.

Kathy took a giant step beyond both Mother and me. For one thing, whatever her rebellion was, it wasn't mine. There was never any question of her having a career if she wanted it. Perhaps her chronology of events was an advantage . . . first marriage, then baby (Nick preceded her degree), then law practice. At any rate, she seemed to grow into her life quite naturally . . . with a beady eye on avoiding my deficiencies in the domestic area. She's always been first of all a woman, a human being . . . free to explore and enjoy *all* her facets and talents. Family, career, home, are equally important and intermingled in her consciousness. Priorities are determined by what the moment requires, without a pressing need to justify the choice.

The progression is fascinating. Mother had to prove that she could be a superb homemaker, and did, to justify giving up her music. I had to prove I was a very good actress come hell or high water, to justify *not* giving up the career. Kathy has just quietly and simply given both areas of life their due. We labeled ourselves, she didn't.

In a way, I'm sorry she doesn't have a daughter. It would be interesting to see what road the fourth generation would follow.

A long prelude to a fish recipe, but really, isn't life fascinating?

London Broil	*259*
Steamed Onions	*229*
Fish with Bacon and Vegetables	*305*

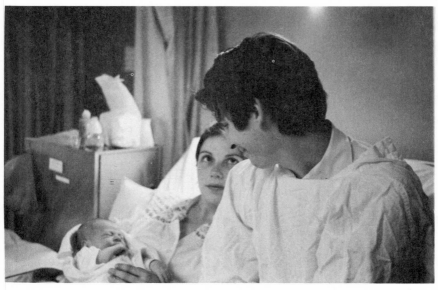

Kathy and David with Nick, one day old

Packing a suitcase is something I've learned to do rather well over the years. Particularly for those frequent trips to work in L.A. It's a simple routine. I put everything out on the bed where I can see at a glance what accessories are needed, then a quick rundown of normal day and night activities keeps me from forgetting something as basic as toothbrush or sneakers.

But *quantity* still has me flummoxed. Those damn "what if's" do it every time. Not wanting to be caught short *if* there should be a dressy weekend party, *if* the weather is balmy enough for the beach, *if* my agent Tom Korman comes up with a second job and I don't get home for weeks. These contingencies rarely materialize, and like as not I return to N.Y. with half the contents of my luggage untouched . . . my arms half out of their sockets from the carrying. (Has anyone done a study of that vanishing breed, the skycap?)

Once, however, I was really proud of myself and packed *light.* The job was "Love, American Style" . . . a 20-minute comedy segment with a two-day shooting schedule. I left New York with a very small case containing a pair of jeans, two makeup shirts, and a few changes of underwear, exactly what I'd need for the work . . . no more, no less. The month was August, so all I carried in the other hand was a purse and a book. Free as the wind. Heaven.

Never has another job turned up so fast. Before the first day's shooting of "L.A.S." was over, Tom had sent me a script for "Young Dr. Kildare" . . . and the third day found me driving to MGM instead of the airport.

Okay. Belle's washing machine did yeoman duty and I managed. But then Tom called again, the day before I was to finish "Kildare."

"Want to go to Australia?"

"Australia?!"

"Day after tomorrow. For two segments of a new half-hour TV series, "Evil Touch." Filming in Sydney."

"You're kidding. On one pair of jeans? I don't even have a coat with me!"

"Don't be so conservative. Mende Brown, the producer, is picking up the tab for Bob, too. Can't he bring a coat from New York? And your passport?"

Conservative, indeed. I called Bob that night. He said, "Why not?", was in Los Angeles the next night with half my wardrobe and part of his, and we were in the air over the Pacific the following night. Inundated with luggage. Not knowing what awaited us on the other side of the globe, Bob had even outdone *me* with "what if's."

As it turned out, clothes were the least of the problems. That flight was the longest night of our lives. We were comatose on arrival from jet-lag and couldn't have cared less if we went starkers.

We finally recovered, somewhere toward the end of the next week. I worked through the first film in a daze, on sheer instinct. But eventually our fogginess dissipated, Australia appeared, and we began to take a look at "Down Under."

Quite a city, Sydney. Protected from the sea by rocky cliffs, the harbour is spectacularly beautiful, with hundreds of coves and inlets. The city proper rises on green-laden hills around the irregular shoreline, which allows almost every building to share in a view of the water. The panorama from the harbour is no less entrancing. Transportation by boat is almost as popular as by auto.

Mende Brown

Courtesy of APA Leisure Time International Limited

165

The film company shot entirely on location, so we got to see a lot of the area even during working hours. But the fun was on the days off. Up to the Blue Mountains, with associate producer Peter Appleton and his girl, Judy. A whole glorious day on the water with production assistant Pam Borain and her actor-husband, Mike Dorsey. Friends of theirs, the Hatfields, took us for a grand tour of the harbour and fed us royally on their splendid power boat. Another day, the first day of "Spring," at the Taronga Park Zoo, charmingly terraced, housing all the usual animals, birds, creatures, as well as indigenous Australian varieties. I never knew there were so many types, sizes, and colors of kangaroos. The koala bears were a bit disappointing. Maybe it was the time of year, but they looked motheaten and scruffy, like beat-up, abandoned dolls stuffed into the crooks of trees. Never batted an eyelash.

We saw interesting theatre, heard good jazz, ate great seafood, and hot Malaysian food, and were introduced to rather pleasant Australian wines. And worked, of course. Even Bob worked. Mende cast him in the second of the films, which gave his frustrated actor's soul a bit of happy release.

The Company was small and efficient. After working in Hollywood, surrounded by crews of 40 or 50 people, it was strange to have only 16 or so doing everything. Doubling in brass was the order of the day. Everyone pitched in, the atmosphere was warm and enthusiastic, even the occasional griping was permeated with good humor.

It's hard to get much further away from "home," but we had to keep reminding ourselves that we were *not* in the States. That we were actually in Australia. There were differences in customs, of course . . . the inevitable British tea-time, and cars driving on the left. God knows the *accent* is distinctive. But we found the look and the spirit of the place much more American than English. Like us, they're an overt, informal, enterprising people. We've lost some of their innocence and optimism; Australia seems younger, the pioneer spirit is still very strong. But I swear we're cut from the same mold.

It seemed a shame we couldn't stay on after the films were completed . . . to travel "Out Back," up to the Great Barrier Reef, to Melbourne, Adelaide, or Perth. One doesn't get to Australia just any old day. But it was well into September by this time, and Sean had need of his parents. Peter arranged our trip home with three stopovers . . . Fiji, Honolulu, and L.A. . . . hoping to beat the return jet-lag.

We arrived in New York some four weeks after I'd left it for a quick two-day TV assignment. Just in time. Thor was on antibiotics for an infection. Sean was minus two years' high school transcripts to clear his admission to Berklee College of Music in Boston.

Somehow we dealt with their problems, and managed to pull *ourselves* together a week or so later. Breaking up the trip was better than not, I suppose, but our bodies weren't fooled one bit.

Still, we fancifully dream of returning "Down Under" someday. What's 10,000 miles? Coming back the flying time was only 24 hours.

We still correspond with Pam and Mike. Mike, a cooking buff, too, gave me a bundle of his recipes to take home, all of which I've tried, and recommend. And Pam sent a cookbook . . . "200 Years of Australian Cooking," by Babette Hayes . . . fascinating recipes for such dishes as Solid Syllabub, Busters, Pupton Pigeon, One-eyed Jack's Bush Rissoles, Oxcheek Soup, Hotch Potch, Pavlova, etc. We kitchen freaks do find each other . . . even halfway around the world.

I haven't packed "light" since. Who knows when Tom will call and say, "What about Singapore?"

Pam Borain and Mike Dorsey, our friends "Down Under"

HIDDEN TALENTS

My agent, Tom, is married to Nadine Korman, a little wisp of a thing who used to be in agentry, too, sort of. She'd been a top-notch secretary to a literary agent in Beverly Hills, and was preparing to move upward, when her boss informed her in no uncertain terms to forget it. He wouldn't dream of grooming her to be an agent because she was female, and women didn't belong in the business, as far as *he* was concerned. So she quit, in equally certain terms, with a few added remarks of her own.

In her spare time, she had been experimenting a lot with chocolate desserts, because she loved chocolate, and didn't have to worry about it changing her dimensions, as most of us do.

One night after she'd told her boss where to go, she served one of her concoctions to a friend who was in the midst of opening a new restaurant called The Green something-or-other. He went into ecstasies, and immediately suggested putting it on his menu. Would she, could she manage it? She could. At least she was very ready to try.

She named the dessert Chocolate Mousse Pie, and turned part of her kitchen over to the project. Tom helped out by delivering the pies to the restaurant. "Here's your mousse." They were a huge success.

That was the beginning of what has turned out to be a thriving operation . . . and the ruin of more figures than could be squeezed into the Colosseum. Gradually other restaurants were clamoring for her Mousse Pies (Mocha Chip was added to the Chocolate), and *all* of her kitchen plus most of the garage were turned over to the business. Her home nearly disappeared in an avalanche of whipped cream.

Something had to give. So her home is now her home again, and her pie-making has been moved into a shop she calls "La Mousse." Nadine has trained people to work for her, has acquired an enormous station wagon with driver, and a business phone that never stops ringing. The Pies are delivered to restaurants galore, private homes, special parties, even to the airport . . . for shipping to El Paso and other foreign parts. Chocolate and Mocha Chip have been joined by Lemon, Raspberry, Strawberry, Orange, Chocolate Almond Fudge, and Pineapple. She is now known as the Queen of the Mousse. And Tom is her willing and proud Prince Consort. And she couldn't care less that she never became a litr'ry agent.

Nadine would sooner turn in her mixing bowl than divulge the recipe for either the Chocolate or Mocha Chip Mousse Pie . . . but with my persistence and her generosity, I've captured recipes for three of the fruit mousses, jewels in their own right.

Of course, when I'm safely home in New York (and reasonably skinny), I have been known to try to figure out the magic that goes into her original creation. Since chocolate is chocolate is chocolate, each attempt has been wickedly edible, but it has yet to turn out like *hers.* And as her fame grows, I'm becoming embarrassed to try anymore. There are certain things in this life that *should* remain private . . . deep, dark, delicious secrets . . . and for Nadine, the Chocolate Mousse Pie is one of them.

Tom and Nadine ("La Mousse") Korman

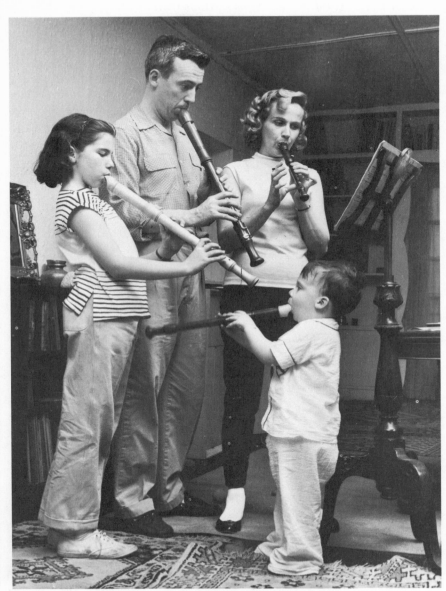

He indicated music might have a place in his life as early as age three.

For a young man who'd avoided scholarly pursuits most of his twelve years in school, Sean settled in at Berklee College of Music with surprising enthusiasm. It surprised him as much as it did us. Of course, all his subjects dealt with music . . . instrumental, theory, composition, arranging, conducting . . . all modern American, mostly jazz. The curriculum was heavy and demanding, and his casual work habits were initially a formidable obstacle . . .but he plowed through and the school was a smashing success.

The food, however, wasn't. What is it about dormitory kitchens? We were getting the same plaintive cries for help from Sean that Kathy had beseiged us with her first year at Radcliffe. Even the same phrases described the food . . . "breaded bread," "boiled vegetable mush." Either the cuisine is traditional, or the student disdain is. A little of both, most likely.

We'd sent Kathy "CARE" packages at college from time to time until she was permitted to abandon the dorm and move into her own digs. Whether she had time for imaginative cooking or not, at least the meat she ate was all meat and not mostly breadcrumbs and fat.

Sean was no less bombarded with boxes of food . . . anything we could think of that wouldn't perish in the mails. Nuts, beef jerky, dried fruits, cookies.

I made a valiant effort to find tasty recipes for "health food" cookies, and sent up dozens containing wheat germ, blackstrap molasses, soybeans, carob powder, etc. His reaction was devastatingly polite. So I settled for his favorite "cooky" cookies, figuring gastronomic morale had its virtues, too.

Like Kathy, Sean could move out of the dorm his second year, and though he ate better food when he ate, I suspect he wasn't as conscientious about cooking as his sister. He's now out West, putting his musical training to the test. He's playing . . . all those bass instruments of his . . . tuba, string bass, electric bass . . . living in an apartment he shares with others . . . and cooking, so he says. At least we haven't been receiving any requests for supplementary goodies these days.

We might have been unprepared for his taking to college, but not to music. He indicated music might have a place in his life as early as age three. He sang an impromptu audition for director Philip Burton (Richard's foster father) at the neighboring Cherry Lane Theatre. Bob and I weren't aware of his stunt at the time, but six months later, Philip and I figured out that the young man who stalked up to the stage and sang "Ragtime Cowboy Joe" for him had to be Sean. The beanie with the flashing light on top was adequate identification.

At eight he asked to learn to play the oboe. At ten, it was the piano. And in the 7th grade at P.S. 3, all other possible careers faded away. Jerry Sheik, the music instructor, assigned him the tuba, for orchestra and band. He fell in love with the instrument . . . at that age they were just about the same size . . . and made it clear, from that moment forward his "major" was music, and English, Math, Science, Languages, History, were all "minors." The next five years' grades backed him up to the letter.

Brownie Drops	*393*
Melba's Cookies	*391*
Date Cookies (Tillie Cole)	*392*
Pecan Balls (Belle's)	*390*

Our son the musician

When I was a child, I didn't think I'd live to reach forty. It seemed forever away. I wasn't even sure I *wanted* to live that long. The prospect of doddering was much scarier than dying, and I was convinced that "Life Begins At Forty" was a phrase whistled in the dark to keep people from admitting that it was really the beginning of the end.

As I got closer to forty, I changed my mind. I wasn't anywhere near doddering. But still that "middle-age" milestone filled me with anxiety. I was becoming *very* nervous about it when Bob said, "Enough of this!" He invited forty friends to a party on "that" night, and turned the preparations over to me. I didn't have *time* to feel sorry for myself. And it was a great party . . . such an exuberant, roaring *blast-off* into the next decade, I lost track of whatever I was fretting about, and haven't been bothered by a birthday since. (I don't exactly stand up and cheer as they pass, but I don't fall apart, either.)

Times have changed. The present Reign of Youth seems to have shifted the beginning of middle-age from forty to thirty. Under-thirties are "with it." Over-thirties are the lost generation, slightly congealed . . . caught up in the success-syndrome, materialism; held responsible for the wars, pollution, prejudice, credibility gaps . . . if not actually the enemy, at least not "where it's at."

Our particular "in" group has been remarkably generous in respect to Bob and me. Once they got to late teenagedom, that is. Perhaps it's because we've never been overly devoted to the standards our "generation" is accused of representing. An unwitting ally might have been our profession, concerned as it is with the exploration and understanding of people, not things. Who knows. Anyway, the necessary rebellion against parents' ideas got a bit muddled in our household. They had a difficult time accusing us of being indifferent to the things they were against . . . wars, pollution, prejudice. And as frustrating as it may have been at the time, it's meant we've been able to get along rather well now they're grown up. Which is very nice.

But they still have their peers' attitudes to cope with. And that "Black-Thirty" milestone can be as much of a beast for *them* to face, as forty was for *us*.

David Rosen hit "that age" in May of '74, and somehow managed to make the transition with equilibrium. If it disturbed him, he didn't let on to us. Kathy's turn came in December of the same year, along with three of their friends. (Two other lawyers, and an administrator of a community health clinic.) This quartet showed no *distressing* signs of apprehension, but they did indicate they could use a little support from their friends.

They, also, decided on a riproaring party . . . to make it a gala, joint *celebration* rather than a wake. They hired the Yale Law School dining room, which is huge, and invited 500 people. (They even included some of us "golden oldies" . . . Herbert and Shirley, Bob and me.) They brought "Bev Grant and the Human Condition" up from New York for music . . . provided ash trays and ice (it was a Bring-Your-Own-Drinks party) . . . and went all out to serve a fantastic midnight buffet. The Xeroxed invitation wistfully signed off with, "We hope you'll be able to come and that you'll still talk to us even after we're thirty!"

Everybody did . . . both. The party was a success, the music was a success, the food was a success, and the birthday folk avoided being unduly traumatized as they joined the "out" generation. (And I came home with two grand recipes of Kathy's!)

They're over the mark now, Kathy and David. And it's hardly the "beginning of the end." I doubt if they're any more likely to join the "status quo set" next year than they were last year. David's dissatisfaction with the evils of the present system isn't going to go up in smoke . . . he'll be working just as hard to correct them in the future as before. And so will Kathy. She's been struggling against injustices ever since Law School. (Even high school.) And often winning.

Take women. Kathy deals with all *sorts* of law cases . . . but somehow, many that wind up in her capable hands are those involving inequities in the treatment of women. She's gone to bat for harassed prostitutes, for matters concerning freedom of choice, against employment discrimination (for minority groups as well as women), against medical malpractice, against anything and everything that smacks of Unfair, or Raw Deal.

Her first big fight was the famed "Mory's" case, one that got quite a bit of press. Mory's, a long-established eating club in New Haven (nationally known thanks to the Yale Glee Club and their Whiffenpoof Song . . . and Rudy Vallee), offered membership and welcome entry to all Yale undergraduates, graduate students, faculty members, anyone who even *looked* as if he belonged to the Yale community . . . as long as he was MALE.

The day when Yale had an all-male population had long since passed, but Mory's chose to ignore the changed character of the University. They refused to allow women students or professors past their portals, except at dinner-time, and then only if escorted by some chap. Reluctantly, evening "dates" were tolerated. But the fact that it was the traditionally favored gathering place at *lunch*-time, particularly for graduate students and faculty members, meant that women were denied a vital participation in the continuing business and social part of the University life.

So in 1971, a group of Yale Law students joined with Women's Movement people and some of Mory's members to protest the situation . . . they tried negotiating with the Club, took their complaint to the University, all to no avail. Finally, with Kathy at the helm, they took the case to the Connecticut Liquor Commission as a remonstrance. They proposed that Mory's liquor license be revoked on two counts: Mory's couldn't properly qualify as a private club, since they served non-members as readily as members (as long as they were *male*, of course); and the Liquor Commission, as a State Agency, couldn't properly extend privileges to an organization that discriminated against women.

Kathy pleaded the case and the Commission revoked the license, on both counts. Mory's took advantage of its right to appeal to the courts, and finally in '74, the Connecticut Supreme Court ruled that the Liquor Commission had responded correctly. The Club was ordered to turn in its license.

Mory's still didn't get the message, though, until two of its members retained Kathy to bring suit on behalf of *all* the members for the thousands of dollars they had been assessed, without authorization, to pay for the Club's court expenses. It took the prospect of another suit, and financial disaster (by this time, even the University had turned against them) to agree to negotiate. At last! And Kathy proved to be a formidable negotiator.

The results: Women are now admitted to membership; four women (acceptable to Kathy's clients) were appointed to the board; the members who had refused to submit to the assessments, and subsequently were dropped from membership, were reinstated; Mory's was compelled to offer money back to those members who were threatened with loss of membership if they didn't comply, and to publish a notice to that effect in the Yale Alumni Bulletin. In exchange, the law suit was dropped and their liquor license was reinstated. And now all the members are allowed voting privileges, which they'd never had before, which was why the members had had no power to decide for themselves whether women could be admitted or not.

Another time, she joined with five other women lawyers to get the Connecticut anti-abortion laws declared unconstitutional. After a long struggle, they won in Connecticut, and the U.S. Supreme Court later backed them up, following the reasoning of their case. But they can't relax on that one yet. Now, she says, the Connecticut

Department of Welfare is making it as difficult as it can for the women on its rolls to *qualify* for abortions.

Nothing changes easily or immediately. But both Kathy and David *pretend* that it can, because if they didn't, things might not change at all. And so long as they can still recognize inequities when they see them, the fear of being an "over-thirty" in *spirit* is pretty unrealistic. I figure they're a long way from settling down into a comfortable, secure, complacency. If they should ever be tempted, they might have us two "lost ones" to reckon with, and that would be just too embarrassing.

Mother had now and then served a "lamb curry" at home, which was nothing more than leftover lamb in a white sauce, liberally seasoned with curry powder. It was flavorsome over rice, and the Major Grey's chutney she served on the side was particularly tasty, and until I went to England to make "Stairway to Heaven," I assumed I knew all there was to know about curry.

My hairdresser on the film was named Ida Mills, and I have many fond memories of our time together. She was a captive of the Daily Telegraph's Puns and Anagrams crossword puzzles, and every free moment on the set was devoted to solving the elusive clues. She undoubtedly was responsible for getting me caught up in the whole puzzle world, too . . . from the New York Times daily and Sunday crosswords, to double crostics.

She also taught me an invaluable trick for setting hair, when a hairdryer isn't available and time is of the essence. Spit. It's a quick-drying solution *par excellence!* She proved it admirably the day we shot the "camera obscura" scene in Surrey. We were headquartered in a 12th century cottage in the village of Shere, and only the minimum of equipment was brought along. It was partially to save trucking fuel in an England still beleaguered by wartime rationing, but it was also a very odd cottage, and the unit manager assumed that much of the usual equipment a film company carries (such as a hairdryer) simply wouldn't be able to function. For instance, the ceilings were so low, even I, as short as I am, had to stoop to walk about. Only one room had been "modernized." A century or so prior, one of the owners had dug up the living room floor in order to make more comfortable head room. And discovered the cottage had once been in the hands of sheep rustlers. They found hundreds of sheep carcasses beneath the floor boards, craftily hidden from the authorities.

Equipment in the studio at Denham was standard, of course, and the "spit" method wasn't necessary. But to this day I still set my hair at the theatre "à la Ida," where such luxury as a hairdryer is rare.

The studio hairdryer was put to unorthodox uses, too. One memorable lunch hour its heat contributed to a grand makeup-department feast . . . and I learned there was more to a curry than I'd dreamed.

Ida was born in Southeast Asia, of an English father and Burmese mother, and had been promising us a sample of her native cooking for weeks. As the filming neared the final days, she gathered food stamp contributions from the eight of us to be fêted, and bought the necessary ingredients.

Cooking in the department was a challenge, but she managed it with great cleverness. The only stove was a one-burner hotplate, normally used for the tea kettle to make "cuppa's." This day, everyone cheerily gave up his tea while Ida prepared her magic meal. The rice was cooked first and set aside until the curry was half done. She then made a sling out of towels and tied it to the hairdryer. The colander of rice was slipped neatly inside, close to the unit, and the dryer was turned to "hot."

When lunch-time arrived, the great pot of fish curry was brought to the improvised party table. The rice had a hard, brown crust on top, but she deftly peeled it off, and the rice underneath was piping hot, fluffy, and perfect.

I wish I'd had the sense to get Ida's recipe at the time. It was truly a marvelous combination of flavors, all adding up to a very hot curry. It certainly was a far cry from Mother's simple version.

I've had many curries since, mostly of the hot variety, but some years ago I happened on a delightful cookbook entitled "Classic Cooking from India," by Dharam Jit Singh. The text is highly informative and laced with charming tales . . . and the recipes, those I've tried, are splendid. Mr. Singh gave me an entirely different concept of curries, and Eastern cookery in general . . . an appreciation of the art of combining spices and herbs to produce refined and delicate flavors, not necessarily hot at all.

In the first place, he is uncompromisingly derisive of commercial curry powder. His argument: Whenever a combination of spices is sold in one jar, you can be certain that the individual spices are of inferior quality. And he has an even stronger objection . . . the artistic limitation it imposes on the dish. The possibilities of variance in flavor are infinite and fascinating if one is selective in the choice of herbs and spices.

His recipes prove his thesis. And very few of them are "hot" . . . but they're dangerous, nonetheless.

The first time I prepared one of his curries, I was absolutely stoned by the time we sat down to eat. Before we reached dessert, Bob had to put me to bed . . . out cold. Grinding the spices with mortar and pestle started the high . . . and the aromas floating up from the cooking pot completed the job. It was quite a trip!

I'm now very cautious with all of his recipes. I keep the windows wide open, and come near the pot only when I absolutely have to. I may still get giddy, but I can stay with the party.

There are times, however, when I ignore Singh's good sense and use curry powder anyway. One recipe, a shrimp curry, is a legacy from a Jamaican maid we had years ago. We'd eaten curried goat on our trips to Jamaica . . . *very* hot indeed . . . and my adaptation of Pearl Phipps' recipe is in that tradition.

My favorite "party" curry is made with chicken, and it's neither unduly mild nor gaspingly hot. Served with rice, tomatoes stewed with coconut, and a wide variety of accompaniments for the curry, it also makes a very pretty buffet spread.

I haven't given up Mother's "left-over" curry, though. It's still a good way to use up the remains of a lamb, beef, chicken, or turkey roast. I've just jazzed up the sauce slightly, and the result is vaguely reminiscent of Ida's marvelous concoction.

Rogan Jaush (Dharam Jit Singh)	*275*
Shrimp Curry	*311*
Chicken Curry	*296*
Saffron Rice	*241*
Curry Accompaniments	*297*
East Indian Stewed Tomatoes	*229*
Curry Sauce for leftover meat or fowl	*335*

Pearl Phipps, our authority on Jamaican cuisine

As Jere Halliday in "The Disenchanted" in Philadelphia, opposite John Baragrey.

I'm often asked in interviews: "What part have you always wanted to play?" And I have to confess I gave up asking myself that question long ago. There was one part, early on ... Miriamne in Maxwell Anderson's "Winterset." I was dying to play her, but was never given the opportunity. And by the time I was established enough to promote a production on my own, I was too old to play her. Miriamne is my symbol of the futility of wishful dreaming.

Most of the parts I've played simply fell into my lap. Wanting a part desperately was almost a sure sign I'd never get it. Take Jere Halliday in "The Disenchanted," Budd Schulberg's heartbreaking portrait of Zelda Fitzgerald. The playwright wouldn't even hear of my reading for it. I did finally play it in stock, and proved to myself and the Philadelphia critics that the part should have been mine on Broadway. But Rosemary Harris played her there, and I'm inwardly convinced my really *wanting* to do it was the snag. I wasn't cool.

I can recall only two occasions when I knew what I wanted, went after it, and got it. But both times there was a guardian angel in the wings with clout who wanted it, too, or it wouldn't have happened.

The first was "Streetcar," the film. Charles Feldman produced it for Warner Brothers. Charles Feldman was also an agent, with other actresses to promote, and ideas of his own as to who should play Stella on the Silver Screen. Kazan was the angel with clout. I made one test in New York, a test rigged to convince the California contingent that I could be sexy enough for their taste. I'd played the part on Broadway to the satisfaction of many, but that wasn't good enough for Hollywood. Kazan dressed me in my skin, threw a sheer nightgown over it because pure nudity wasn't cinemaphotographic yet, and it titillated them enough to allow me to come to Lotus Land for a second test. The argument had now switched to: "She's a brunette. She won't look as if she could be Vivien Leigh's sister when Leigh is wearing her blonde wig." All sisters have the same coloring? I bleached my hair blonde and they finally gave in. Not because I wanted to play Stella. They gave in because *Kazan* wanted me to play Stella.

Landing my role of Sylvia in the Broadway play, "The Tender Trap," was a little different, but not much. Producer Clinton Wilder was the persistent one there. No one else thought I could play a sophisticated, witty, 33-year-old. I *was* 33 at the time, and I could act ... but director Mike Gordon, and playwrights Max Schulman and Robert Smith, saw me in person as a 23-year-old sweet thing.

So I went to the shoppers' service department at Bonwit Teller and said, "Do me." They took up the challenge with verve. Three hours later, I was dressed in a chic black sheath, accessoried to the hilt with shoes, hat, and jewelry. And was about to trip off to the theatre to convince the skeptics I could behave as worldly-wise as I looked, when a salesgirl across the way in Furs yelled: "Wait! You need a stole to top it off!"

She had an aesthetic point, but I didn't have that kind of money. Also, it was August, and very hot in New York.

She said, "To hell with the weather and who asked you to *buy* it? Wear it! Just bring it back for God's sake."

So I walked into the theatre looking like a million dollars, concealing the drips of perspiration as best I could, and read Sylvia as if I *were* Sylvia. And they said, "Hmmm." It was an interested "Hmmm" but they weren't waving any contracts.

Clint was still in there punching, though, and a week later they called for me to do it again.

I did it again . . . exactly the same. Same dress, same hat, same jewelry . . . and courtesy of Bonwit's, same stole. I got the part. It may not have been sophisticated to have only one outfit . . . but no one could say it wasn't witty.

Normally, I take what comes, and rise to the challenge of that. But I try to keep my irresistible desires in line. Those determined angels are rarely in the lineup when I could use them. I love well-meaning people who say, "Why aren't *you* playing that part?" I'm not playing that part because I wasn't *cast* in that part.

That's what's nice about cooking. I'm my own Producer and Director. I can cast myself in any "role" I please, whether I'm an obvious choice or not. I can even goof it, and I don't throw myself on the scrap heap. I go on to something else . . . or better, I give myself a second chance. Even a third and fourth.

It was so with pies. I was really a bad risk to tackle the role of "pie-maker." Mother had taught me a great deal about cakes, and nothing whatever about pies. All I knew was the inhibiting mystique . . . "there's a knack to the crust and good luck if you aren't born with it." Like a green thumb. My sister-in-law Tillie baked a legendary Apple Pie, and Bob made one helluva Lemon Meringue Pie. But me? I avoided the test for years.

And then I was made "an offer I couldn't refuse" the second Thanksgiving after Mother died. Her Pumpkin Pie had become a tradition at our Holiday table, and we all missed it a lot. Not just out of nostalgia . . . they were the best we'd ever tasted. I was her direct descendant, the logical reviver of the treat.

So I took a deep breath and plunged. And fell flat on my face. That damn pie-crust mystique. I was so careful to follow the instructions: "Just enough water to hold the dough together, *no*

As Sylvia in "The Tender Trap" at the Longacre, with Ronny Graham

more." It disintegrated into a thousand crumbles when I tried to roll it out. And if that weren't bad enough, the can of pumpkin in the larder (left over from Mother's cupboard) had spoiled, and all the stores were closed.

But Bob was in the wings, and with his Lemon Meringue experience (using Flako mix), he patched and patted my pathetic dough with flicks of water here and there and miraculously managed to get two crusts on two pie plates. They had all the expert look of kindergarten ceramics, but he'd done it. I baked the crusts without mishap, and whipped up a Chocolate Cream filling . . . and with freakish luck the pies were flaky, tender, and Thanksgiving dessert that year was a smash. It wasn't *Pumpkin* pie, but it was pie.

And a new culinary challenge was out in the open. I went through a long and frustrating apprenticeship following that initial "turkey," but I've developed enough expertise finally to put myself up for piemaker any time there's a call. (*Mother's Pumpkin Pies* are back on our holiday table.)

One never knows until one tries. Or is given the chance to try. Of course, it's harder for theatrical producers. Plays and films cost more to produce than pies . . . and what if an actor falls all of a heap on stage! They tend to play it safe. Cast to type. The mavericks who are willing to go with an off-beat notion are rare. So I do my thing and know it's mostly luck if I get to do another of my things that no one's seen before. Only when there's some adventurous soul, with clout, who has an idea that maybe . . . ?

In the meantime, there's a certain release in the kitchen where I can count on *me* to take a chance on me. And if I come through in splendor? Well, there's no Oscar for a gorgeous pie, but the applause is very nice.

P. S.

A small, final paragraph to sneak in a few recipes we've become very fond of, and you may enjoy . . . recipes that call up no special memories except the pleasures of preparing and eating. (There are many more such, of course, in my collection of books by Julia Child, Craig Claiborne, James Beard, Michael Field, Gourmet, etc., etc.) Some of the following were donated by friends. Others were originally kitchen experiments of mine, encouraged to become recorded recipes by popular demand.

the Collection

THE RECIPES

ENTREES

BEEF

VEAL

LAMB

DESSERTS

EGGNOG (Grandmother Cole)

3 quarts heavy cream
2 cups sugar (scant measurement)
12 eggs, separated
1½ pints French brandy
1 pint Madeira wine
½ pint dark Jamaica rum

Half-Recipe

3 pints heavy cream
1 cup sugar (scant)
6 eggs, separated
1½ cups French brandy
1 cup Madeira wine
½ cup dark Jamaica rum

Freshly grated nutmeg

Whip the cream and add the sugar gradually. Beat the egg yolks lightly and add. Add the liquors slowly, beating all the time. Lastly, fold in the stiffly beaten egg whites. Chill an hour or two before serving. Top each punch cup of Eggnog with a grating of fresh nutmeg.

The recipe on the left is Grandmother's verbatim. God knows what sort of bowl she possessed to be able to deal with the quantity — about 10 quarts or more. If you're having a large Christmas-Winter party, you'll probably want that much, but I suggest making only half at a time.

Even the Half-Recipe is a bit tricky for most electric mixer bowls, but I manage by gradually adding the liquor until the contents are ready to overflow — then scooping out about ¼ or ⅓ of the mixture into another bowl, an enormous bowl. Continue adding the liquor to the remainder in the mixer bowl, beating constantly until well-blended, and then turn it all into the enormous bowl. Use a rotary hand-beater to finish blending the lot. Fold in the beaten egg whites, and either refrigerate the large bowl or divide the Eggnog into jars to chill.

SANGRIA

    2   bottles dry red wine
    ½ cup brandy
    ½ cup sugar, or to taste
    1   navel orange, unpeeled, thinly sliced, center core removed, and each slice then quartered
    1   unpeeled lemon, thinly sliced, seeds removed
    1   cup fresh pineapple, chunked
    1   cup small cantaloupe balls
    1   red apple, unpeeled, cored and chunked
    1   (10-ounce) bottle club soda (optional)
    Ice cubes

Combine the wine, brandy, and sugar in a very large pitcher. Stir well until the sugar dissolves. Add all the fruit, stir, and cover the pitcher with plastic wrap. Refrigerate until very cold, preferably overnight.

Just before serving, add the optional club soda and ice cubes. Serve in tall glasses with portions of fruit in each.

If you like it fizzy, do add the soda. But it's just as tasty without.

LELAND HAYWARD'S BREW

To each quart of whiskey (a good Bourbon), add

    10   cubes of sugar
    7   drops Angostura Bitters
    6   coffee spoons Maraschino cherry juice
    The rind of one whole orange

Store in bottles in a dark closet. The rind of the orange is removed after 36 hours. Do not stir or drink for *three* weeks.

Serve in old-fashioned glasses . . . poured over ice.

I suggest using mason jars. The wide top makes it easier to remove the orange rind.

SWEDISH GLOGG (Al and Lillie Tins)

A "warming cup." To be served comfortably hot.

1   tablespoon cardamom pods
½ teaspoon whole cloves
3   sticks cinnamon (½-inch each)
1   quart red wine (Claret or Burgundy)
1   quart white wine (Sauterne)
1   quart rye whiskey or Akvavit
¾ cup seedless raisins
   Orange peel from 1 whole orange, dried
1   cup almonds
½ cup lump sugar

Just crack open the cardamom pods and put them with the cloves and cinnamon sticks in a cheese cloth bag. Simmer the tied-up bag in a cup of the wine, about 3 to 5 minutes, long enough to release the fragrant aromas.

Put the rest of the wine and whiskey in a large pot. Add the raisins, orange peel and almonds. Add the bag of spices, and the wine it was simmered in. Heat to almost a boil.

Put the lump sugar in a strainer. Dip it into the pot mixture and *turn off the burner.* Holding the strainer over the pot, set fire to it. Let the sugar burn for a few seconds, then dump it into the pot. The whole mixture will flame. Let it burn for a few seconds, then put a cover on the pot.

Add more sugar to taste. Before serving, take the bag of spices out, and serve with a few raisins and almonds in each glass.

To double the recipe, no need to double the spices . . . just simmer them a little longer.

STEBBINS STINGER

1 jigger (1½ ounces) light Bacardi Rum
   Juice of ½ lime
1 teaspoon brown sugar, rounded (or a heaping teaspoon raw sugar*)
   Cracked ice

The drinks should be frosty cold, so put your cocktail glasses in the freezer a couple of hours early.

Multiply the rum, brown sugar, and lime juice to the number of drinks you want to serve, and put it all in a large cocktail shaker. Add one more jigger of rum "for the pot."

Add lots of cracked ice and shake vigorously. Pour through a strainer into the frosted glasses and serve immediately.

> *Raw sugar is not quite as sweet as brown sugar. It's not a bad idea to prepare the cocktail shaker (minus ice, of course) ahead of time and refrigerate. When you're ready to serve, add the ice and continue as above.*

Bill Baldwin and me (2nd and 3rd from right) with friends at Laguna Beach in those early years

200

DEVILED EGGS (Bob Emmett)

10 eggs
 5 tablespoons mayonnaise
 1 tablespoon finely minced onion
 1 teaspoon lemon juice
    Dash Tabasco sauce
    Dash Worcestershire sauce
    Generous dash paprika
 ½ teaspoon onion salt
 ¼ teaspoon dry mustard
 ¼ teaspoon salt, or to taste
    Chopped chives
    Paprika

Put the eggs in a pot and cover with cold water. Bring the water to a boil and then set a timer for 20 minutes. Turn the heat down so the water barely moves while the eggs cook. At the end of 20 minutes, pour off the hot water and cover the eggs immediately with cold water. Drain again, and let the eggs cool a bit before refrigerating.

When thoroughly chilled, peel the eggs and slice them very carefully in half, lengthwise. Remove the yolks and put in a mixing bowl. Mash the yolks with a fork and add the mayonnaise. When the mixture is blended and smooth, add the minced onions, lemon juice, Tabasco, Worcestershire sauce, paprika, onion salt, mustard, and salt. Blend thoroughly and adjust the seasoning to taste.

Gently fill the holes of the eggwhite halves with the yolk mixture. Pipe it through a decorating tube if you wish. Garnish each half with a dash of paprika and chopped chives. Chill before serving.

To refrigerate, put the stuffed eggs on a plate, stick a toothpick upright into the center of each, and cover the plate gently and completely with plastic wrap.

HORS D'OEUVRES, CANAPÉS

SOUR CREAM DIP

1   cup sour cream
½ cup small curd cottage cheese
2   or 3 scallions, finely chopped, including the green
1   teaspoon dill weed — more if you prefer
¼ teaspoon onion salt
   Salt to taste
   Dash Tabasco sauce
   Freshly ground black pepper
   Paprika

Beat the sour cream and the cottage cheese together until nearly smooth. (You can put it in the blender.) Add everything else except the paprika, adjust the seasoning to taste, and chill thoroughly. Garnish with the paprika before serving. Serve with chilled raw vegetables, or potato chips, Fritos, etc.

> *Raw vegetable suggestions:*
> *Carrot, celery, cucumber sticks*
> *Sweet red or green pepper strips*
> *Cauliflower, broccoli flowerets*
> *Mushrooms: whole, quartered, or sliced*
> *Cherry tomatoes*
> *Scallions*
> *Radishes*

> *To make cucumber sticks, peel the cuke, trim the ends, and cut it in half crosswise. Then slice it lengthwise in quarters. Scoop out the seeds, and slice each strip (lengthwise) in half or thirds, depending on the thickness of the cuke.*

MINCED CLAM DIP

1   can (approximately 10 ounces) minced clams, drained (save some of the juice)
2   (3-ounce) packages cream cheese

2   tablespoons grated (not chopped) onion
¼ teaspoon Tabasco sauce
⅛ teaspoon Worcestershire sauce
½ teaspoon lemon juice
1   teaspoon clam juice
    Salt and freshly ground black pepper to taste

Soften the cream cheese and beat until smooth. Add the remaining ingredients and blend thoroughly. Adjust the seasonings to your taste, and chill. Serve as with the Sour Cream Dip.

This dip is good on crackers, too.

GUACAMOLE

4   fully ripe avocados
½ cup mayonnaise
¼ cup onion, finely chopped
1½ teaspoons salt, or to taste
2   teaspoons chili powder
1   teaspoon garlic powder
½ teaspoon Tabasco sauce
2   tablespoons lemon juice, or more to taste

Peel, seed, and mash the avocado meat. Mix thoroughly with the rest of the ingredients, and taste for seasoning. Chill, and serve as with the Sour Cream Dip.

HOT STUFFED MUSHROOMS

12 mushrooms, each about 1½-inch diameter
1 link hot Italian sausage
3 tablespoons butter
1 large clove garlic, finely chopped
¼ cup dry bread crumbs
2½ tablespoons freshly grated Parmesan cheese
Salt and freshly ground black pepper
1 tablespoon freshly chopped parsley

Wash the mushrooms and carefully remove the stems. Finely chop the stems and reserve.

Melt 1 tablespoon butter in a skillet. Remove the casing from the sausage and add the meat to the skillet, breaking it up into crumbles. Sauté the sausage, stirring frequently, about 5 minutes. Add the chopped mushroom stems and chopped garlic, and continue to sauté, stirring occasionally, about 10 more minutes. Add the bread crumbs, grated cheese, parsley, and salt and pepper to taste. Stir to blend, cook a few more minutes, and turn off the heat.

In another skillet, melt the remaining 2 tablespoons butter and sauté the mushroom caps briefly on both sides. Fill each cap with stuffing, pressing down into the well and piling as high as possible. Put the caps on a foil-lined baking sheet (or into a lightly buttered shallow casserole), and bake at 350° about 15 minutes. Serve hot.

To increase the recipe, double or triple everything, including the butter.

STUFFED MUSHROOMS (Leo Lotito)

24 mushrooms (1½ to 2 inches in diameter)
1 (8-ounce) package cream cheese, softened
4 scallions, finely chopped with the green
¼ green pepper, finely chopped

3   drops soy sauce, or more to taste
10   drops Worcestershire sauce
      Garlic salt
      Salt and freshly ground black pepper
1   (4½-ounce) can chopped, black olives or half of a 3-ounce jar of pimiento-stuffed green olives chopped (approximately and to your taste)

Wash the mushrooms quickly and carefully remove the stems. Cream the cheese until smooth, and add the scallions and green pepper. Add salt, pepper, and garlic salt to taste. Add Worcestershire and soy sauce. Add the chopped olives last.* Stuff the mushrooms with the mixture and chill in the fridge at least 30 minutes before serving.

> *For some mysterious reason, the whole thing is ruined if the olives don't go in* last. *I've never tested it to find out how or why, but Leo says it's so and I trust him.*

SHRIMP CANAPÉS

  ½ cup mayonnaise
1   teaspoon curry powder
    Salt to taste
1   (8-ounce) package frozen, cooked baby shrimp, defrosted
      and thoroughly dried
    White sandwich bread
    Thinly sliced cherry tomatoes (optional)
    Paper-thin slices lemon, cut in quarters
    Chopped chives or parsley

Combine the mayonnaise with the curry powder and season to taste with salt.

Cut 1½- to 2-inch rounds from each slice of sandwich bread. Toast one side lightly under the broiler. Spread the untoasted side with the curried mayonnaise. Top with as many baby shrimp as the toast will accommodate, pressing them gently into the mayonnaise.

Garnish each round with a slice of tomato, if you wish, a lemon quarter, and chives or parsley. Serve immediately.

These canapés don't refrigerate too well.

MIKE DORSEY'S FAKE PÂTÉ

  ½ pound imported liverwurst
6   tablespoons sweet butter, softened
2   tablespoons finely chopped onion
1   scallion, finely minced with the green
2   tablespoons finely chopped pitted green olives
  ½ teaspoon dry mustard
  ¼ teaspoon paprika
    Salt and freshly ground black pepper to taste
1   hard-boiled egg, finely chopped

Mix everything together with a fork. It should be blended, but not a smooth paste. Serve on hot, buttered toast squares, or with crackers. (Makes about 2 cups.)

206

COCKTAIL SHRIMP

Two ways to cook the shrimp. The first is spicier.

For 1 pound shrimp, shelled and deveined:

The First Way

1   quart water
1   clove garlic, minced
½ teaspoon thyme
1   bay leaf
    Generous dash cayenne pepper
    Freshly ground black pepper

The Second Way

1   quart water
½ stalk celery, sliced
1   carrot, sliced
1   white onion, sliced
    Juice of ½ lemon
6   black peppercorns

In both cases, use a large saucepan and bring all the ingredients, except the shrimp, to a boil. Simmer 15 minutes, then bring the pot to a full boil and add the shrimp. Cook, uncovered, over high heat for about 2 minutes, or until the shrimp are pink and firm.

Add salt to taste to the pot, and let the shrimp cool in the broth. Drain, and refrigerate until well chilled.

COCKTAIL SAUCE

1   cup catsup
2   to 3 teaspoons horseradish, or more to taste
¼ to ½ teaspoon lemon juice
    Salt and freshly ground black pepper to taste
    Tabasco sauce to taste

Blend the ingredients thoroughly, and adjust the seasonings to taste. Chill.

207

CRABMEAT DIABLE (Bellevernon Shapiro)

  3   tablespoons butter
  ½ cup chopped fresh mushrooms
  2   tablespoons flour
  ¾ cup plus 2 tablespoons milk
  ½ teaspoon salt
  ¼ teaspoon chili powder
  ⅛ teaspoon Tabasco sauce
  1   (6-ounce) package frozen crabmeat, defrosted and drained
      (or canned or fresh), coarsely chopped
24   croustades (see recipe following)

Melt 1 tablespoon butter in a small skillet and sauté the mushrooms, stirring, about 2 minutes. Set aside.

Melt the remaining 2 tablespoons butter in a saucepan. Add the flour and blend well. When the flour begins to brown, gradually add the milk, stirring constantly. When the sauce is smooth, stir in the salt, chili powder, Tabasco, and sautéed mushrooms. Cook 3 to 5 minutes, stirring, adjusting the heat so the sauce doesn't boil. Fold in the crabmeat, and cool.

Fill the croustades and bake 10 to 15 minutes in a 350° oven, until thoroughly hot, and not too browned. Then put briefly under the broiler till the filling begins to bubble. Serve hot.

> *The filling may be made in advance and refrigerated. Also, the shells may be filled in advance if set in a covered container in the fridge. They may also be frozen.*

CROUSTADES

  2   tablespoons *very* soft butter (soft, not melted)
24   slices very thin white bread

Coat the insides of 24 tiny muffin tins with the butter, using a pastry brush, and *all* the butter. (The bottoms and sides should be heavily coated.)

Cut 3-inch rounds from the bread slices (make sure none of them have holes in the dough), and carefully fit each into a muffin cup. Push the center of the bread into the well and gently mold it around the bottom and sides with your fingertips. (Be careful not to tear the bread. If your nails are longish, the tip of a round-handled wooden spoon is useful to help you.) The idea is to form perfect little cups.

Bake the cups at 400° for about 10 minutes, or until they brown lightly on the rims and outsides. (Don't let them get too brown — they will brown further when baked with the filling.) Remove the cups from the tins and let cool.

> *They freeze well. Fill and bake without defrosting. Be careful when putting under the broiler. They burn easily. Also, don't ever use too liquid a filling, or the bread cases will get soggy.*

TUNA AND CUCUMBER CANAPÉS

  1   (8½-ounce) can tuna fish
  1   rib celery, chopped
  2   scallions, chopped with the green
  ¼ cup mayonnaise, approximately
      Paprika
      Salt and freshly ground black pepper to taste
  1   cucumber
      Pimiento, cut in narrow strips, each about an inch long

Drain the canned tuna thoroughly, and flake into small bits with a fork. Add the chopped celery and scallions. Add the mayonnaise, enough to hold the mixture together, but not too moist. Season to taste with paprika, salt, and pepper. Chill thoroughly.

Wash the cucumber and leave unpeeled. Cut off the ends and slice it into rounds (straight up and down or on the diagonal), about ¼-inch thick or a little less. Spread the rounds generously with the tuna mixture. Garnish each canapé with strips of pimiento, another dash of paprika, and serve chilled.

One can of tuna makes approximately 15 canapés.

PIQUANT SHRIMP

¾ cup olive oil
3   cloves garlic, finely chopped
2   small white onions, finely chopped
2   pounds raw shrimp, shelled and deveined
½ cup white wine vinegar
2   small white onions, thinly sliced (separate the rings)
1   teaspoon salt
½ teaspoon freshly ground black pepper
1   teaspoon dry mustard
¼ teaspoon cayenne pepper
1   tablespoon capers

Sauté the garlic and chopped onions in ¼ cup of the oil for 10 minutes over moderate heat, stirring constantly. Turn the heat down to low and add the shrimp. Cook, stirring, until the shrimp are pink all over, about 5 minutes or more. Cool the mixture.

If it's accumulated liquid in the sautéing, drain the mixture through a fine sieve when cooled, before adding to the marinade.

Make a marinade with the remaining oil and all the rest of the ingredients. Put the cooled shrimp mixture in a large bowl, add the marinade, and stir to coat the shrimp thoroughly. Refrigerate the bowl for about 6 hours, stirring occasionally. (Overnight is fine, too.)

Serve very cold with cocktail picks — and napkins, or on small plates with cocktail forks.

SHRIMP OMELETS (Bill Casey)

¼ cup pastina
3   strips bacon, diced
½ cup onion, finely chopped
½ pound raw shrimp, shelled and deveined
½ tablespoon bouillon

2   eggs
½ quart hot fat

Cook the pastina according to package directions, and drain.

Cook the bacon until golden brown. Remove the bacon bits with a slotted spoon, and add the onions to the bacon skillet. Sauté until tender. Slice the shrimp thinly and add to the onions along with the reserved bacon. Add the beef bouillon and cook over low heat for 2 to 3 minutes. Place in a bowl and add the pastina. Mix and cool.

Beat the eggs lightly with a fork and add to the shrimp mix. Heat the fat to 300°. Drop the shrimp mixture carefully by spoonsful into the hot fat, and cook until golden. Serve hot.

CHOPPED CHICKEN LIVERS (Nina Fonaroff)

1   pound chicken livers
2   tablespoons butter, more or less
2   or 3 medium onions
2   hard-boiled eggs
1   tablespoon chicken fat
    Salt and freshly ground black pepper

Chop the onions and parboil them in water for 5 minutes. Drain the onions through a sieve, pressing them down with the back of a wooden spoon to get rid of all the water. Leave them in the sieve to continue draining, while you sauté the livers.

Sear the livers quickly in hot butter, so they're brown on the outside and rare in the middle. Remove them from the skillet and set aside.

Add a little more butter if necessary and sauté the onions in the liver skillet slowly, until thoroughly tender.

Chop the livers, onions, and eggs together until thoroughly blended. (The largest grind on a food chopper is useful for this.) Melt the chicken fat and add. Add salt and pepper easily . . . don't over-season. Stir with a fork. The mixture shouldn't be a smooth paste.

Serve at room temperature with sweet butter and black Russian bread.

CRABMEAT CANAPÉS (Nina Fonaroff)

6 ounces crabmeat (fresh, frozen, or canned), bones and cartilage removed
3 ounces cream cheese, softened
2 tablespoons butter, softened
2 scallions, finely chopped with the green
Salt and freshly ground black pepper to taste
Paprika
Freshly chopped parsley

Cream the butter and cheese together, and then mix with the crab-meat, scallions, and salt and pepper. If prepared ahead, keep in fridge, but before serving bring to room temperature. Serve on toast rounds, garnished with paprika and parsley.

You may also run the canapés under the broiler briefly. If you do, save adding the garnish until they come out.

DEE BAKER'S COCKTAIL SPREAD

David Baker, pianist-composer, is her son. The recipe was passed on by Emory Bass, an actor friend.

1 (8-ounce) package cream cheese
1 (2½-ounce) package walnut chips (chop a little more with a knife — they should be very small pieces, but not pulverized)
1 small can pitted black olives, finely chopped
2 ounces Bleu cheese, or more to taste
4 tablespoons butter (½ stick)
¼ cup Sherry, approximately — enough to loosen and mix

Soften the cheeses and butter, and mix everything thoroughly to blend. The flavor develops the longer it stands. Keep in the fridge, but take it out a little before serving so the spread can soften up. Serve with crackers, toasts, black bread, etc.

MARINATED RIPE OLIVES (Bob Emmett)

1 (7¼-ounce) can "large" black olives with pits
  Olive oil
1 teaspoon salt
1 to 2 garlic cloves, minced or crushed
  Freshly ground black pepper
  Large pinches each: basil, oregano, and rosemary

Drain the olives and put them in a glass jar with a screw top. (A 12-ounce peanut butter jar is perfect.) Add olive oil to cover. Add the rest of the ingredients. Shake the jar well and let stand at room temperature at least *three* hours. The jar may be refrigerated then, but always serve at room temperature. Drain off the marinade before serving.

> *It's Bob's feeling that the giant, colossal, super-colossal olives are not as flavorsome as the smaller variety. Any size will do, of course.*

STUFFED CELERY

1 tablespoon butter, softened
1 tablespoon Roquefort cheese, softened
1 (3-ounce) package cream cheese, softened
  Salt to taste
1 teaspoon caraway seeds
  Paprika
  Dwarf celery ribs or celery hearts

Mix the butter, cheeses, salt, and seeds thoroughly. Mound in the scrubbed and dried celery ribs. Sprinkle with paprika and chill.

> *Also try stuffing celery with Guacamole, Minced Clam Dip, Crabmeat Canapé mix, or a combination of cottage cheese, salt, pepper, minced clams, and Tabasco. Garnish with paprika.*

CHEESE AND BACON CANAPÉS (Bellevernon Shapiro)

1 pound sharp Cheddar cheese (or sharp Tillamook)
½ pound lean bacon
½ green pepper
½ medium onion
  Garlic salt
  Worcestershire sauce
  Sourdough French bread, sourdough English muffins, or regular English muffins

Grind the cheese, bacon, green pepper, and onion together in a meat grinder. (It's easier if everything is chopped up a bit first.) Add garlic salt and Worcestershire sauce to taste.

Cut the bread slices or muffin halves in half or quarters, to make canapé-sized pieces. Spread each generously with the cheese-bacon mixture, and put under a very hot broiler for 5 minutes, until browned on top. Serve hot.

Everything can be done ahead of time up to the broiling.

I prefer using sourdough English muffins, but I've been able to get them only in California. It's your preference as to the other two. The sourdough flavor is the best, but the texture of English muffins is very nice, too.

MARINATED MUSHROOMS STUFFED WITH TARTAR STEAK

36 mushrooms (approx. 1½ inches in diameter)
6 tablespoons oil
2 tablespoons cider vinegar
1½ teaspoons salt
  Freshly ground black pepper

Wash the mushrooms, remove the stems carefully, and dry.

Mix the rest of the ingredients in a large bowl. Toss the mushrooms in the dressing and chill at least 30 minutes . . . preferably longer. Toss them again once or twice. Before stuffing them, drain on paper towels.

TARTAR STEAK STUFFING

½ pound good steak (round or sirloin), trimmed of *all* fat and
    freshly ground
1 egg yolk
½ cup minced sweet onion, more or less
   Salt and freshly ground black pepper to taste
   Capers, drained
   Watercress or parsley sprigs

In a bowl, mix the ground steak, raw egg yolk, minced onion, salt, and pepper thoroughly. Roll into balls, large enough to fit the mushroom caps generously. Garnish each stuffed mushroom with a few capers. Chill thoroughly in the fridge before serving on a bed of watercress or parsley sprigs. (They tend to skid a lot without the greens, so the addition is not purely aesthetic.)

Nina Fonaroff directing her dance-drama "Lazarus" in 1952

STUFFED GRAPE LEAVES (Regina Ress)

Regina and I were in "The Women" together at the 46th St. Theatre. The recipe originated with her friend Arisdene Krikorian. It makes about 50 pieces.

4 large onions, finely chopped
   Olive oil
1 cup raw rice
½ bunch parsley, finely chopped
½ cup currants
½ teaspoon cinnamon, or more to taste
2 tablespoons pignola nuts
   Salt and freshly ground black pepper
1 jar vine leaves
½ cup water
   Juice of 1 lemon
   Parsley sprigs
   Lemon wedges

Sauté the chopped onions in the oil 10 minutes. Add the rice, minced parsley, currants, cinnamon, pignolas, and salt and pepper to taste. Cook another 10 minutes, stirring.

Pour the brine off the grape leaves. Unroll them, and put in boiling water 5 minutes, to soften and cleanse.

Cut off the stems of the leaves, and lay them out shiny side down. Adjust the amount of filling to the size of the leaf (use two leaves if they're very small), tuck the sides in and roll like cigars.

Pack the rolls tightly, in layers, in a casserole. Put parsley sprigs between each layer, and cover the top layer with left-over grape leaves. Mix the water and lemon juice, and pour over all. Then put an oven-proof plate on top to keep the rolls from floating.

Bake at 350° for 1 to 1½ hours, or until done. Serve them cold with lemon wedges.

They keep well in the fridge, and improve with age.

LENTIL SOUP

2   cups lentils, picked over and washed thoroughly (if the package directions insist, soak overnight in water to cover)

1   large, or 2 medium onions, coarsely chopped

2   or 3 leeks, coarsely chopped (white part only)

2   carrots, scraped and cut in dice

1   large stalk celery, diced

2   cloves garlic, finely chopped

4   tablespoons butter

⅓ ham hock

Salt and freshly ground black pepper

¼ teaspoon thyme

1   bay leaf

1   tablespoon chopped fresh parsley

Dash or two of cayenne pepper

6   cups liquid (4 cups chicken broth plus 2 cups water)

Hot, cooked, skinless frankfurters, cut in ½-inch slices (optional)

Melt the butter in a heavy casserole and add the onions, leeks, carrots, celery, garlic, and ham hock. Toss in the butter over moderately low heat for 20 minutes, without browning.

Stir in the drained lentils. Season with salt and pepper, and add the thyme, bay leaf, parsley, and cayenne. Add the liquid and stir to mix thoroughly. Bring the pot to a boil, cover, and simmer gently for 1½ hours, or until the lentils are quite soft. Stir occasionally during the cooking.

Correct the seasoning, remove the ham hock and bay leaf, and serve piping hot. Top each serving with a handful of the hot frankfurter chunks. Serves 6.

This soup is quite thick. If you prefer to serve it as a first course, add just one cup lentils.

BORSCHT (Nina Fonaroff)

*Nina asked me to mention that
this is her adaptation of Vera
Fonaroff's recipe, fully approved
by Vera. (Her mother didn't
hand out such kudos readily.)*

6   or 7 bunches of beets
1   dozen big, fat, soft red tomatoes
5   big Spanish onions
1   medium green cabbage
     Water
2   or 3 potatoes
     Salt to taste
1   dozen lemons, juiced (you may use less, but have this
        much ready)
     Sugar to taste
½ dozen eggs

Scrub the beets thoroughly and trim the ends. Save the roots, but make sure they're very clean. Peel the beets, and put the peelings with the roots in a saucepan. Cover them with water, bring the pot to a boil, and turn the heat down to a simmer. Keep the pot at a gentle simmer until ready to use. Leave the beets whole and tie them up in cheesecloth. Put them in the bottom of a *very* large pot. (I find it's easier to use two 10-quart pots, and divide everything in half.)

Peel and core the tomatoes with a paring knife. (It's not necessary to be meticulous when cutting away the skin.) Save the tomato peelings, tie them up in cheesecloth, and add to the main pot. Quarter the tomatoes and add. Peel the onions and chop very coarsely. Discard the core of the cabbage and chop the rest very coarsely. Add the onions and cabbage to the main pot.

Measure the water as you add it to the pot, pushing the vegetables down with your hand or a large spoon, and add just enough to barely cover the vegetables, no more. (Make a note of how much water you added.) Bring the pot to a boil and turn the fire to very low. Cook *very* gently until the vegetables are tender but not mushy. Approximately 2 hours.

Peel the potatoes, cut in quarters, and then slice them about ¼-inch thick. Add the potatoes to the pot about ½ hour before you think the beets will be done. Also add salt, a scant teaspoon for each quart of water you put in.

When the vegetables are tender, pull out the cheesecloth bags. Squeeze the tomato-peeling bag over the pot so none of the juice is lost, and discard the peelings. Cut the beets up in small cubes or julienne, and return them to the pot. As soon as the potatoes are tender, take the pot off heat. Pour the hot liquid of the beet-peeling pot through a sieve into the main pot.

Add the lemon juice, a little at a time, stirring all the while, and add sugar slowly, tablespoon by tablespoon, taking it easy. Keep tasting after each addition of lemon juice and sugar. Perhaps add more salt. This part is the most difficult, to balance the lemon juice, sugar, and salt to reach the proper sweet-sour flavor. Take great care not to get it too sweet. When you're satisfied with the seasoning, let the soup cool a bit. (Not too cool, or the eggs won't blend.)

Beat the eggs. Add some of the soup broth to the eggs, stirring. Then turn it all back into the soup pot, stirring constantly so the eggs won't curdle and they're thoroughly blended.

Serve the Borscht cold, with a large dab of sour cream on top. It *may* be served hot, but traditionally it should be cold.

> *The liquid from the beet peelings and roots is basically for the deep, rich, red color, but it also adds extra nourishment.*
>
> *The recipe makes approximately 4 gallons, and freezes well.*

NINA'S WINTER BORSCHT

2   or 3 pounds or *more* (as many as possible) veal knuckle bones, chopped up very small
1   large onion stuck with 2 cloves
4   leeks, chopped very coarsely
1   stalk celery with the leaves, cut in half
3   or 4 carrots, cut in lengths
1   bunch parsley

Put the veal bones in a heavy pot and cover with at least 5 quarts of water. Simmer *very* gently for 8 hours. Keep removing the scum as it accumulates on the surface. After a minimum of 8 hours, add the vegetables and simmer 3 more hours. Strain the liquid through a sieve lined with cheesecloth.

Follow the instructions for regular Borscht, starting with 1½ to 2 pounds brisket of beef, as lean as possible, cut in 1½-inch cubes. (Remove all visible fat before weighing.)

Instead of adding water to the main pot, add the stock from the knuckle bones, measuring the amount as in the master recipe. (You shouldn't need more liquid, but if you do, supplement with water.)

Keep skimming fat and scum off the surface of the soup liquid as it simmers.

Serve the Winter Borscht hot only, with sour cream.

Vera Fonaroff's original recipe included chicken feet, cleaned and boiled before being added to the brisket and vegetables. Since it's nearly impossible to buy chicken feet in New York City, Nina eliminated them from her adaptation. But she remembers with pleasure the very special flavor they added to the soup, and how delicious they were to eat.

CHICKEN AND CHINESE CABBAGE SOUP (Bob Emmett)

1   2½- to 3-pound chicken, cut up
2   teaspoons salt
5   whole peppercorns
1   onion, quartered
1   bay leaf
    A few parsley sprigs
1   small Chinese cabbage, trimmed and cut crosswise into
        ½-inch shreds
    ½ cup sliced water chestnuts (or sliced red radishes)
    Dash or two of soy sauce
    Chopped chives or scallions

Put the chicken, salt, peppercorns, onion, bay leaf, and parsley sprigs in a heavy pot with 6 cups of water, enough to cover. Bring the pot to a boil, reduce the heat, and simmer for 45 minutes, or until the chicken is tender. Cool.

Take the chicken from the broth, remove the skin and bones, and cut the meat into strips. Strain the broth, and reserve the onions.

If you can, cook the chicken a day ahead and refrigerate the strained broth overnight, so the fat can be thoroughly removed before making the soup.

Add enough water to the broth to measure 5 cups. Bring the broth to a boil, add the cabbage and allow to wilt. Add the chicken, reserved onions, water chestnuts, and soy sauce, and correct the seasoning. More salt, possibly.

When thoroughly hot, serve the soup garnished with chopped chives or scallions.

TOSSED SALAD SUGGESTIONS

I suppose there is no sort of lettuce we don't enjoy in a salad, as long as it's young, tender, and fresh.

Listing all the varieties would be an exercise in futility. Just from Manhattan to Los Angeles to East Hampton, lettuce may look alike but isn't named alike. Our choices are what *we* call Boston, Romaine, Curly, Red Tip, Field, Bibb, Garden, Chicory (if *very* young). And other greens such as Watercress, young Spinach (stems removed), Arugula (an Italian green similar to watercress, with a bite all its own).

Generally we toss two or three different textures and flavors together and then add a few "extras." Not too many . . . a salad can get cluttered. (Unless the entrée is very light and we feel like a "zoftig" salad to go with it. Of course, the opposite happens, too. There's nothing like Bibb lettuce, when it's in season, all by itself.)

A few suggestions for the "extras":

> Belgian Endive . . . either whole leaves, or broken up.
> Scallions . . . sliced with the green, or sometimes they're thrown in whole.
> Raw Mushrooms . . . sliced, or chunked.
> Onion Rings . . . red Italian, or sweet white, sliced very thin.
> Tomatoes . . . in wedges or chunks; or cherry tomatoes, whole or halved.
> Green Pepper (or sweet Red Pepper) . . . sliced in thin strips.
> Cucumber . . . either sliced very thin, peeled or not; or peeled and chunked.
> Mung Bean Sprouts . . . we grow our own from the seeds.
> Avocado . . . sliced lengthwise, or cut in bite-sized chunks.
> Artichoke hearts or bottoms . . . canned, sometimes packed in oil, sometimes in brine . . . whole, halved, or quartered, depending on size.
> Baby Alaskan Shrimp . . . cooked, of course.
> Garbanzos . . . drained.
> Pitted Black Olives . . . whole or halved.
> Cheese . . . small chunks of Roquefort, bleu, Gruyère, whatever.
> Croutons . . . garlic or plain.
> Toasted Wheat Germ . . . sprinkled on at the last minute.

Everything seems to stay fresh longer if washed, spun dried, and put in plastic bags in the crisper as soon as it's brought home. My friend, Belle Shapiro, passed on a marvelous suggestion. If you have a *lot* of lettuce to dry, and you have a washing machine handy . . . put it all in a lingerie bag and run it through the short-cycle "Spin Dry." Saves a lot of time and energy.

TOMATO AND ONION SALAD

For a smaller platter, use fewer tomatoes and onions. The dressing will keep in the fridge for other occasions.

4   large, ripe, red tomatoes, sliced
4   red Italian onions, or Spanish onions, sliced
 ¾ cup olive oil
 ¼ cup wine vinegar
2   tablespoons capers
2   teaspoons basil
1   teaspoon salt, or to taste
 ¼ teaspoon freshly ground black pepper
    Parsley sprigs
    Finely chopped fresh parsley or chives

Alternate tomato and onion slices in overlapping circles on a platter. Blend the oil, vinegar, capers, basil, salt, and pepper. Pour about half the dressing over the tomatoes and onions. Cover with plastic wrap and chill thoroughly.

When ready to serve, decorate the platter with parsley, and sprinkle the tomatoes and onions with chopped parsley or chives. Serve with the remaining dressing.

BOB'S SALAD DRESSING (Bob Emmett)

    9   tablespoons oil (mixed half and half . . . olive and peanut)
    3   tablespoons cider vinegar
    ¾ teaspoon salt, or to taste
    ¼ teaspoon freshly ground black pepper
    ⅛ teaspoon dry mustard
        Dash Worcestershire sauce
        Dash Tabasco sauce
    1   clove garlic, sliced into 4 pieces, lengthwise
    5   capers
    ⅛ teaspoon salad herbs (optional)

    or (also optional)

Pinches of:
        Dried basil, oregano, parsley, chervil, rosemary
    4   green peppercorns (optional)

Put everything into a cruet, or a jar with a screw top, and shake vigorously.

If the weather isn't too hot, and you use the dressing daily, there's no need to refrigerate it.

If you do refrigerate the dressing, be sure to bring it to room temperature before using it.

Always shake the bottle well before gently tossing the dressing with the salad. Use enough to coat the greens, but they should never swim in it. Add at the very last minute before serving.

> *Bob will also vary the vinegar as well as the "optionals." He's been known to use red or white wine vinegar, plain white vinegar, lemon juice, or a mixture of lemon juice and vinegar. For example, lemon juice makes a gentler dressing for something as delicate as field lettuce.*
>
> *Of course, tarragon vinegar is splendid, too. It's not in the list only because Bob isn't too keen about it. He rarely uses it.*

224

CELERY SEED DRESSING

*A bit of family competition. Bob's
oldest brother, George McMenamin,
contributed this one when he was
padre of Our Lady of Refuge Church
in Castroville, Calif. He got it from
his housekeeper, Lucy Poor, who
got it from Margaret Romero.*

½ cup sugar
1   teaspoon dry mustard
1   teaspoon salt
1   teaspoon grated onion
1   teaspoon paprika
¼ cup wine vinegar, or ⅓ cup cider vinegar
1   cup oil (half olive, half peanut)
1   teaspoon to 1 tablespoon celery seeds

Mix the sugar, mustard, salt, onion, and paprika together.

Alternately add the vinegar and oil, a little at a time, the vinegar first. Beat well. Add the celery seeds last. Pour the dressing into a jar, cover tightly, and store in the fridge.

Bring it out of the fridge about an hour before ready to use. Shake the jar vigorously, and serve the dressing on almost any kind of salad . . . fresh greens, vegetables, or fruit.

*You can also put everything at once into a mixer
bowl, and beat on medium speed until thoroughly
blended, about 5 minutes, or longer, until the sugar
is dissolved.*

COLE SLAW (Grandmother Cole)

½ large head green cabbage
1 tablespoon butter
1 teaspoon salt
1 teaspoon dry mustard
1 tablespoon sugar
¼ teaspoon freshly ground black pepper
2 eggs
1 cup milk
3 tablespoons vinegar

Slice the cabbage in wedges, cut out the core and discard. Then finely chop the cabbage and put in a bowl.

Melt the butter in the top of a double boiler. Add the salt, mustard, sugar, and pepper, and blend thoroughly. Beat the eggs with the milk, and add to the butter mixture slowly, stirring constantly.

When the mixture is hot, slowly add the vinegar, stirring all the while. Cook until the dressing masks the spoon (do *not* let it boil), and then pour hot over the chopped cabbage.

Toss to mix thoroughly, let cool, and refrigerate.

BLUEBERRY MOLD (Bellevernon Shapiro)

Step I.

2 packages lemon Jello
2 large cans blueberries
½ large banana, mashed — or 1 medium can drained, crushed pineapple — or both
½ pint heavy cream, whipped

Lightly brush a 2½-quart mold with vegetable oil, preferably a ring mold, and turn it upside down on paper toweling to drain.

Pour the cans of blueberries into a sieve placed over a saucepan large enough to capture all the juice. Drain the blueberries thoroughly and set aside.

Heat the liquid from the cans with enough water to make 3 cups. Dissolve the Jello in this hot liquid. Cool, and let set until it begins to firm, then whip. Fold in the crushed banana or pineapple or both. Fold in the whipped cream, and then pour the mixture into the prepared mold.

Let set long enough so that when you pour in the second part it won't run into the first.

Step II.

2	packages lemon Jello
2	cups hot water
3	teaspoons sugar
1	teaspoon vanilla
1	pint sour cream, beaten until smooth

Dissolve the Jello in the hot water, cool, and let set until it begins to firm. Whip the Jello, add the sugar, vanilla, and sour cream, and blend. Let set long enough so it won't weep too much into the blueberry mixture, and then pour gently into the mold.

Sprinkle the drained blueberries over the top, and put in the fridge to set thoroughly. Preferably overnight.

When ready to serve, unmold on a large platter.

> *I suppose this could work for a dessert, but both Belle and I serve it as a buffet salad. It's handsome, and has much more character than any gelatin mold I've ever eaten.*
>
> *A ring mold is especially attractive if you have a small bowl to set carefully inside the center when the Jello is unmolded. Fill it with a few fresh flowers . . . roses, camellias . . .*

CHERRY TOMATOES IN GARLIC

2 pints cherry tomatoes
½ cup olive oil
2 tablespoons red wine vinegar
3 large cloves garlic, finely chopped
   Dash marjoram
   Dash tarragon
   Salt and freshly ground black pepper to taste
1 tablespoon finely chopped fresh parsley

Put the washed tomatoes in a pot, and cover with boiling water. Let stand 10 to 15 seconds, and drain immediately. When cool enough to handle, peel. Combine the remaining ingredients and pour over the tomatoes in a bowl. Chill.

Remove the bowl from the fridge a half hour or so before serving, so the dressing will loosen.

George McMenamin when pastor of the Old Mission in San Juan Bautista

EAST INDIAN STEWED TOMATOES

¼ pound butter
2 medium onions, chopped
1 clove garlic, finely chopped
½ teaspoon freshly grated ginger
½ teaspoon chili powder
8 ripe, red tomatoes, peeled, cored, and chopped
2 teaspoons salt
2 tablespoons flaked coconut

Melt the butter in a large skillet. Add the onion, garlic, ginger, and chili powder. Sauté for about 5 minutes, stirring occasionally. Add the tomatoes, salt, and coconut. Simmer over moderately low heat for 15 minutes, or until most of the liquid is absorbed.

This recipe will serve 6 to 8. If you're doubling the recipe for a large group, 12 tablespoons butter are sufficient. Also, test 3 teaspoons salt before adding 4.

STEAMED ONIONS

3 large onions, Spanish or Bermuda
4 tablespoons butter
1½ teaspoons salt
1½ teaspoons paprika

Slice the onions very thin and separate into rings. Melt the butter in a large skillet with a top. Add the onions, salt, and paprika, and stir gently to blend. When the butter is sizzling, cover the skillet and turn the heat to very low. Steam the onions in the butter about 20 minutes, or until they are soft.

A variation is to add 1 tablespoon brown sugar when the onions are done, and cook 1 minute longer.

If you wish, eliminate the butter and substitute a small amount of water, just enough to cover the bottom of the skillet.

ARTICHOKES

> 4 medium to large artichokes
> 1 small onion, sliced
> 1 garlic clove, cut in half
> 1 or 2 ribs celery with leaves, cut in 2-inch lengths
> ½ lemon, juiced
> 1 tablespoon salt
> 4 teaspoons olive oil

Wash the artichokes by holding the stems and plunging them up and down in a large pot of cold water. Remove the tough bottom row of leaves. Slice off the stems, and with scissors, cut off all the thorns. Also slice ½ to ¾ inch off the tops.

Place the artichokes in a pot that will hold them upright in one layer . . . in 1½ inches of boiling water containing all the remaining ingredients except the oil. Dribble 1 teaspoon of the oil on top of each choke.

Sprinkle more salt on top of the artichokes, and simmer covered, for about 45 minutes . . . or until tender. Pull out one of the lower leaves to test . . . if it feels right to your teeth, it's done. Lift the artichokes carefully from the pot with tongs, and drain.

Serve hot, warm, or cold . . . with mayonnaise or melted butter on the side.

> *If you're fond of garlic, slip thin slices here and there between the leaves before putting the artichokes in the pot to cook.*

BROCCOLI WITH GARLIC

Peel the stems of the broccoli and slice them on the diagonal into 1-inch sections. Separate the flowerets into 2 to 4 pieces, according to size.

Sauté the broccoli in hot oil, with several cloves of garlic cut in half, for 2 minutes in a covered skillet. Add 2 to 4 tablespoons water, salt to taste, freshly ground black pepper, and a sprinkle of lemon juice. Cook over low heat, covered, for 10 more minutes, or until tender. Do not overcook. Serve as is, or sprinkled with freshly grated Parmesan cheese.

STEWED TOMATOES À LA AGNES McMENAMIN (Bob Emmett)

1   tablespoon butter
1   small onion, chopped coarsely
¼ green pepper, chopped coarsely
1   large can tomatoes
1   clove garlic, cut in half
¼ teaspoon sugar
¼ teaspoon basil
¼ teaspoon oregano
1   bay leaf
   Salt and freshly ground black pepper to taste
2   slices French or Italian bread, toasted and cubed with the crusts

Heat the butter in a large skillet and sauté the onion and green pepper 10 minutes. Add everything else except the croutons, and simmer 15 minutes.

Adjust the seasoning. Add the croutons, and cook 2 to 3 minutes longer.

VEGETABLES IN FOIL (Jane Warwick)

Cut Italian red onions and ripe, red tomatoes into wedges, and cut zucchini and yellow squash into ½-inch slices. Place the vegetables in the center of a doubled layer of heavy foil.

Add salt and pepper to taste, and generous chunks of butter. Wrap the foil securely, and either put on the rack over a charcoal fire, or in a preheated 350° oven. Let cook 15 to 30 minutes. Test for doneness. The vegetables should be slightly crisp.

This makes a wonderfully easy and delicious accompaniment to an outdoor barbecue, but is equally fine for any meal, anyplace.

FRIJOLES (Bob Emmett)

    4   cups dried Mexican beans, or red kidney beans
    6   cups water
    4   teaspoons salt

Wash the beans. Heat the water to lukewarm in a heavy pot and add the beans. Cover and cook slowly until the beans are tender, about 2 hours. Add salt 30 minutes before the beans are done. Drain off 2 cups bean liquid and spoon out 1 cup beans for making the sauce.

SALSA DE FRIJOLES

    ½ cup bacon drippings or cooking oil
    1   clove garlic, finely chopped
    ½ cup chopped onion
    ½ cup chopped green pepper
    1   cup cooked beans
    2   cups bean liquid
    1½ teaspoons chili powder
    ½ teaspoon freshly ground black pepper

Heat the bacon drippings in a skillet. Add the garlic, onions, and green pepper, and cook until limp. Add ½ cup of the beans and mash thoroughly. Add 1 cup of the bean liquid. Repeat with the rest of the beans and liquid. (This thickens the sauce.) Cook until the mixture is thick, and add the seasonings. Pour over the frijoles, mix well, and serve.

SWEET AND SOUR CABBAGE

    1   red cabbage
    3   apples
    3   medium onions
    ¼ pound butter

3   tablespoons brown (or raw) sugar
¼ to ½ teaspoon freshly grated nutmeg
The rind of one orange, grated
Salt and freshly ground black pepper to taste
Bouquet garni, tied in cheesecloth (thyme, parsley, and bay leaf)
3   ounces red wine (optional)

Cut the cabbage in wedges and discard the core. Slice the wedges. Peel, core, and chop the apples coarsely. Halve the onions, and slice.

Melt the butter in a very large, heavy casserole. Add the cabbage, apples, onions, and rest of the ingredients except the wine. Toss to mix well.

Cover the casserole tightly and cook very gently for at least 2 hours, or until the cabbage is very soft. Add the optional wine, and cook another 5 minutes. Remove the bouquet garni and serve.

BELLE'S RICE (Bellevernon Shapiro)

3   cups cooked rice
3   pints sour cream
2   cans diced Ortega green chiles (seeds removed and rinsed under cold water first)
¾ pound Monterey jack cheese, thinly sliced
½ cup grated sharp Cheddar cheese
Salt and freshly ground black pepper to taste

Butter a large casserole. Mix the sour cream, chiles, salt, and pepper in the blender. Mix the rice and sour cream mixture in a large bowl. Put a layer of this mixture in the casserole, strips of jack cheese on top, another layer of rice, jack cheese, etc. When ready to cook, bake in a 350° oven for 30 minutes, or until it bubbles. Add the Cheddar cheese on top, and bake another 5 minutes, or until the cheese melts.

The casserole can be prepared and arranged a day ahead. Simply keep it in the fridge until half an hour before baking time.

RATATOUILLE

*The definitive recipe is probably Michael Field's.
But this is quite a respectable version, developed
in a household that's usually pressed for time.*

1 onion, chopped coarsely
1 green pepper, cut julienne (in thin strips)
1 sweet red pepper, cut julienne
1 medium-size zucchini, sliced in ½-inch rounds
1 yellow squash, sliced in ½-inch rounds
1 small eggplant, sliced in ½-inch rounds
2 tomatoes, peeled, cored, and cut up coarsely
   Freshly chopped parsley
2 or 3 large garlic cloves, chopped finely
   Salt and freshly ground black pepper
   Olive oil

Layer the vegetables in the order listed in a heavy saucepan or casserole. On top of each layer, add a sprinkle of chopped parsley, chopped garlic, salt, and pepper. When the casserole is fully assembled, lightly sprinkle a little olive oil on top. *Very* little.

Bring the pot to a sizzle, cover, and turn the heat low. Simmer 30 to 45 minutes, or until all the vegetables are tender. Every 10 minutes, with a bulb baster, withdraw the liquid that accumulates in the bottom of the pot. Put the liquid in a small saucepan and reserve. When the ratatouille is done, reduce the liquid in the saucepan over high heat until it is a brownish glaze. Pour over the ratatouille.

It can be served either hot or cold.

STUFFED ARTICHOKES (Marilyn Weitz)

    4   artichokes — cook as in Artichokes (P. 230) and drain
    ½ cup mayonnaise
    ¼ cup sour cream
    2   tablespoons French mustard
    1   tablespoon Bavarian-style mustard
    1   tablespoon brown sugar
        Capers
        Celery seed
        Onion salt
        Table salt and freshly ground black pepper
    ½ pound tiny Bay shrimp

When the artichokes are cool, remove the center leaves and scoop out the choke.

Mix the mayonnaise, sour cream, mustards, and brown sugar together until well blended. Add capers, celery seed, onion salt, table salt, and pepper to taste. Stir in the shrimp and fill the center of each artichoke with the mixture.

Serve to four, and dip the leaves in the center sauce to eat.

BAKED OR BROILED EGGPLANT

Cut off the stem end and slice the eggplant into ½- to ¾-inch slices, crosswise. (It's not necessary to peel them, but you may if you prefer.) Spread both sides of the slices generously with soft butter or oil, and season with salt, pepper, paprika, grated onion, and lemon juice.

Place them on a foil-lined baking sheet and broil, or bake in a 400° oven, until tender. Turn them once with a wide spatula. (If broiling, put the pan at least 5 inches from the flame.) It should take no more than 5 minutes on each side broiling, and 8 minutes on each side baking.

> *A tasty variation is to mix a few crushed blanched almonds with the soft butter before spreading on the slices.*

CHINESE FRIED RICE

> 1   cup rice
> 2   cups water

Early in the day, or the day before, put the rice and water in a deep, heavy saucepan. Cover with a tight-fitting lid. Set over high heat and bring to a boil. After steam appears around the lid, cook for 3 minutes. Reduce heat to medium and cook 5 minutes. Reduce heat to very low and cook 12 minutes longer. Turn off the heat and let the rice stand 5 to 10 minutes still covered. Remove cover, cool, and chill well. (This method produces good *dry* rice.)

> 2   tablespoons peanut oil
> 1   clove garlic, finely chopped
> 1   slice fresh ginger, minced . . . or ½ teaspoon powdered ginger
> 2   scallions, chopped, including the green
> 1   tablespoon freshly chopped parsley
> 1   egg beaten lightly
> ⅛ teaspoon ground white pepper
> 2   tablespoons soy sauce
>   Salt to taste

Optionals:

> ¼ to ½ cup sliced mushrooms
> ¼ cup thinly sliced water chestnuts
> ¼ cup celery, diced small
> 1   cup cooked, diced pork, ham, chicken, shrimp, beef, what you will

Combine the scallions, parsley, and any combination of the optionals (or all, or none) in a bowl. In another bowl, combine the egg, soy sauce, and pepper.

Heat a wok or skillet hot and dry. Add the oil. Brown the garlic and ginger slightly, then add the rice, stirring to break up the lumps and coat evenly with the oil. Cook 3 to 5 minutes, or until the rice is thoroughly heated.

Add all the rest of the ingredients except the egg mixture and the salt. Fry and stir constantly until thoroughly mixed and hot.

Add the egg mixture, and stir to mix well. Cook, stirring, about 2 more minutes. Add salt if desired.

Serve immediately while hot.

RICE WITH ALMONDS AND MUSHROOM SAUCE (Louise Welty)

Louise is an old friend of Bob's from his youth. She and husband Dan are the guiding lights of the Gaslight Troupers in Folsom, California.

⅔ cup rice
¼ pound mushrooms, sliced or quartered
4 tablespoons butter
2 tablespoons flour
1 cup strong beef stock (or more)
¼ cup blanched slivered almonds
    Salt, freshly ground black pepper, paprika, Tabasco sauce, lemon juice, mixed herbs, Sherry

Steam the rice in 1½ cups water until done. Sauté the mushrooms in 1 tablespoon of the butter.

Melt 2 tablespoons butter and stir in the flour. When the flour is brown, add the beef stock gradually, stirring constantly, and heat to boiling. If too thick, add more stock . . . the sauce should be thin. Season with the last 7 items to taste. Add the sautéed mushrooms to the sauce.

Sauté the almonds in the remaining tablespoon of butter. Mix the almonds with the rice. The sauce may be poured over the rice when serving, or stirred in.

This reheats well in a covered casserole, so may be made early in the day.

LENTILS

2   cups dried lentils
2   medium onions, halved and thinly sliced
2   tablespoons chopped fresh parsley
2   ounces salt pork, half a ham hock, or a fat piece of corned
     beef
1   bay leaf, crumbled
     Pinch of ground cloves
2   garlic cloves, thinly sliced
 ½ teaspoon freshly ground black pepper
1½ teaspoons salt, or more to taste
2   to 3 tablespoons butter

Pick the lentils over carefully and wash them in cold water. If the package suggests soaking overnight, do so, in 4 cups water. If not, put them in a heavy pot and add water to cover. Add all the rest of the ingredients except the salt and butter. (If the lentils have been soaked and too much water has evaporated, add more just to cover, and cook in the soaking water.)

> Lentils tend to produce a kind of gas while soaking, so if they've been standing overnight, it's best to cook them in the morning and reheat later when ready to use.

> To vary the recipe, try adding 1½ to 2 cups sliced carrots (cut in ½-inch rounds) with the lentils. Add water just to cover, and then the remaining ingredients (except salt and butter as above).

Bring the pot to a boil, cover, and turn the heat to very low. Simmer gently for about 30 minutes, stirring occasionally to keep the lentils from sticking to the bottom. Add more water if necessary, but try to regulate the quantity so the water is absorbed when the lentils are done.

After 15 minutes, add the salt, stir, and continue simmering. When the lentils are tender (but not mushy), remove the salt pork or ham hock, correct the seasoning, and add the butter.

RICE PILAF

- 1 cup rice
- 2 cups beef bouillon
- 1 tablespoon butter
- ½ cup white raisins
- ½ teaspoon salt
- ¼ cup blanched slivered almonds, toasted until golden under the broiler

Combine the rice, bouillon, butter, raisins, and salt in a saucepan. Bring the pot to a boil and stir. Cover, and simmer gently for 14 minutes, or until the liquid is absorbed. Add the almonds, mix lightly with a fork, and serve.

SPANISH RICE

- 2 tablespoons butter
- 2 tablespoons oil
- 1 cup finely chopped onion
- ½ cup finely chopped green pepper
- 1 clove garlic, finely chopped
- 1 cup rice
- 1 bay leaf
- 2 cups chicken broth
- ½ cup tomato juice
- ½ teaspoon brown sugar
- 1 teaspoon chili powder
- ½ teaspoon leaf saffron, crushed in your fingers
- ¼ teaspoon thyme
- Salt and freshly ground black pepper to taste

Heat the butter and oil in a casserole. Add the onions, green pepper, and garlic. Cook until the onion wilts, and add the rice. Cook the rice, stirring, about 2 minutes, and then stir in the remaining ingredients.

Bring the casserole to a boil, cover tightly, and bake in a 375° oven for 30 minutes, or until the rice is tender.

LAUREL RICE

    2   tablespoons butter
    1   tablespoon finely chopped onion
    ½ teaspoon finely chopped garlic
    1   cup rice
    ½ bay leaf
    ¼ teaspoon thyme
    ⅛ teaspoon cayenne pepper (optional)
  2⅛ cups chicken stock
    2   sprigs fresh parsley

Melt the butter in a saucepan and cook the onion and garlic until wilted but not brown. Add the rice, bay leaf, thyme, and cayenne. Cook, stirring, about 2 minutes.

Meanwhile bring the chicken stock to a boil. Add it to the rice with the parsley sprigs, stir once, cover tightly, and simmer about 15 minutes or until the liquid is absorbed. Remove the bay leaf and parsley sprigs before serving.

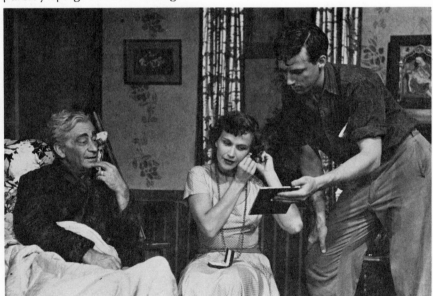

J. Peter Happel

Bob and me on tour with Art Smith in "They Knew What They Wanted" — Summer, 1952

BROWN RICE SOUFFLÉ

    2   cups cooked brown rice (add salt to the water when
           cooking)
    ¼ cup chopped watercress
    ¼ cup chopped raw spinach
    ¼ cup chopped parsley (preferably Italian, for sturdier
           flavor)
    ¼ cup scallions, chopped with the green
    1   cup grated Gruyère or imported Swiss cheese
    ½ teaspoon thyme
    3   eggs, separated

Combine everything except the eggs in a mixing bowl. Beat the egg
yolks lightly and stir into the rice mixture. Beat the egg whites until
stiff, but not dry, and fold into the rice.

Turn the mixture into a greased 1-quart soufflé dish. Set in a pan
with hot water coming half-way up the sides of the dish. Bake at
350° for 30 minutes, or until set. Test with a silver knife. If it comes
out clean, the soufflé is done. Serve immediately.

SAFFRON RICE

    ¼ teaspoon saffron, crumbled
    2   tablespoons olive oil
    2   tablespoons butter
    1½ cups rice
    1½ teaspoons salt

Mix the saffron with 1 tablespoon hot water and set aside. Heat the
oil and butter in a saucepan and add the rice and salt. Cook, stirring,
about 5 minutes. Add the saffron mixture and 3 cups water. Bring
the pot to a boil, reduce the heat, and simmer, covered, 15 to 20
minutes, or until the liquid is absorbed.

PICADILLO

   2   tablespoons olive oil
   1   cup onions, coarsely chopped
   ½ green pepper, chopped
   ¼ teaspoon finely chopped garlic
  2½ pounds lean ground beef
   1   cup canned Italian plum tomatoes, drained and chopped
   3   canned green chiles, drained, seeded, rinsed, and chopped
   ½ cup seedless raisins
  12   stuffed green olives, cut in half
   ⅛ teaspoon cinnamon
   ½ teaspoon freshly ground black pepper
   1   teaspoon salt, or to taste
   ½ cup blanched slivered almonds, toasted under the broiler
      until golden brown

Heat the olive oil in a large, heavy skillet or casserole. Sauté the onions, green pepper, and garlic until lightly browned. Add the ground beef and cook until the red is gone, breaking up the lumps with a wooden spoon.

Add all the remaining ingredients, except the almonds, and simmer, uncovered, over low heat for 30 minutes. Stir the pot occasionally.

Add the toasted almonds, stir, and serve with plain rice, black beans, and sautéed bananas. (Recipes for the beans and bananas follow.)

BLACK BEANS

  1   pound dry black (turtle) beans
  ½ cup olive oil
  1   large green pepper, finely chopped
  2   large onions, finely chopped
  2   cloves garlic, finely chopped
  2   bay leaves
  1   tablespoon salt

½ teaspoon freshly ground black pepper
¼ teaspoon oregano
¼ teaspoon thyme
1 tablespoon finely chopped fresh parsley
3 tablespoons cider vinegar
1 (4-ounce) can pimientos, drained and chopped

Wash the beans and pick them over. Place in a large, heavy pot and cover with water. (If the package says soak overnight, do.) Cook them until barely tender (at least 2 hours), adding more boiling water if necessary, to keep the pot from going dry.

Sauté the green pepper, onions, and garlic in 2 tablespoons of the oil about 15 to 20 minutes. When the beans are barely tender, add the sautéed vegetables and the bay leaves, salt, pepper, oregano, thyme, and parsley. When the beans are thoroughly tender (3 hours or longer), add the vinegar, remaining oil, and chopped pimientos. Simmer 30 minutes longer. Remove the bay leaves before serving.

SAUTÉED BANANAS

6 bananas
Lemon juice
Flour seasoned with salt and pepper
2 tablespoons butter, more as needed

Peel the bananas. If they're large, cut them in half. Then slice them once lengthwise. Sprinkle them all over with lemon juice and dredge them lightly in the seasoned flour. Melt the butter in a large skillet, and sauté the slices until they're lightly browned. Serve at once.

GOO DU JOUR

  2   medium onions, halved and thinly sliced
  ½ medium green pepper, chopped
  1   large clove garlic, minced
  1   tablespoon butter
  1   tablespoon oil
  1   pound ground beef, lean
  3   mushrooms, chopped coarsely
  1   (35-ounce) can Italian plum tomatoes
  1   can green chiles, chopped (rinsed and seeded first)
  ¼ teaspoon oregano
  ½ teaspoon basil
  1   bay leaf
  1½ teaspoons salt
      Freshly ground black pepper to taste
  2   tablespoons dry red wine

Heat the butter and oil in a large, heavy skillet. Add the onions, green pepper, and garlic, and sauté about 20 minutes, until soft. Add the ground beef, break it up with a wooden spoon, and cook until the red is gone. Add the mushrooms, stir, and cook 5 minutes.

Add all the rest of the ingredients and stir to blend well, breaking up the tomatoes. Bring to a simmer, cover the skillet, and turn the heat low. Simmer gently for 30 minutes, remove the cover, and cook 10 more minutes.

Discard the bay leaf, and serve over rice, or any kind of pasta.

> *This Goo is slightly "hot." If you like it less so, eliminate the chili peppers, and substitute 1 teaspoon chili powder.*

> *The dish is adaptable to almost any combination of seasoning. The basics are — onions, green pepper, garlic, beef, tomatoes, salt, and pepper. The rest is up to your taste and experimental fancies.*

MEXICAN STEW (the Coles)

- 1½ tablespoons butter
- 1½ tablespoons oil
- 1 large Spanish onion, finely chopped
- 1 medium green pepper, finely chopped
- 1 large clove garlic, minced
- 1½ pounds lean ground beef
- 1 (28-ounce) can Italian plum tomatoes packed in puree
- 1 teaspoon chili powder
- ½ teaspoon basil
- ½ teaspoon oregano
- 1 tablespoon freshly chopped parsley
  - Salt and freshly ground black pepper to taste
- ½ pound elbow macaroni
  - Freshly grated Parmesan cheese

Heat the butter and oil in a large skillet. Add the onions, green pepper, and garlic, and sauté 30 minutes.

Add the ground beef to the onion mixture, break it up with a wooden spoon, and cook on medium heat until most of its redness is gone. Crush the tomatoes and add them to the skillet. Add the chili powder, basil, oregano, parsley, salt, and pepper, and mix thoroughly. Simmer, covered, for 30 minutes. Correct the seasoning.

Cook the macaroni according to package directions. Drain thoroughly, and return to the pot.

Pour the meat mixture into the macaroni pot, and stir gently with a wooden spatula to blend. Pass the grated Parmesan cheese at the table.

It's really better to make the dish early and reheat, allowing the flavors time to blend. To reheat, put the stew pot over a pan of boiling water, and take care not to mush up the macaroni by over-stirring.

245

MEAT LOAF

1   cup each: finely chopped onion, celery, and green pepper
2   cloves garlic, finely chopped
2   tablespoons oil
1½ pounds lean ground beef
1   can (28-ounce) Italian plum tomatoes, drained thoroughly
    in a sieve without actually mashing the pulp (reserve the
    juice)
1   tablespoon catsup
1   tablespoon chili sauce
1   teaspoon dry mustard
 ½ cup dry bread crumbs
 ½ teaspoon garlic seasoning
 ¼ teaspoon oregano
 ¼ teaspoon basil
    Salt and freshly ground black pepper to taste
1   can tomato sauce (either an 8-ounce can mixed with ½ cup
    or more reserved juice from the tomatoes; or a 15-ounce
    can alone; or 1½ to 2 cups homemade Tomato Sauce —
    there's a recipe on page 336)

Optionals:
1   to 3 links hot Italian sausage
1   cup mushrooms, chopped
1   (4-ounce) can green chiles, rinsed, seeded, and chopped
    Whole green and/or black olives, pitted
    Mushroom caps, for garnish

(Directions assume all the optionals are being used. Just ignore the ingredients you prefer to eliminate.)

Stab the sausages all over with a fork and sauté in a small skillet until nearly cooked. Remove the casing and crumble the meat.

*One or two of the sausages may be sliced in ½-inch
rounds after the sautéeing, and used for garnishing*

the top of the loaf along with, or instead of, the mushroom caps.

As the onions, green pepper, celery, mushrooms, and green chiles are chopped, divide them in half. Put one half in a large mixing bowl. Heat the oil in a skillet, and sauté the other half with the chopped garlic for 20 minutes.

To the vegetables in the mixing bowl, add the ground beef, tomatoes, sausage meat, catsup, chili sauce, mustard, bread crumbs, garlic seasoning, oregano, basil, salt, pepper, and olives. Mix well with your hands until thoroughly blended.

Put the meat mixture into an 8 x 12 x 2-inch baking dish and shape into a loaf. Distribute the sautéed vegetables around the sides, and pour the tomato sauce over all. Decorate the top of the loaf with the mushroom caps, and bake at 350° for 60 minutes. Baste once or twice with some of the leftover plum tomato juice.

Spoon the sauce over the slices of meat loaf when serving, and top with a bit of the garnish.

SWINGERS (Bellevernon Shapiro)

    2   pounds lean ground beef
    1½ teaspoons salt
        Freshly ground black pepper
    ½ pound fresh mushrooms, chopped
    1   green pepper, chopped
    1   onion, chopped
    ½ pound grated sharp Cheddar cheese
    15 to 20 stuffed green olives, chopped
    15 to 20 pitted black olives, chopped
    ½ cup freshly chopped parsley
    1   tablespoon toasted wheat germ (optional)

Mix everything together to blend, and shape into hearty patties. Pan fry in a little butter . . . rare, medium, well-done, to your taste . . . and serve immediately. Makes approximately 10 patties.

TAMALE PIE (the McMenamins)

1½ cups yellow cornmeal
6   cups water
1½ teaspoons salt

Boil the cornmeal in salted water 10 to 15 minutes, or until thick and bubbly. When cool enough to handle, line a greased 3½- or 4-quart casserole with the cooked cornmeal, using no more than necessary to cover the bottom and sides to a thickness of ¼ to ⅜ of an inch. Save ½ cup or more for the topping later. Bake the shell in a 375° oven for 20 minutes, or until the cornmeal dries and slightly toasts at the edges. Set aside.

1   large Spanish onion, chopped
1   medium green pepper, chopped
1   small jar pimientos, drained and chopped
2   cloves garlic, crushed
2   tablespoons cooking oil, more as needed
1   tablespoon chopped fresh parsley
1   bay leaf
1   can (approximately 8-ounce) ripe olives, drained ("large", not jumbo . . . and *not* pitted)
1   (1-pound-13-ounce) can Italian plum tomatoes
2   tablespoons chili powder, or more to taste
4   chili tepines,* ground in mortar with pestle (or ¼ to ½ teaspoon crushed red peppers)
2   pounds ground beef (1 pound chuck for flavor, 1 pound round for lean)
    Salt and freshly ground black pepper
    Flour seasoned with parsley, oregano, basil, salt, and pepper

Put the chili powder in ¼ cup water and let soak. Roll the meat into 1-inch balls and then roll them in the seasoned flour.

In a large, heavy skillet, sauté the onions, green pepper, garlic and pimientos in the cooking oil until the onions are golden brown. Remove the vegetables with a slotted spoon to a bowl, leaving as much oil in the skillet as possible.

Add more oil to the skillet if necessary, and brown the meat balls, a dozen or so at a time. As browned, remove them to drain on paper towels. Keep adding oil as needed, and be gentle with the meat balls so they don't break up. When they're all browned and drained, wipe the oil out of the skillet.

Return the meatballs and onion mixture to the skillet, and add tomatoes, parsley, bay leaf, tepines, olives, and salt and pepper to taste. Add the chili mixture, stir gently to blend, and simmer 30 minutes, uncovered.

Adjust the seasoning (you may well need more salt), and pour the mixture into the cornmeal-lined casserole. Top it with poker-chip-sized dabs of the reserved cornmeal. Bake in a 350° oven for 30 minutes, or until the pie is thoroughly hot, bubbly, and the top is slightly browned.

> *The pie can be prepared ahead to the final baking stage. It can also be frozen at that point. And, as with Chili, it's even better the second day, warmed up — the flavors have more time to blend.*

> ** In some areas, chili tepines are called chili piquines. They're tiny, round, dried hot peppers. If not available in any of your markets, Italian crushed red peppers will do nicely as a substitute.*

Our summer home after Mother married Govie — Juniper Lodge at Grand Lake Resort Hotel, Presque Isle, Michigan

CHILI WITH BEANS

2   large Spanish onions, finely chopped
1   large green pepper, finely chopped
3   cloves garlic, finely chopped
2   tablespoons butter
2   tablespoons cooking oil
2   pounds ground beef (1 pound chuck for flavor, 1 pound round for leanness ... coarsely ground together just once)
2   (28-ounce) cans Italian plum tomatoes, drained well and chopped up (reserve some of the juice)
2   (8-ounce) cans tomato sauce
½ teaspoon celery seeds
½ teaspoon cayenne pepper
2   teaspoons crushed or ground cumin seeds
¼ teaspoon basil
1   tablespoon freshly chopped parsley
4   tablespoons chili powder, or more to taste (I usually use 2½-3 tablespoons chili powder and 1½ tablespoons chili con carne powder . . . or if using *all* chili powder, I add ¼ teaspoon each, coriander seeds and oregano, ground together in a mortar)
2   teaspoons salt, or to taste
Freshly ground black pepper
2   (20-ounce) cans red kidney beans, well drained in a sieve
Crushed red peppers (optional)
Tabasco sauce (optional)

Put chili powders in a small bowl with ½ cup of the drained plum tomato juice. Stir, and let soak.

Heat the butter and oil in a large, heavy casserole (at least 5-quart capacity), and sauté the onions, green pepper, and garlic until very soft, about 30 minutes. Push the onion mixture to the sides of the pot and add the meat. Turn the heat to medium, and cook until most of the red is gone. Try not to crumble the meat too much.

Add 1 teaspoon salt and several turns of the peppermill and stir. Now add the tomatoes, tomato sauce, and all the spices (except the optional red peppers and Tabasco), including the soaked chili powder. Add one more teaspoon salt and more pepper, and mix thoroughly. Bring the pot to a boil, turn the heat down very low, and simmer gently, uncovered, for at least 2 hours. Stir occasionally, but try to keep the meat lumpy.

After 2 hours, test for seasoning. Add more salt if necessary. If not "hot" enough, add dashes of crushed red peppers and/or Tabasco. Continue simmering another ½ hour, or until the chili is the desired consistency. It should not be "juicy."

Add the drained kidney beans, stir gently to blend, and simmer another half hour or so. Total simmering time can be anywhere from 3 to 4 hours. Don't add the beans until the last half hour, or they'll get mushy.

Throughout, gently stir the pot once in a while so the chili doesn't stick to the bottom of the casserole.

The recipe makes about 2½ quarts, and doubles or triples splendidly for large crowds. What's left over freezes well.

It's at its best reheated . . . time for all the flavors to blend.

CHILI AND EGGS (Bob Emmett)

Allow at least two eggs per person, and scramble as many as you need for the number of people to be served. Preferably they should be cooked "soft" . . . not underdone, or runny, but soft. Top each portion with thoroughly heated Chili (homemade or canned . . . if canned, Gebhardt's Chili with Beans is recommended), and serve with a bowl of chopped raw Spanish onion on the side . . . to be passed. (Sprinkle the chopped onion on top of the Chili, or, for a change, top with a dab of sour cream.) Toasted buttered English muffins make a pleasant accompaniment.

TAMALE LOAF (Maryesther Denver)

Maryesther, like Bellevernon, is a dear friend inherited from Bob's college days in Berkeley. M'est is an actress, a statuesque redhead, the unlikely owner of a tiny Cockapoo named Dudley-Do-Right. Her recipe, although in the same vein, is quite different from the McMenamin Tamale Pie. And if you don't have a lot of time, it's certainly quicker to prepare.

    Cooking oil
1   pound ground beef
1   medium to large onion, chopped
2   large cloves garlic, minced
1   teaspoon ground cumin
1   teaspoon chili powder
    Salt and freshly ground black pepper to taste
1   (1-pound) can tomatoes (chop up the tomatoes)
1   (12-ounce) can whole kernel corn, liquid and all
  ½ to 1 cup pitted ripe olives, drained
  ½ jar (4-ounce jar) pimientos, chopped coarsely
  ½ cup oil
1   egg
  ¾ cup milk, approximately
1   cup yellow cornmeal

Brush the bottom of a 3-quart casserole lightly with oil. Add the beef and break it all up with a wooden spoon. Add the onions and garlic, cover the pot, and cook over medium-low heat for 20 to 30 minutes, until the onions are soft. Stir every now and then, so the meat loses all its red color.

Add the cumin, chili powder, and salt and pepper to taste. Then add the tomatoes, corn, olives, pimientos, and ½ cup oil. Stir to blend, and continue cooking, uncovered.

Drop the egg into a 1-pint measuring cup, and add enough milk to reach the 1-cup level. Beat with a fork until blended, and add to the casserole, stirring constantly.

When the casserole is bubbling hot, add the cornmeal, stirring constantly. Cook over medium-low heat for about 5 to 10 minutes, until the cornmeal is well-integrated and beginning to get thick. Check again for salt. You'll need more after the cornmeal is added. Stir all the while.

Cover the casserole, and bake at 350° for 30 minutes. Serves about 6.

If you have leftovers, and the loaf seems dry after being refrigerated, add a bit of tomato juice to it when reheating. It shouldn't be goopy, but it shouldn't be as dry as a loaf you'd cut with a knife.

NORWEGIAN MEAT BALLS

2   tablespoons minced onion
1   tablespoon butter
1   pound lean ground beef ⎫
½ pound ground veal   ⎬ (Have the butcher chop them together)
½ pound lean ground pork ⎭
1   teaspoon salt
½ teaspoon nutmeg, freshly grated
¼ teaspoon freshly ground black pepper
1   (13¾-ounce) can chicken broth
2   egg whites
6   tablespoons butter
8   cups celery, sliced on the diagonal in ½-inch pieces
1   (10½-ounce) can cream of celery soup, undiluted

In a small skillet, cook the onion in 1 tablespoon butter until transparent, about 3 minutes.

In a large bowl, put the onion, meats, salt, nutmeg, pepper, and ½ cup of the chicken broth. Mix thoroughly. Beat the egg whites into soft peaks and mix lightly into the meat mixture. Shape into 18 balls.

Melt 3 tablespoons butter in a large, heavy casserole and brown 9 of the meat balls all over. Remove them to drain on paper towels. Add the remaining 3 tablespoons butter and brown the remaining meat balls. Remove and drain.

Add the celery to the casserole with the remaining chicken broth. Cover and simmer 10 minutes. Stir in the celery soup. Put the drained meat balls on top of the celery. Cover, and continue cooking until the celery is tender and the meat balls are done, approximately 30 minutes.

STUFFED ZUCCHINI

- 4 fat zucchini, about 9 inches long
- 1 pound lean ground beef
- 1 cup chopped onions
- 1 clove garlic, finely chopped
- 2 cups cooked rice (best cooked in beef broth)
- ¼ cup pignolas
- 2 tablespoons freshly chopped parsley
  Salt and freshly ground black pepper to taste
- 2 tablespoons cooking oil
  Grated Parmesan cheese
  Oil
  Butter
  Homemade Tomato Sauce (see recipe, p. 336)

Scrub the zucchini and trim the stem ends. Place them in a large pot and cover with water. Salt the water and bring to a boil. Simmer gently for about 10 minutes, or until crisp-tender.

Drain the zucchini and dry with paper towels. When cool enough to handle, split them evenly lengthwise. Place them cut-side down on paper towels to drain.

With Paul Langton —
the young lovers in
"Arsenic and Old Lace"
at the Pasadena Playhouse

Heat 2 tablespoons oil in a skillet and sauté the onions and garlic about 15 minutes, until lightly browned. Add the beef, breaking it up with a wooden spoon. Cook until the red is gone.

Scoop out the center pulp of the zucchini halves with a spoon, and put in a sieve. Mash out the excess liquid and chop the pulp. Add to the meat mixture along with the rice, pignolas, parsley, salt, and pepper. Cook another 5 minutes, stirring occasionally.

Pour a *thin* layer of oil in a shallow baking dish large enough to hold the zucchini halves in one layer. Roll the skin side of each half in the oil as you place them in the dish. Sprinkle the cut sides with grated Parmesan cheese.

Fill the shells with the stuffing, piling it high. Sprinkle more grated Parmesan on top, and add dots of butter. Bake in a 350° oven for 30 minutes. Serve immediately, topped with Tomato Sauce.

> *Serving with the Tomato Sauce is optional, but very pleasant.*
>
> *A variation is to top each zucchini half with a thin strip of Swiss or mozzarella cheese before the final sprinkling of Parmesan and dots of butter.*

STUFFED ZUCCHINI — VEGETARIAN STYLE

Use the same method as above, for 4 zucchini, but with the following ingredients in the *stuffing:*

- 1 cup chopped onions
- 1 clove garlic, finely chopped
- 3 to 4 cups cooked brown rice
  Zucchini pulp, drained and chopped
  Salt and freshly ground black pepper
- ¼ cup each: pignolas, toasted sesame seeds, and freshly chopped parsley
- ½ cup coarsely chopped walnuts

TILLIE'S "NEVER-FAIL" PRIME RIB ROAST (Tillie Cole)

Always buy the first 3 or 4 ribs from a cut — they're really the best and the leanest. (You can buy as many or as few as you choose, although *one* rib would be more a steak than a roast.) Have your butcher crack the bottom bone.

It doesn't matter whether the roast is 4 pounds or 12, the directions are the same and must be followed exactly.

Have the roast at room temperature. This is very important. Season it any way you wish.

Preheat the oven to 375°. Place the roast on a rack in a shallow pan, fat side up. (Do not cover it.)

Roast *1 hour* at 375°. Then turn the oven off. Do not look in or open the oven door for 2½ hours when the oven should be completely cold. (This is called the "resting period.") After the 2½ hours, turn the oven on to 375° (again, without opening the door), and roast:

     40 minutes for rare
     50 minutes for medium
     60 minutes for well-done

Start the timing as soon as you turn the oven back on. The timing is for the whole roast, not per pound. Don't peek, no matter how much you're tempted.

After taking the roast out of the oven, let it stand about 15 minutes. Easier to carve.

Tillie with Gordon

MIKE'S PEPPER STEAK (Mike Dorsey)

    4   filets, or other good steak, cut 1 to 2 inches thick
          Whole white peppercorns
          Butter
   ½ cup brandy
   1   cup sour cream

Trim the steaks well. Crack the peppercorns in a tea towel with a mallet. Coat the steaks completely on both sides with the cracked pepper. Heat butter in a skillet large enough to hold the steaks, and when the foam begins to subside, add the steaks. Pan-fry to your pleasure — rare, medium, well-done. Remove the steaks to the warming oven.

Add the brandy to the skillet and cook a couple of minutes, stirring with a wooden spoon to scrape up the brown bits. Stir in the sour cream, mixing well and heating thoroughly till the sauce is piping hot but not boiling. Serve the steaks immediately, topped with the sauce, to four.

257

HEAVENLY POT ROAST

This recipe takes two days to prepare properly, but can be done in one.

4   pound bottom round of beef, well-trimmed
¼ pound salt pork
     Salt and freshly ground black pepper
1   medium onion, coarsely chopped
1   clove garlic, sliced
2   carrots, coarsely chopped
     Bouquet garni: 10 sprigs parsley, 1 bay leaf, 1 teaspoon
     thyme, tied together in cheesecloth
1½ cups water
1   cup dry white wine
3   cups chicken broth
6   tablespoons tomato paste
1   teaspoon cornstarch
1   tablespoon cold water

The First Day

Cube the salt pork, and sauté the cubes in a large, heavy skillet until all the fat is rendered. Remove the bits of pork with a slotted spoon.

Dry the meat well, and rub it with salt and pepper. Brown the beef all over in the fat in the skillet. When the meat is a rich, deep brown, transfer it to a heavy casserole, and surround it with the onion, garlic, and carrots. Cook, stirring, until the onions start to brown, and then add the bouquet garni.

Pour all the fat out of the skillet and add the water. Bring it to a boil, stirring with a wooden spoon to scrape up all the brown bits. Add the wine, chicken broth, tomato paste, and stir to blend.

Pour the liquid from the skillet over the beef in the casserole and cover tightly. Bake at 350° for 2½ to 3½ hours, or until the meat is tender. Transfer the roast to a plate. When it's cooled, wrap it tightly in a double layer of foil, and refrigerate.

Bring the liquid in the casserole to a boil on top of the stove, and simmer 15 minutes. Then strain it into a large saucepan and return to a boil. Simmer, uncovered, 45 minutes to reduce the sauce. Let it cool, and refrigerate overnight.

The Second Day

Next day, remove the roast from the fridge *at least* 2 hours before you'll be ready to serve. About an hour or more before, put it in a 300° oven, still wrapped tightly in its foil, and reheat until piping hot all the way through.

Remove all the fat from the top of the cooking liquid and discard. Bring the sauce to a simmer on top of the stove. Blend the cornstarch with the cold water, then with some of the hot sauce, and add this to the pot, stirring constantly.

When the roast is hot, put it in a warmed casserole, and pour the boiling sauce over it.

Carve the roast on a heated platter, and serve with some of the sauce over each portion. Serves 6 to 8.

LONDON BROIL

Buy boneless sirloin, the first cut if possible . . . 2 to 4 inches thick. Take the steak out of the fridge an hour before cooking. Trim off most of the fat and wipe dry with paper towels. Peel a couple of garlic cloves and slice them thinly lengthwise. Rub these well into both sides of the steak, and then press them into one side until you're ready to broil.

Prepare a charcoal fire or preheat the broiler to very hot. If broiling in the stove, put steak on a dripping pan lined with heavy foil. Remove the garlic slices, and discard. Adjust distance from heat according to the thickness of the steak.

London Broil should always be cooked *rare.* When it's ready to be turned, season with salt and pepper on both sides.

Carve in thin slices on the diagonal . . . across the grain . . . and serve. Spoon the natural juices over the meat.

> *Variation . . . combine 1 tablespoon oil, 2 teaspoons chopped parsley, 1 crushed garlic clove, 1 teaspoon salt, 1 teaspoon lemon juice, and ⅛ teaspoon pepper. Brush half the mixture on the steak before placing in broiler. Brush on the other half after turning.*

> *Very good served with baked potatoes, Steamed Onions (p. 229), and tossed green salad.*

STUFFED FLANK STEAK

1   flank steak, well trimmed of fat, with a pocket (have your butcher cut as large a pocket as possible without tearing holes)

⅓ to ½ package Pepperidge Farm Stuffing, prepared according to package directions (using slightly less water than package suggests)

    Salt

    Paprika

    Ground ginger

1½ tablespoons butter

1½ tablespoons cooking oil

1   medium onion, chopped coarsely

2   tablespoons flour

1   cup beef bouillon

1   cup dry white wine

    Salt and freshly ground black pepper

Prepare the stuffing, let it cool, and then fluff it up. Put it in the steak's pocket loosely. Fold up both ends of the steak and secure them with skewers (or tie with string). Season it all over with salt, paprika, and ginger. Rub the seasoning into the meat well.

Heat the butter and oil in a skillet, add the onions, and the steak. Sear the steak over high heat until brown all over. Place the steak in a casserole.

Stir the flour into the fat and onions in the skillet with a wooden spoon and blend well. Add the stock and the wine gradually, and stir until smooth, scraping up the brown bits. Season with salt and pepper to taste.

Pour the sauce over the steak, and bake the casserole in a 275° oven, closely covered, for 1½ hours.

Remove the skewers (or string), carve the meat in slices against the grain, and spoon gravy over each portion.

Mother's Cranberries are delicious with this. See page 337 for the recipe.

I make no apology for using Pepperidge Farm Stuffing. You're welcome to use your own, naturally.

BEEF STROGANOFF (Nina Fonaroff)

3   pounds boneless sirloin or round steak, cut 1 inch thick and then sliced in slender strips (3 pounds when all fat is removed, that is)

1   cup butter (½ pound)

4   to 5 medium onions, finely chopped

2   cloves garlic, finely chopped

  ¼ cup flour (or more, if you like a thicker gravy)

3   cups chicken broth

1   pound fresh mushrooms, sliced

1   pint sour cream

    Salt and freshly ground black pepper

Melt the butter in a large, heavy casserole. When the foam begins to subside, add the strips of beef and coat them all over with the butter. Simmer for 20 to 30 minutes, until all the red is gone. Remove the meat to a bowl with a slotted spoon.

Add the onions and garlic to the casserole and simmer 10 minutes. Add the flour, a little at a time. Blend well, and cook 5 to 10 minutes, stirring constantly. Gradually add the chicken broth, stirring, and when blended and smooth, season to taste with salt and pepper.

When the sauce begins to bubble, return the beef strips to the casserole.

> *The dish can be prepared a day ahead up to this point. After returning the beef to the casserole, let it cool and refrigerate.*
>
> *Before continuing, remove the casserole from the fridge and allow it to reach room temperature. Then heat gently to a simmer.*

Add the sliced mushrooms and stir gently but thoroughly. Bring to a boil, turn down the heat, and simmer 30 minutes, or until the beef is tender.

Just before serving, fold in the sour cream and cook long enough to heat thoroughly. No more than 5 minutes.

Serve over rice or noodles. Serves 10.

BEEF AND EGGPLANT CASSEROLE (Kathy Emmett)

- 1 tablespoon oil
- 1 tablespoon butter
- 1 medium onion, chopped
- ½ medium green pepper, chopped
- 2 cloves garlic, finely chopped
- 1 pound lean ground beef
- 2 (8-ounce) cans tomato sauce (or 2 cups homemade — see p. 336)
- ¼ teaspoon allspice
- ¼ teaspoon oregano
- ¼ teaspoon basil
- 2 tablespoons chopped fresh parsley
- Salt and freshly ground black pepper
- 1 large eggplant
- 2 eggs, beaten lightly with 1 tablespoon water
- 1 cup dry bread crumbs, mixed with 2 tablespoons grated Parmesan cheese
- 1 to 1½ cups grated Parmesan cheese
- 1 (8-ounce) package mozzarella cheese, thinly sliced
- 2 large ripe tomatoes, peeled, cored, and thinly sliced
- Olive oil

Heat the 1 tablespoon oil and butter in a skillet, and sauté the onion, green pepper, and garlic for 10 minutes. Add the ground beef, and cook until the red is gone, breaking it up with a wooden spoon.

Add the tomato sauce, allspice, oregano, basil, parsley, and salt and pepper to taste. Stir to blend, and simmer gently for 30 minutes. Stir occasionally.

While the meat sauce cooks, wash the eggplant and cut off the ends. Then cut it crosswise into ½-inch slices. Put the eggs in a pie plate with 1 tablespoon water and beat with a fork until blended. In another pie plate, combine the bread crumbs with 2 tablespoons grated Parmesan cheese. Heat olive oil in a large skillet. Coat the eggplant first in the egg mixture, then lightly in the bread crumb mixture, and lightly brown the slices on both sides in the olive oil, a few at a time. Add more oil as necessary. Remove the slices to drain on paper towels as they're browned.

Lightly oil a casserole, about 8 x 12 x 2½ inches, and layer half the eggplant slices in the bottom. Sprinkle generously with grated Parmesan cheese. Next layer slices of one of the tomatoes, and cover them with half the mozzarella slices. Spoon half the meat sauce on top, spreading it over all. Place the rest of the eggplant slices in one layer on top of the meat sauce and sprinkle with the rest of the Parmesan. Spoon the remaining meat sauce on top evenly, and bake the casserole for 15 minutes at 350° uncovered.

Now layer the remaining tomato slices on top, and cover with the rest of the mozzarella. Bake another 15 minutes (at 350°), and then run under the broiler briefly until the cheese is melted and browned.

Depending on appetites, the dish will serve 4 to 6. (More likely 6.)

PEPPER STEAK (Tillie Cole)

Unlike Mike's, this is quite like Chinese, and should be served with rice.

1½ pounds sirloin, cut in small bite-size pieces
2   tablespoons oil
1   large green pepper, cut in thin strips
3   scallions, chopped with the green
2   tablespoons molasses
2½ tablespoons soy sauce
 ½ cup celery, cut in julienne strips
1   large tomato, peeled, cored, and chopped
 ½ teaspoon salt
 ¼ teaspoon thyme
1½ teaspoons candied ginger, crumbled — or a pinch of powdered ginger. If you don't use the candied ginger, add ½ teaspoon sugar.
2½ teaspoons cornstarch mixed with ½ cup water or beef bouillon

Brown the beef in the oil and cook until tender. Add vegetables (all but the tomato). Add the molasses mixed with the soy sauce, salt, thyme, and ginger. Now add the tomatoes, and cornstarch mixture. Cover and simmer 5 to 7 minutes. The vegetables should be crisp-tender.

TOMATO BREDIE

Picked this up in London. Bredie very simply means "meat cooked with veg."

2 pounds good stewing steak, cut in 1-inch cubes
2 tablespoons olive oil
3 pounds ripe, red tomatoes, peeled, cored, seeded, and quartered
2 large onions, halved and thinly sliced
1 tablespoon tomato paste
½ teaspoon curry powder
¼ teaspoon cinnamon
1 bay leaf
  Salt and freshly ground black pepper
1 tablespoon brown sugar

Dry the meat cubes well. Heat the oil in a large skillet, add the beef, a few pieces at a time, and cook quickly over high heat until browned on all sides. Remove the meat with tongs to a heavy casserole.

Add the onions to the oil and cook until light golden, about 10 minutes. Combine onions, tomatoes, tomato paste, curry powder, cinnamon, and bay leaf with the meat, season with salt and pepper, and mix in the sugar. Cover tightly and simmer very slowly for about 2 hours, or until the meat is fork–tender and the tomatoes have melted into a thick, aromatic puree. Stir occasionally. Remove the bay leaf before serving.

CARNE CON GARBANZOS (Tillie Cole)

1½ pounds beef, cut in 1-inch cubes
⅓ cup flour
¼ teaspoon celery salt
2 tablespoons oil
1 medium onion, chopped
1 cup chopped celery
1 beef bouillon cube, dissolved in ½ cup water
1 can (about 1 pound) garbanzos, drained
1 cup canned tomatoes with juice
½ cup pitted ripe olives, drained

¼ teaspoon oregano
½ teaspoon salt, or to taste
  Freshly ground black pepper
3   whole cloves garlic, peeled
1   cup dry red wine (or less, depending on how much sauce you want)

Dust the beef cubes with flour and sprinkle with celery salt. Heat the oil in a heavy casserole and brown the beef, a few pieces at a time. Remove them to paper toweling, and add the onions to the casserole. Cook the onions until soft. Return the beef to the pot along with the celery, bouillon, garbanzos, olives, tomatoes, oregano, salt, pepper, garlic cloves, and ½ cup of the wine. Cover and simmer 1½ hours. Add remaining wine and let simmer an hour longer, or until the beef is fork-tender.

TARTAR STEAK   *To serve 2.*

¾ pound freshly ground round or sirloin steak, *all* fat removed before grinding (bully your butcher if he doesn't seem to get the message — or trim and grind it yourself, using the coarse blade, and putting it through just once)
1   egg yolk
    Salt and freshly ground black pepper
    Capers, drained
    Rye bread, buttered
    Chopped sweet onion

Be sure to buy the beef and grind it (or have it ground) the same day you plan to serve it.

In a bowl, thoroughly mix the beef, egg yolk, and salt and pepper to taste. Spread the mixture thickly on buttered rye bread, and sprinkle each serving with capers. Pass the chopped onions.

Anchovies, of course, are traditional. We just prefer it without.

BEEF STEW WITH BEER

3 pounds top round, cut in 2-inch cubes, fat removed
¼ cup bacon drippings, or oil
5 cups onions, sliced
3 cloves garlic, finely chopped
   Salt and freshly ground black pepper
2 tablespoons flour
4½ cups light beer (or half light and half dark beer)
   Bouquet garni: 2 allspice, bay leaf, ¼ teaspoon thyme, 4
      peppercorns — tied in cheesecloth.
6 slices Italian or French bread, cut 1-inch thick
   Dijon-type mustard

Heat the bacon drippings in a heavy casserole. Dry the meat thoroughly with paper towels, and brown a few pieces at a time over high heat. Remove them as browned to drain on paper towels. Add the onions to the pot and cook until they begin to brown. After 15 minutes, add the garlic as well. Stir frequently. When lightly browned, season with salt and pepper, and stir in the flour. Stirring constantly, gradually add the beer. Bring to a boil and simmer slowly, uncovered, for 20 minutes.

Return the browned beef to the pot. Sprinkle with salt and pepper, and add the bouquet garni. Cover, and simmer gently for 1½ hours. Remove cover, and simmer 30 minutes longer, or until the meat is fork-tender.

Toast the bread, and spread each slice generously with mustard. Place the toast, mustard side up, on top of the stew. Bake the pot in a 375° oven for 20 minutes, uncovered.

Remove the bouquet garni, and serve each portion topped with a slice of the mustard bread.

VEAL CHOPS SAUTÉED WITH GARLIC

Veal steaks are splendid cooked this way, too. Have them sliced the same thickness as the chops. It's also a marvelous way to cook Chicken Breasts that have not been boned. The same directions apply exactly. (Chicken legs are fine, too, but take slightly longer to cook.)

4   veal loin chops, each 1½ inches thick, all fat removed (if enough meat is left on the tail, skewer it to the chop)
   Flour
2   tablespoons oil
2   tablespoons butter
4   whole cloves garlic, peeled
2   bay leaves
   ¼ to ½ teaspoon thyme
   Salt and freshly ground black pepper
2   tablespoons wine vinegar
1   cup chicken stock

Dredge the chops lightly on all sides with flour. Heat the oil and butter in a heavy skillet and brown the chops on both sides. Scatter the garlic cloves around the chops, and sprinkle both sides with thyme, salt, and pepper. Cut the bay leaves in half and top each chop with a piece.

Cover the skillet tightly, and cook the chops over very low heat for about 30 minutes, or until cooked through and tender. Remove the chops to the warming oven.

Add the vinegar to the skillet and cook, stirring, over moderately high heat until it has evaporated. Add the stock and cook, stirring, about 3 to 5 minutes, or until the sauce is slightly reduced and syrupy. Check the seasoning.

Remove the skewers, pour the sauce over the chops, and garnish each with a garlic clove and piece of bay leaf. Serve immediately.

You can brown the chops ahead of time, season them, and add the garlic cloves and bay leaves. Cover the skillet, and just let it sit until you're ready to continue.

VEAL PICCATA

    1½ pounds veal cutlets, pounded very thin
        Salt and freshly ground black pepper
        Flour
    2   tablespoons butter
    3   tablespoons olive oil
    1   cup beef bouillon
        Paper thin slices of lemon, one for each cutlet
    1½ tablespoons lemon juice
        Finely chopped fresh parsley

Season the cutlets with salt and pepper. Dredge them lightly with flour and shake off the excess. Heat the oil and butter in a heavy skillet and sauté the veal until golden brown, about 2 to 3 minutes on each side. As they brown, transfer them to paper towels.

Pour off almost all the fat from the skillet, leaving just a thin film on the bottom. Add ½ cup of the bouillon and boil over high heat a minute or two, stirring to scrape up the brown bits. Turn the heat down and return the veal to the skillet. Arrange lemon slices on the top of each. Cover the skillet and simmer over very low heat for 10 to 15 minutes, or until the veal is tender. Remove the cutlets to a warming oven and top with the lemon slices.

Add the remaining ½ cup bouillon to the juices in the pan and boil quickly until the stock is slightly syrupy. Add lemon juice and cook, stirring, 1 minute. Pour the sauce over the cutlets, sprinkle with parsley, and serve immediately.

VEAL PARMIGIANA

    6   veal cutlets pounded very thin
    1   egg, beaten, and seasoned with salt and pepper
    ¾ cup dry bread crumbs
    3   tablespoons grated Parmesan cheese
    2   tablespoons olive oil, or more as needed
    1   cup tomato sauce
        Thin slices mozzarella cheese
        Freshly grated Parmesan cheese

Combine the bread crumbs with 3 tablespoons Parmesan cheese in a pie pan. Put the seasoned, beaten egg in another pie pan. Dip the cutlets first in the egg and then in the crumbs, and sauté in hot oil until golden brown . . . a few minutes on each side. Put the cutlets in a shallow baking pan in one layer. Pour the tomato sauce on top, arrange slices of mozzarella over each cutlet, and sprinkle grated Parmesan over all. Bake in a 350° oven for about 15 minutes, or until the cheese melts and browns.

> *In spite of all the camouflage, Parmigiana can only be as good as the veal it covers. It should be pale in color, and sliced so that all membrane is discarded. Fat, too, should be removed.*

Bill Doll & Company

With Melvyn Douglas in "Two Blind Mice"

269

VEAL WITH PASTA AND PESTO (Coleman Dowell)

4   pound piece of boneless veal, trimmed and larded (see note at end of recipe)
4   cups dry white wine
1   cup thinly sliced onions
6   cloves garlic, mashed
1   large bay leaf, or 2 small
    Olive oil
1   cup finely chopped carrots
1   cup finely chopped onions
⅓ cup flour
    Grated rind of 1 lemon
¼ cup thick tomato puree
1   tablespoon Rose paprika
2   cups water
    Pasta (spaghetti or macaroni, cooked al dente)
    Pesto (see recipe following)

Make a marinade of 2 cups of the white wine, the sliced onions, 4 of the mashed garlic cloves, and the bay leaf. Marinate the veal overnight in this mixture.

After the meat has marinated about 16 hours, take it out of the marinade and cut it into large cubes. Strain the marinade and reserve. Brown the veal in olive oil with the chopped carrots and chopped onions.

When the meat is brown all over, blend in the flour, the remaining 2 cloves of garlic, the grated lemon rind, tomato puree, and paprika. Add the strained marinade, the remaining 2 cups of wine, and the water. Bring the casserole to a simmer, and cook for 2 hours, or until the meat is fork-tender.

Serve the veal with the hot pasta and the Pesto.

PESTO

2   large bunches of arugula (see below)
½ cup chopped parsley
2   cloves garlic, chopped
½ cup freshly grated Parmesan cheese
½ cup slivered almonds
¼ to ½ cup olive oil

Wash the arugula thoroughly and strip the leaves. Put leaves in a blender with the next four ingredients. Turn on the blender and add olive oil until the right consistency is reached. (The amount of oil will vary.)

> *Have your butcher lard the meat, or do it yourself, if necessary. Thread a larding needle with a long, thin strip of salt pork and push it carefully into the veal at right angles to the grain. Let about 1 inch of the strip hang out of the meat at each end. Repeat the process at several intervals throughout the meat.*
>
> *If you are unable to get arugula where you live, the pesto can be made with watercress. But arugula is best.*
>
> *Arugula, a member of the mustard family, is the Italian version of the French* roquette *or* rocket *as Anglicized.*

**With Coleman Dowell
and Bob at East Hampton**

SHASHLIK

        2   pounds lamb from the leg, weighed when trimmed of all
                fat
       ½ cup olive oil
       ¼ cup lemon juice
       ¼ cup dry red wine
        2   cloves garlic, crushed
        2   teaspoons salt
              Freshly ground black pepper
        2   teaspoons dried mint leaves
        1   teaspoon oregano
              Mushroom caps
              Tomato wedges, or cherry tomatoes
              Green pepper squares
              Red or white onion squares, 2 or 3 layers each
              Eggplant cubes (optional)

Cut the well-trimmed lamb into 2-inch squares. Combine the oil, lemon juice, wine, garlic, salt, pepper, mint, and oregano in a large bowl and mix well. Add the lamb cubes and coat all over with the marinade. Marinate in the refrigerator at least overnight, giving it a stir occasionally.

Preheat the broiler.

String the lamb alternately with the vegetables on skewers and brush with some of the marinade. Broil them 5 minutes about 3 inches from the flame. Turn the skewers, brush again with marinade, and broil another 5 minutes.

Serve immediately with rice. (Serves 6 to 8.)

> *I try to plan the arrangement of the skewers ahead of time, so I don't cut up more vegetables than necessary. My skewers are such that I can get about 4 pieces of meat and 3 groups of vegetables on each. You have to judge what's possible on your own.*
>
> *Of course, Shashlik is ideal cooked on an outdoor grill over charcoal.*

MARINATED BROILED LAMB (May Katz)

In the summer, May has the advantage of her outdoor grill. The recipe is super over charcoal, but it's fine broiled normally, too.

6- to 7-pound leg of lamb (have your butcher bone, trim, and butterfly it)
⅔ cup olive oil
3 tablespoons lemon juice
1 teaspoon salt
½ teaspoon freshly ground black pepper
2 tablespoons chopped fresh parsley
1 teaspoon oregano
3 bay leaves, crushed
2 cups thinly sliced onions, the rings separated
3 cloves garlic, thinly sliced

Remove all excess fat from the lamb.

Combine the oil, lemon juice, salt, pepper, parsley, oregano, and bay leaves, and blend thoroughly. Add the onions and the garlic.

Put the marinade in a shallow baking dish large enough to hold the lamb. Add the lamb and spoon some of the marinade on top. Marinate it at least 12 hours, preferably 24, turning the lamb over every few hours. It's best to do it at room temperature, but if the weather is hot, put the pan in the fridge.

When ready to cook, preheat the broiler to very hot. (If the lamb has been in the fridge, bring it to room temperature.)

Lift the meat to the broiler pan without drying it, and broil about 4 to 5 inches from the flame. When the top is browned, in about 15 minutes, salt the meat and turn. Salt again, and finish broiling . . . about 10 more minutes. (The lamb should vary in doneness from rare to medium-well, because of the unevenness of the butterflying.)

To serve, carve against the grain in ½-inch slices. Spoon the natural juices over each portion.

You can brush some of the marinade over the meat as it's broiling, if you wish, or if it seems to be getting dry.

The lamb will serve about 6 to 8 people.

MIKE DORSEY'S LAMB DINNER

This is Mike's answer to the working family's dilemma. The cooking instructions are geared to those who can get home for lunch, pop the roast in the oven, then have the pleasure of facing only minimal preparations at the end of the day.

Thinly sliced, peeled potatoes, enough for the number being served
4 cloves garlic, finely chopped
   Salt and freshly ground black pepper
3 cups white wine, more or less
1 (6-pound) leg of lamb, well-trimmed
   Garlic slivers
   Rosemary
   Lemon juice

Butter your roasting pan, and layer the sliced potatoes on the bottom. Sprinkle with the minced garlic, salt, and pepper, and cover with the wine.

Insert garlic slivers at various points in the lamb, using the sharp point of a paring knife to make the incisions. Rub lemon juice, salt, pepper, and rosemary all over the roast. Place the roast on a rack, fat side up, over the potatoes. Make sure the rack is high enough, so the potatoes aren't squashed.

Bake in a slow oven, 275°, for 5 hours or so. (Use a meat thermometer.) When done, remove the roast to a platter and the potatoes to a serving dish and keep warm. Make gravy as usual.

Serve with Broccoli with Garlic (page 230), or if the fresh broccoli isn't looking too good in your market, Mike's frozen version, and the Minted Pears.

BROCCOLI — Put frozen broccoli in a saucepan with plenty of butter and minced garlic (*no* water), and cook gently until crisp tender.

MINTED PEARS — Drain canned Bartlett pears, one half per person. Put a generous teaspoon of mint jelly in the hole of each half and run under the broiler for about 10 minutes.

*If you prefer, the lamb may also be roasted in a 300°
oven, at 30 to 35 minutes per pound. (For a
six-pound leg, 3 to 3½ hours.)*

ROGAN JAUSH (Dharam Jit Singh)

*Translated, it means "Color-Passion Curry." This
recipe is from "Classic Cooking from India."*

5 tablespoons butter
6 medium yellow onions, finely chopped
2 pounds lamb, preferably from the leg
 ¾ tablespoon turmeric
1½ tablespoons coriander
 ½ tablespoon cumin seed
 ¾ tablespoon freshly grated ginger
 ¼ teaspoon chili powder
   Salt to taste
6 tablespoons yoghurt
3 ripe tomatoes, peeled and cored

Remove all the fat from the lamb and cut into 2-inch pieces.

Melt the butter in a heavy casserole. Add the onions, and cook over
medium heat until an even brown. Stir frequently.

Crush the coriander and cumin seeds together in a mortar. Add the
grated ginger and turmeric and blend.

Add the lamb, coriander, cumin, ginger, and turmeric to the onions,
and fry over medium-high heat for 12 minutes. Stir all the time,
taking care not to burn or scorch the meat. (Scrape the bottom of
the pot with a wooden spoon whenever brown bits start
accumulating.)

Add the chili powder, salt to taste, and yoghurt. Crush the tomatoes
on the meat, and stir well. Cover the casserole, and simmer on low
heat about 2 hours, or until the lamb is fork-tender. Stir the pot
occasionally. Cook uncovered over very low heat for the last five
minutes.

The Curry will serve 4 to 6.

BRAISED LAMB SHANKS

4 lamb shanks, well trimmed of fat (if the shanks are large, have the butcher crack them . . . easier to bend and fit in the pot)
   Salt and freshly ground black pepper
   Flour
2 or 3 garlic cloves, peeled and cut in half crosswise
1 tablespoon butter
1 tablespoon oil
1 medium onion, halved and sliced thin
2 cups boiling liquid — half water, half beef broth
   Salt and freshly ground black pepper
1 bay leaf
8 carrots, scrubbed and cut in half, crosswise

Really be ruthless when you trim the shanks of fat . . . get rid of as much as humanly possible.

Sprinkle the shanks all over with salt and pepper, and then dredge them in flour. Shake off the excess.

Rub a large, heavy casserole with the cut ends of the garlic, and reserve the garlic pieces. Heat the butter and oil in the pot, and sear the shanks in the hot fat all over, until richly browned. Toward the end of the searing, strew the onion slices around the meat. (If they go in too early, they'll get burned rather than browned.)

Remove the lamb to paper toweling, and pour off the fat, trying not to lose the onions.

Return the shanks to the casserole and add the boiling liquid, garlic pieces, bay leaf, and sprinkle generously with salt and pepper. If the carrots are very fat, add them now. If not, wait until after the first or second 20 minutes of cooking before distributing them among the shanks.

Bring the liquid to a boil, cover the casserole, and put it in a preheated 325° oven. Bake 1½ hours, or until the shanks are buttery tender.

Set your timer, and turn the shanks over in the liquid every 20 minutes during the baking. *Very important.*

Serve the shanks and carrots with rice, spooning the juice over the meat and rice.

> *Even with judicious trimming, lamb is so naturally fatty, I often cook the shanks a day ahead. Remove the shanks and carrots from the pot and refrigerate, tightly covered. Refrigerate the sauce as well, and next day scrape off the fat that will have accumulated on the surface. Recombine the shanks, carrots, and sauce and put in a 325° oven, closely covered, for 30 to 40 minutes, or until the sauce is bubbling and the lamb is thoroughly hot. (Turn the shanks over once or twice during the time.)*

Courtesy of Otterbein College Theatre

Photo by Donal

As the Dowager Empress in "Anastasia," presented by the Otterbein College Theatre; Dr. Charles W. Dodrill, Producer; Ortha Stambaugh, Director.

HAM

HAM-IN-PASTRY (Bellevernon Shapiro)

    1   whole pre-cooked ham
    1   cup soft bread crumbs
    ¼ cup lemon juice
    1   teaspoon thyme
    1   teaspoon dry mustard
    ½ teaspoon nutmeg

Mix the bread crumbs with the lemon juice, thyme, mustard, and nutmeg, and rub well into the fat of the ham. Bake for 1 hour at 350°. Remove ham and immediately turn the oven up to 450°. Cover the ham with the following pastry, return to the very hot oven, and continue baking for about 30 minutes, or until the pastry is golden brown.

PASTRY

    1   cup plus 2 tablespoons butter
    3   cups flour
    ⅔ cup ice water, approximately
         Melted butter

The pastry may be made several days ahead.

Cut the butter into the flour until well blended. Add ice water until the mixture holds together. Chill the dough for ½ hour.

Roll the dough out on a slightly floured board into a rectangle. Brush lightly with melted butter and fold over in thirds. Roll, brush, and fold the dough again and return to the fridge to chill another ½ hour.

When ready to cover the ham, roll the dough into a sheet large enough to hold it, wrap well, and seal by moistening the edges with water. If you want to, cut out fancy shapes of the pastry with a cooky cutter and decorate. Secure these with a little water also.

STUFFED PORK CHOPS (Bellevernon Shapiro)

4   pork chops, cut about 2 inches thick, with pockets
¼ pound pork sausage, or 2 links Italian sausage (sweet and/or hot)
2   tablespoons chopped walnuts
2   tablespoons chopped apple (peeled and cored)
½ cup cooked rice
    Salt and freshly ground black pepper

If you're using the Italian sausage, slit the casings, peel off, and discard. Crumble the sausage meat, be it the conventional pork or the Italian, and sauté gently in a skillet until it's cooked through, but not browned. (You may need a bit of oil to keep it from sticking to the pan, but if you keep stirring you might be able to get by without it. Use a Teflon skillet if you have one.) When done, remove the sausage meat with a slotted spoon to a bowl.

Trim the chops of excess fat and brown lightly in the sausage skillet. (This is so they won't turn lavender while baking.)

Blend the sausage meat with the walnuts, apples, and rice. Fill the pockets of the chops with the stuffing, and secure each opening with 2 or 3 toothpicks. (Don't try to close the openings — the toothpicks should act as bars to a cage. If you handle the chops gently, the stuffing won't escape.

Place the chops on a foil-lined baking pan and bake at 350° for 1 hour. After 45 minutes, sprinkle the chops with salt and pepper. There's no need to turn them.

Serve with apple sauce, or Mother's Cranberries, page 337.

PORK

PEARL BUCK'S SPARERIBS

    5   pounds lean spareribs, cracked
    4   cups water
    8   tablespoons soy sauce
    2   teaspoons salt

After removing as much fat as possible from the ribs, cut in separate pieces and put in a large pot. Add the water, soy sauce, and salt. Bring to a boil and turn down the heat. Simmer 1 hour, and drain. This can be done ahead of time.

    6   tablespoons honey
    6   tablespoons vinegar
    2   tablespoons cornstarch (optional)
    4   tablespoons sherry or brandy
    2   teaspoons freshly grated ginger
    1   cup water

Blend the above ingredients. Transfer the ribs to two large skillets. Divide the honey mixture, and add half to each skillet. Fry the ribs, turning them frequently, until the gravy becomes translucent.

5 pounds ribs will usually serve 6 people.

SPARERIBS NUMBER TWO

    5   pounds lean spareribs, cracked (excess fat removed)
    1   jar (12-ounce) damson plum preserves
    ¼ cup soy sauce
    2   tablespoons cider vinegar
    2   tablespoons catsup
    ½ teaspoon finely chopped garlic
    ¼ teaspoon dry mustard

Put the ribs, whole, on a rack in a large roasting pan. Bake 1 hour at 350°. Pour off the fat.

Mix the rest of the ingredients together and brush thickly on the ribs. Bake at 400° about 45 minutes longer, until dark and well-glazed. Baste often with the sauce.

Cut into single ribs, and serve.

> *These ribs can be cooked and sliced ahead. Reheat just before serving.*

SPARERIBS NUMBER THREE

Prepare 5 pounds spareribs and bake as in Number Two, but use the following marinade:

1½ cups orange marmalade
½ cup vinegar
1 teaspoon dry mustard
Salt and freshly ground black pepper to taste

CHINESE MUSTARD SAUCE

Dry mustard
Dry vermouth (or water)
Ground cumin

Put several teaspoonsful mustard in a small bowl. Add enough vermouth to make a loose paste, blending thoroughly. Add a pinch or two of cumin, to taste. The mustard sauce should be very "hot," and about the consistency of a thick gravy. (A touch thinner than ordinary bottled mustard.)

How much mustard you start with depends on how many you're serving. It's much better if made up fresh each time. Also remember that a little goes a long way, unless everyone you're serving is just wild about "hot."

CHOP SUEY (Tillie Cole)

⅓ cup oil

3 pounds lean pork and veal (2 pounds pork to 1 pound veal, cut in 2-inch long, *narrow* strips)

1 pound mushrooms, sliced

4 cups celery, sliced thinly on the diagonal

2 cups onions, halved and thinly sliced

2 cloves garlic, minced

2 teaspoons ginger

1 to 2 teaspoons salt, to taste

2 tablespoons molasses

6 tablespoons soy sauce

4 cups beef broth

2 pounds fresh bean sprouts

1 can water chestnuts, sliced thin

6 tablespoons cornstarch

½ cup cold water

Hot, cooked rice or Chinese noodles

Heat the oil in a large, heavy casserole. Add the strips of meat and cook over medium heat until brown (be patient, it takes a while).

When the meat is lightly browned, and the liquid is nearly absorbed, add the mushrooms. Stir gently and sauté for 3 minutes. Then add the celery, onions, garlic, ginger, salt, molasses, soy sauce, and beef broth. Stir, and cook for 5 to 10 minutes.

Dissolve the cornstarch in the cold water, add some of the hot broth from the pot to it, and when smooth, turn it all into the casserole, stirring. When blended, add the bean sprouts and water chestnuts. Stir and cook 3 to 5 minutes or until thoroughly hot.

Serve piping hot over hot rice or on Chinese noodles warmed and crisped in the oven. The casserole will serve 8 to 10.

The recipe divides in half quite happily for less, and doubles or triples just as easily. Just make certain the meat is nearly done before adding the mushrooms.

MARINATED ROAST PORK (Mike Dorsey)

Skin the roast, and save the skin for Crackling if you wish. Marinate the roast in white wine, lemon juice, crushed garlic, and lemon slices for 36 hours, turning every now and then. Roast in a slow oven, about 275°, for 5 hours or more. Use a meat thermometer.

For Crackling, sprinkle the skin with salt and pepper and broil 5 minutes on each side.

> *See comments at the top of Mike's Lamb Dinner, page 274.*

> *It can also be roasted the ordinary way. A 4-pound center cut loin roast should take about 2 hours and 40 minutes in a 350° oven.*

One of my roles at the Theatre of the Fifteen was opposite Lou Nova, the ex-prizefighter, in "Is Zat So!"

CHICKEN FLORA

Katherine Popper gave this recipe to Flora Roberts, who gave it to us, who gave it its name. All apologies to Katherine.

Wash a 3- to 3½-pound broiler, cut up in serving pieces, and dry thoroughly. Place the chicken, skin side up, in one layer in a shallow baking pan. Sprinkle with:

> **Salt**
> **Freshly ground black pepper**
> **Paprika**
> **Onion salt**

Turn the pieces over, skin side down, and repeat the seasoning. Put small dabs of butter on each piece of chicken, and then sprinkle them with a very thin stream of olive oil.

Bake in a 350° to 375° oven for 45 minutes. Turn the chicken pieces, and continue baking another 45 minutes. 1½ hours in all. Serve immediately. soon. or cold.

Flora Roberts

MAX'S CHICKEN (Max Showalter)

Lightly butter a large, heavy casserole, and cover the bottom with a half-inch layer of sliced onions. Over the onions, place a layer of sliced apples, pitted prunes, dried peaches, apricots, raisins, or whatever . . . cook's choice.

Wash and dry thoroughly the cut-up pieces of a 3½-pound chicken. Season with salt and pepper, and layer on top of the fruit. Dot generously with butter, and sprinkle 1 to 1½ tablespoons curry powder over all.

Bake in a 350° oven, uncovered, for 1½ hours.

MARGE'S CHICKEN (Marge Champion)

- 1 chicken, about 3 to 3½ pounds, cut in serving pieces
- 3 potatoes
- 3 hot Italian sausages
- 3 sweet Italian sausages
   Oregano
   Basil
   Garlic salt
   Paprika
   Freshly ground black pepper

Generously butter the bottom of a heavy casserole.

Peel the potatoes and cut them into wedges. Slice all the sausages in ½-inch pieces, mix them together, and divide the lot in half.

Layer the potato wedges on the bottom of the casserole. Distribute half the sausages over the potatoes. Sprinkle with the last five ingredients. Layer the chicken pieces on top. Add the rest of the sausage, and another sprinkle of the spices.

Bake at 400° for 1 hour, covered, and then ½ hour uncovered.

CHICKEN CACCIATORE (Tillie Cole)

- 6 tablespoons olive oil
- 2 chickens (2½ to 3 pounds each), cut in serving pieces
- 1½ cups finely chopped onions
- 1 cup finely chopped green pepper
- 4 cloves garlic, minced
- 3½ cups canned Italian plum tomatoes
- 1 (8-ounce) can tomato sauce
- ½ cup Chianti
- 1 tablespoon salt, or to taste
- ½ teaspoon freshly ground black pepper
- ½ teaspoon allspice
- 2 bay leaves
- ½ teaspoon thyme
- Dash cayenne pepper

Heat the oil almost to smoking in a large, heavy casserole. Add the chicken pieces, a few at a time, and sauté until golden brown on all sides. Remove to paper toweling to drain as they're browned. Pour off all but a small amount of the oil and add the onions, green pepper, and garlic, and brown lightly.

Return the chicken pieces to the casserole and add all the rest of the ingredients. Stir gently to mix up thoroughly. Simmer, partially covered, approximately 40 minutes, or until the chicken is fork-tender. (Serves 8.)

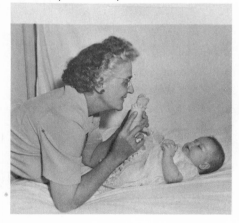

Mother with Kathy at the Encino house

"CAPE SCOTT" CHICKEN

Developed and named in honor of Sean. Cape Scott, Vancouver Island, is where his devotion to brown rice first saw light of day.

1   (3-pound) chicken, cut in 8 pieces
    Garlic salt
    Freshly ground black pepper
    Paprika
3   cups chicken broth
1   teaspoon salt
 ½ teaspoon freshly ground black pepper
1   cup brown rice
1   pound carrots, scraped and cut in 1-inch slices
2   to 3 medium onions, peeled, and cut into 8 wedges each
2   tablespoons finely chopped fresh parsley
 ½ teaspoon saffron (optional)
3   tablespoons seedless raisins (optional)
 ½ pound fresh peas (optional)

Wash and dry the chicken pieces thoroughly, cutting away excess fat. Sprinkle the chicken liberally with garlic salt, pepper, and paprika. Place the pieces, skin side up, on a shallow baking pan large enough for them to lie in one layer, not touching. Bake 10-15 minutes in the hottest oven — 550°, preheated. When they're brown and crispy on top, and well-rendered of fat, remove the pieces with tongs to paper toweling.

Bring the chicken broth to a boil in a casserole that's large enough to hold the chicken pieces in one layer. Add the salt, pepper, optional saffron, and rice. Stir well. Mix in the carrots, onions, parsley, and optional raisins. Place the chicken pieces on top, skin side up, in one layer. (Don't overlap them.) Cover the casserole and bake at 325° for 1½ hours.

If you're adding the peas, remove the casserole from the oven after an hour. Lift out the chicken and scatter the peas over the vegetables. Put the chicken back (skin side up), cover the casserole, and continue baking ½ hour longer.

Serve immediately.

CHICKEN AND SAUSAGE CASSEROLE

3	slices bacon, diced
2	cups finely chopped onions
3	cloves garlic, finely chopped
1	green pepper, finely chopped
1	sweet red pepper, finely chopped
1	pound sweet Italian sausage
1	pound hot Italian sausage
1	(3½-ounce) can pitted ripe olives, well-drained
1	tablespoon capers
1	teaspoon leaf saffron, crushed (or ½ teaspoon powdered)
	Salt and freshly ground black pepper
	Paprika
1	(3½-pound) chicken, cut in serving pieces
¼	cup olive oil
2	cups raw rice
4	cups chicken stock, or more if necessary
1	cup green peas, cooked until just tender (optional)

Slice all the sausages into ½-inch lengths, and combine with the bacon, onions, garlic, and green and red peppers in a large skillet. Sauté all together until the onion is wilted, stirring occasionally, about 20 to 30 minutes.

Spoon the mixture into a large casserole and add salt and pepper to taste. Also add the olives, capers, and saffron.

Wipe out the skillet and add the oil. Sprinkle the chicken pieces with salt, pepper, and paprika, and brown them all over. As the pieces are browned, drain them for a few minutes on paper toweling, and then add to the casserole.

Add the rice and the chicken stock to the casserole. Bring the pot to a simmer, cover, and bake in a 400° oven for 35 to 40 minutes, or until the rice and the chicken are tender. Stir once during the baking. If the liquid absorbs too soon, add a little more stock.

When the rice is tender, turn the heat down to 300° and uncover the casserole. Add the peas and cook 10 minutes longer.

The casserole serves about 6 to 8.

288

BAKED CHICKEN WITH ONIONS (Grace Stebbins)

I've added a little to Mother's recipe . . . the wine, shallots, broth instead of water . . . but it's basically the same. (I also subtracted . . . she always put large dabs of butter on top of the chicken. I figure the broth is less caloric without altering the flavor drastically.)

1   (3-pound) chicken, quartered
1   or 2 large Spanish onions, sliced ½- to ¾-inch thick
    Salt and freshly ground black pepper
1   tablespoon lemon juice
1   cup chicken broth, or more if necessary
2   shallots, finely chopped
1   tablespoon finely chopped fresh parsley
1   large bay leaf cut in quarters (or 2 small leaves, cut in half)
1   ounce dry white wine, or vermouth (optional)

Use an oven-proof baking dish with 2-inch sides, just large enough to hold the chicken quarters in one layer. Line the bottom with the onion slices. Sprinkle the chicken with salt and pepper and arrange, skin side up, on top of the onions. (The onions should be close together and act as a rack, so the chicken doesn't hang in the sauce.)

Sprinkle with the lemon juice.

Add the minced shallots and parsley to the chicken broth in a saucepan. Bring to a boil, and then pour over the chicken. The level of the broth should reach to the top of the onions. Add more broth if necessary. Put one piece of bay leaf on each chicken quarter.

Bake the casserole for 1 hour at 375°. Baste with the juices every 15 minutes (using a bulb baster). After the second basting, sprinkle the optional wine over the chicken.

Serve the chicken with rice, the onions on the side, and spoon the sauce over all.

LEMON CHICKEN

Melt ¼ cup butter in a skillet, and brown a cut-up 3-pound broiler all over. When it's golden brown, sprinkle with salt and freshly ground pepper, and pour on ½ cup lemon juice. Reduce the heat to very low, cover the skillet, and simmer 45 minutes. Baste once or twice with the liquid.

289

CHICKEN VERONIQUE

1 (3-pound) chicken, quartered (or 2 whole chicken breasts, not boned, split in half)
¼ pound sweet butter
2 tablespoons cooking oil
Salt and freshly ground black pepper
1 large Spanish onion, chopped coarsely
¼ teaspoon rosemary
¼ teaspoon thyme
1 teaspoon chopped fresh parsley
1 cup dry red wine
1 cup seedless white grapes (8¼-ounce can, drained)

Dry the washed chicken thoroughly with paper towels. Heat 2 tablespoons of the butter with the oil in a skillet, and brown the chicken on both sides over high heat. Remove the pieces with tongs to a casserole and sprinkle with salt and pepper all over. Wipe out the skillet and add the remaining butter. When it melts, add the onion and sauté over low heat until golden. Cover the chicken with the onions and butter. Sprinkle the rosemary, thyme, and parsley all over, and pour on the wine. Bring the pot to a boil, cover, and simmer very gently for 45 to 55 minutes. After the first 10 minutes, keep the lid slightly ajar. Ten minutes before the chicken is done, add the grapes to the casserole.

BAKED CHICKEN BREASTS WITH WILD RICE DRESSING

1 (6-ounce) package long grain and wild rice mix
½ cup dry vermouth
3 tablespoons finely chopped shallots or scallions with the green
¼ pound mushrooms, coarsely chopped
2 tablespoons butter
1 egg, well-beaten
Salt and freshly ground black pepper
6 tablespoons butter
2 whole chicken breasts, split (not boned)
Flour
Salt and freshly ground black pepper

Cook the rice according to the package directions. While still hot, stir in the vermouth. Cool.

Sauté the shallots (or scallions) and mushrooms in 2 tablespoons butter for 5 minutes, and then stir into the cooled rice. Add salt and pepper to the beaten egg and add to the rice. Stir with a fork. Turn into a lightly buttered baking dish just large enough to hold the split breasts in one layer.

Melt the 6 tablespoons butter in a large skillet. Coat the chicken breasts with flour seasoned with salt and pepper, and lightly brown them on both sides in the butter.

Place the breasts, skin side up, on top of the dressing. Cover with foil, and bake 15 minutes in a 350° oven. Remove the foil, and bake 20 to 30 minutes longer, or until the chicken is done.

> *Variations for the dressing — Try adding sliced, cooked Italian sausage (hot and/or sweet); raisins; toasted nuts (almonds, sliced or slivered; pignolas; chopped walnuts). Add with the shallots and mushrooms.*

CHICKEN BREASTS SAUTÉED WITH GARLIC

See page 267. For two whole chicken breasts, split, the directions are the same as for Veal Chops Sautéed with Garlic.

CHICKEN AND NOODLES CASSEROLE (Kathy Emmett)

As with the Pot Roast, this recipe requires two days to prepare properly.

2	cut-up chickens, 2½ pounds each
1	carrot, cut in ½-inch slices
2	ribs celery, cut in 2-inch slices
1	onion stuck with 2 cloves
12	peppercorns
	Chicken stock
	Tomato Sauce (see recipe p. 294)
5	tablespoons butter
¼	cup flour
	Salt and freshly ground black pepper
¾	cup heavy cream
	Tabasco sauce
½	pound broad noodles
¼	cup chopped chives
1	egg yolk, beaten
¾	cup freshly grated Parmesan cheese

1st Day: Put the chicken pieces in a large pot and add the carrot, celery, onion, peppercorns, and chicken stock to cover. Bring it to a boil and simmer until the chicken is tender, 30 to 45 minutes. Remove the chicken with tongs, and continue boiling the broth until it is reduced to about 2 cups. Strain the broth, cool, and refrigerate overnight.

When the chicken is cool enough to handle, remove and discard the skin and bones, and cut the meat into strips. Refrigerate, covered.

The Tomato Sauce may be prepared the first day, too. At any rate, when ready to assemble the dish, have the tomato sauce ready.

2nd Day: Skim the fat from the broth and discard. Melt 2 tablespoons of the butter in a saucepan, and add the flour. Stir until it is well blended, about 2 or 3 minutes, and then add the broth gradually, stirring constantly. (The broth may be jellied — no matter.) When the sauce is blended and smooth, simmer over low heat, stirring occasionally, for about 30 minutes.

Melt 2 tablespoons of the butter in a large skillet, add the strips of chicken, and sprinkle with salt and pepper. Add ½ cup of the cream and a dash or two of Tabasco to 1 cup of the chicken broth sauce. Blend thoroughly, and then stir into the chicken. Set aside.

Cook the noodles al dente, according to package directions, adding salt and a tablespoon or so of olive oil to the water. Do not overcook. Drain, rinse in cold water, drain again, and return to the pot. Add the remaining tablespoon of butter and toss.

Generously butter a lasagne-type baking dish and layer the noodles on the bottom. Pour the Tomato Sauce over the noodles, sprinkle the chives on top, and then spread the chicken in cream sauce over all.

Add the remaining ¼ cup of cream and the beaten egg yolk to the remaining chicken broth sauce, and heat. (Do *not* boil.) Spread this over the chicken layer, and sprinkle the Parmesan cheese all over the top.

Bake 35 to 45 minutes at 350°, until bubbling and golden brown on top.

This will serve 6 to 8. It also lends itself to doubling and tripling. Needs an enormous *pan for tripling, but I've done it.*

If refrigerated, the whole casserole can be prepared the day before you plan to serve it. Just be sure to bring it to room temperature before baking.

TOMATO SAUCE

3 large, ripe, red tomatoes
3 tablespoons butter
¼ cup finely chopped onion
  Salt and freshly ground black pepper
1 bay leaf
½ teaspoon thyme

Drop the tomatoes, one by one, in boiling water for 10 to 12 seconds. Then peel them, cut out the stem end, and chop coarsely.

Melt the butter in a saucepan and add the onion. Saute until the onion is soft, then add the tomatoes and remaining ingredients. Simmer about 5 minutes. Discard the bay leaf.

If you prepare the sauce the day before, refrigerate it overnight. Reheat before adding to the casserole.

CREAMED CHICKEN (Grace Stebbins)

1 (3½-pound) chicken, quartered (or two 2¼- to 2½-pound broilers)
1 onion, quartered
1 to 2 stalks celery with leaves, cut in large pieces
1 carrot, trimmed, scrubbed, and cut in 4 or 5 pieces
1 tablespoon salt
6 peppercorns
  Chicken stock

Put everything in a heavy pot and cover with the chicken stock. Bring it to a boil, cover, and turn the heat down low. Simmer gently for 35 to 45 minutes, or until the chicken is tender but not falling apart. Let it cool in the broth.

Remove the chicken pieces (squeeze gently over the pot to rid of excess juice) and discard the skin, bones, and visible fat. Cut the meat into good-sized chunks and reserve.

Strain the broth and refrigerate until the fat rises to the top and solidifies (overnight is best). Skim off the fat and discard.

- 4 tablespoons butter
- 4 tablespoons flour
- 2 cups chicken broth (from the chicken)
- ¼ teaspoon freshly grated nutmeg
- 1 teaspoon sherry (optional)
     Salt and freshly ground black pepper
- ½ to ¾ cup sliced mushrooms, sautéed in a little butter (optional)
- ½ cup sliced water chestnuts (optional)

Melt the butter in the top of a large double boiler over direct heat. Add the flour and cook, stirring, until well blended and the flour is nicely browned. Add the broth gradually, stirring constantly. Gradually raise the heat to medium as more and more broth goes in. When all is blended and smooth, add the nutmeg, optional sherry, and salt and pepper to taste. Bring the sauce just to a boil, stirring, and then add the reserved chicken chunks, and optional mushrooms and/or water chestnuts.

If serving soon, keep warm over hot water in the double boiler. Otherwise let cool, and refrigerate until ready to reheat (over hot water).

Keep stirring to a minimum when the chicken is in the sauce, or the large chunks will break up too much.

If the sauce becomes too thick, thin it with a little of the leftover broth, and recheck the seasoning.

Serve the Creamed Chicken over rice, mashed potatoes, baking powder biscuits (see p. 341), or toast. The recipe should serve 6.

Leftover broth can be saved for stock; or correct the seasoning, add cooked rice, and it's a fine soup.

CHICKEN CURRY

The recipe serves 8 and will
double and triple well.

4   whole chicken breasts, split
¼ cup butter
1   (13¾-ounce) can chicken broth

Skin the chicken and wipe dry. Brown the chicken, a few pieces at a time, in hot butter in a large skillet, about 5 minutes on each side. Return all the breasts to the skillet, add the chicken broth, and bring to a boil. Reduce the heat, cover, and simmer 20 to 30 minutes, or until tender. Remove the chicken breasts. When cool enough to handle, remove the bones and discard. Cut the chicken into bite-sized pieces and reserve. Measure the liquid in the skillet and add water to make 3 cups. Reserve.

3   tablespoons butter
1   clove garlic, finely chopped
1   cup onion, finely chopped
2   to 4 teaspoons curry powder, or more to taste
1   cup chopped pared apple
¼ cup flour
¼ teaspoon ground cardamom
1   teaspoon ginger
1   teaspoon salt, or to taste
¼ teaspoon freshly ground black pepper
3   cups reserved chicken liquid
2   teaspoons grated lime peel
2   tablespoons lime juice
¼ cup chopped chutney

Heat the butter in a casserole and sauté the garlic, onion, curry powder, and apple until the onion is soft. Stir in the flour, cardamom, ginger, salt and pepper, and mix well. Cook 5 minutes, stirring. Gradually add the reserved liquid, stirring constantly. Add the lime juice and grated peel. Bring to a boil, stirring. Reduce heat, cover the casserole, and simmer 20 minutes, stirring occasionally. Add the reserved chicken and the chopped chutney. Heat gently just to boiling. Serve with Saffron Rice, page 241; East Indian Stewed Tomatoes, page 229; and Curry Accompaniments in small bowls, as many as you choose, or all.

CURRY ACCOMPANIMENTS

Chopped green pepper
Chutney
Whole salted peanuts
Flaked coconut
Sliced banana, dipped in lemon juice
Raisins
Kumquats
Sliced scallions
Chopped unpeeled cucumber
Yoghurt (plain)
Pineapple chunks
Coconut chips

May Boehlert (Katz) with Kathy, summer of '51

GRILLED CHICKEN BREASTS (Jane Warwick)

Allow half a large, skinned, boned chicken breast per person, or one whole breast if they're small. Place the breasts in a shallow pan just large enough to hold them in one layer. Saturate them with olive oil, and squeeze a generous portion of lemon juice on top. Roll the breasts around in the mixture, and marinate at room temperature for several hours. Turn them every now and then.

To cook over a charcoal fire: Using a pair of tongs, lift the breasts out of the marinade, one by one, and place on the grill. Have handy a lemon cut in half. Turn the breasts frequently as they cook, squeezing lemon juice on them at each turning. When nearly done, sprinkle both sides with salt and pepper. It should take 15 to 20 minutes, depending on the size of the breasts. Test the thickest part of the chicken with the tip of a sharp knife. All the pink should be gone.

To grill on the stove: Cover the bottom of a skillet with a thin layer of the marinade. Halve and slice an onion or two (I use one small onion for two breast halves), and distribute the slices around the edge of the skillet. Turn on the heat. When the skillet is hot, lift the breasts with tongs and place inside the ring of onion slices. Proceed as for charcoal grilling, turning frequently and squeezing lemon juice. You may need to add a bit more marinade to the pan to keep the breasts from sticking to the bottom, but the oil clinging to the meat is usually sufficient.

When serving, top each breast with a few of the onions.

If you wish, you may also add any one of the following to the marinade: finely chopped garlic or shallots; freshly chopped parsley; freshly chopped or dried rosemary or tarragon; grated ginger; curry powder; et cetera, et cetera, et cetera.

TUNA CASSEROLE (Bellevernon Shapiro)

A delicious, low-calorie change of pace. Or forget that it's low-calorie and enjoy anyway.

3   eggs, separated
2   tablespoons minced onion
1½ cups cottage cheese
1   (7-ounce) can light chunk tuna
1   tablespoon minced parsley
    Paprika
    Salt and freshly ground black pepper to taste
    Grated Parmesan cheese (optional)

Beat the egg yolks. Stir in the onion, and fold in the cottage cheese. Drain the tuna, flake with a fork, and fold into the egg mixture. Season with salt and pepper to taste. Beat the egg whites stiff, not dry, and fold in. Pour into a lightly buttered 1½-quart casserole or soufflé dish. Sprinkle the top with the parsley and paprika (and Parmesan if you wish). Bake 45 minutes at 325°. Test with a silver knife . . . if it comes out "clean," the casserole is done.

Barney Shapiro deep sea fishing at Baja

299

FISH

BARBECUED FISH STEAKS (Mike Dorsey — Pam Borain)

*This is really Pam's. She brought it with her to Australia
when she emigrated from South Africa.*

Cream together butter and dry mustard to taste, and spread on both sides of fish steaks . . . halibut, swordfish, kingfish, etc. Cook on an open fire over charcoal. The fish is done when it flakes easily with a fork.

COLD POACHED SALMON (Bellevernon Shapiro)

8- to 10-pound salmon (have fishmonger filet and butterfly it)
3 to 6 medium onions, sliced
4 stalks celery, cut in 2-inch slices
4 carrots, cut in ⅛-inch slices (save after the fish is done for decoration later)
2 bouquets garni (1 teaspoon peppercorns, 2 large bay leaves, fresh dill sprigs in each) tied in cheesecloth bags
1 cup salt
Water
1½ cups white wine (sauterne)

Put onions, celery, and carrots in a large fish poacher, or a large, deep roasting pan (long enough to span two burners). Place the cheesecloth bags at each end. Add the salt and enough water to come two-thirds up the sides of the pan. Bring to a boil and simmer gently for about 15 minutes.

Meanwhile, wrap the fish in a big double square of cheesecloth, skin side up. Tie with "ropes" of cheesecloth at each end, about 4 or 5 inches from the end. (To help you lift fish out of the water when the time comes.) Lay fish gently in the water and pour the wine over. Add more boiling water if necessary to completely cover the fish. Cook, uncovered, on medium-low heat about 10 minutes after the liquid returns to a simmer. Pierce with a fork or knife. If it slides in easily, the fish is done.

Cool the salmon in the liquid. When cool, and not before, lift it out with the cheesecloth ropes. Untie, and open cheesecloth. Carefully pull off the salmon skin. Discard it, and with the help of the cheesecloth, transfer the fish to a platter. Discard the cheesecloth. If the fish should break up when doing this, push the pieces back together to resemble the original. (The sauce will cover the cracks.) Cover with plastic wrap and put the platter in the fridge. Don't forget to save the carrot rounds before throwing out the stock.

SAUCE

1   cup mayonnaise
1   pint sour cream
2   tablespoons each: finely chopped parsley, and finely
      chopped scallions
2   tablespoons lemon juice
1   tablespoon chopped fresh tarragon
¼ teaspoon white pepper
     Generous pinch snipped fresh dill
     Pinch curry powder
     Salt to taste

(Actually, all the proportions are "to taste.") Mix everything together thoroughly, and adjust the seasoning to please your palate. If you want lots of extra sauce, increase the recipe by half . . . or double it.

Before serving, ice the salmon with the sauce. Then decorate it with carrot slices, capers, sliced stuffed green olives, thin lemon slices, cherry tomato slices, whatever occurs to you that's edible. Decorate the platter with fresh parsley and dill sprigs. Serve the extra sauce in a gravyboat on the side. An 8-pound salmon will serve about 20 people, probably more.

FISH IN FOIL (Mike Dorsey)

The recipe is for two. Increase proportions to serve as many as you wish.

2 to 4 fish fillets (about 1 pound), all the same size and shape (sole, flounder, cod, haddock, whiting, whatever)
1 to 2 large shallots, peeled and finely chopped
2 to 3 mushrooms, finely chopped
1 or 2 garlic cloves, finely chopped
  Paper thin lemon slices
  Lemon juice
1 to 2 tablespoons soy sauce

Cut 1 or 2 sheets heavy aluminum foil large enough to completely enclose each pair of fillets. Lightly butter an area in the center of the foil the size of the fish. Lay one fillet on the buttered area. Sprinkle it with chopped shallots and mushrooms. Lay a fillet to match on top, and sprinkle with chopped garlic. Cover with a couple of lemon slices. Sprinkle with the lemon juice, and then soy sauce. Pull the surrounding foil up and seal the fish in so none of the juice can escape.

Put foil case (or cases) on a shallow baking pan, and bake at 450° for 15 to 30 minutes, depending on the thickness of the fish. Serve one whole, or one half "stuffed" fish per person. Spoon the juice from the foil over each portion.

SOLE AU BEURRE

1½ pounds fillet of sole
   Juice of one lemon
6 tablespoons butter
2 tablespoons finely chopped shallots
2 tablespoons finely chopped fresh parsley
   Salt and freshly ground black pepper to taste

Rinse the sole fillets under cold water and dry thoroughly with paper toweling. Put on a lightly buttered baking dish (or foil-lined dish) in one layer. Brush with a little of the lemon juice.

In a small skillet, saute the shallots in the butter for 3 to 5 minutes, until lightly browned. Add the parsley, salt, pepper, and rest of the lemon juice, and blend. Spoon the sauce over the fillets, and broil about 4 or 5 inches from the flame until the fish flakes easily with a fork — 5 to 8 minutes. Serve immediately to 4.

Add sliced almonds, lightly sautéed in butter, the last few minutes of broiling, and you have Sole Amandine, of sorts.

NUTTY SOLE AND BROWN RICE

The name isn't meant to be "cutesy." It just happened.

1   pound fillet of sole or flounder
    Flour
6   tablespoons butter
½ cup toasted slivered almonds
¼ cup toasted pignola nuts
2   tablespoons freshly chopped parsley
½ lemon, juiced
    Hot, cooked, buttered brown rice for three
    Lemon wedges

Lightly flour the fish fillets. Bring 4 tablespoons butter to bubbling stage in a large skillet. Saute the fillets about 3 minutes on each side, or until done. Remove them to a hot platter.

Divide about ¼ cup of the toasted almonds over half of each fillet and fold the fillets in half. Add the rest of the almonds and all the pignola nuts to the hot, buttered brown rice, and stir lightly with a fork.

Add the 2 remaining tablespoons of butter to the skillet and bring to a sizzle. Add the parsley and lemon juice, and stir, scraping into the sauce the brown bits from the fish.

Pour the sauce over the fillets, serve with lemon wedges, and of course, the brown rice.

FIRE ISLAND FISH

Buy Sea Squabs (blowfish) cleaned and prepared for cooking by your fishmonger . . . allowing at least two per portion. At home, rinse and dry them thoroughly. Dip them in Bob's Salad Dressing (see page 224), sprinkle very lightly with salt and pepper, and roll them in cornflake crumbs. Place the fish on a foil-lined baking sheet so they're not touching each other. Bake at 350° for 12 minutes. Then put under the broiler, 6 to 8 inches from the flame, until nicely browned, turning them once. Eat like a drumstick.

STEAMED FISH

- 1 quart water, more or less
- 1 teaspoon salt
  Freshly ground black pepper
- ½ teaspoon thyme
- ¼ teaspoon paprika
- 1 bay leaf
  Generous dash cayenne pepper
- ½ teaspoon fine herbs

Pour water into the steamer to a level just short of the rack when it's in place. Add the rest of the ingredients. Place the steamer on the stove so it spans two burners. Cover, bring to a boil, and simmer for 15 minutes.

Lightly butter the fish rack. Wash and thoroughly dry the fish, either fillets or whole fish, and place on the rack. If possible, arrange the fish so the thickest parts will be over the burners when lowered into the steamer. Lightly season with salt, pepper, paprika, and fine herbs. Dot with butter if you wish.

Lower the rack into the steamer, cover it, and cook the fish over gently simmering liquid until it flakes easily with a fork. Sole fillets should take no longer than 6 to 8 minutes. One large fillet, about 20 minutes. A whole fish can take up to 30 minutes or more, depending on size.

The fish should be served immediately. Sprinkle with freshly chopped parsley, and serve with lemon wedges on the side. Or top with melted butter to which a generous squeeze of lemon juice has been added. Tartar sauce, if you wish.

If you're feeling festive, sprinkle a large fillet with cooked baby shrimp the last few minutes of steaming. Add toasted, slivered almonds when the fish is on the platter, and top with Mornay Sauce (see page 334). Sprinkle with paprika and freshly chopped parsley to give it color.

FISH WITH BACON AND VEGETABLES (Kathy Emmett)

Referring to Kathy as "Emmett" is not a mindless slip. As many professionals do, she practices law under her maiden name. And as many of her contemporaries do, she also uses it socially.

Allow ⅓ to ½ pound fillet of fish per person. Buy as much as you need . . . sole, flounder, turbot, halibut, haddock, etc.

Wash the fish and dry thoroughly. Butter a baking dish that will accommodate the fillets in one layer. Salt and pepper the fish lightly. Cover with layers of the toppings below, and then dot with butter. Bake in a preheated 350° oven for 15 minutes, or until the fish flakes easily with a fork. (Some fillets are so slender, they will take less time. Don't overcook.)

TOPPINGS

3 slices bacon, sautéed until just crisp, and crumbled
¼ cup scallions, chopped fine with the green
¼ cup green pepper, chopped fine (optional)
½ cup tomatoes, peeled, cored, and chopped fine

The above quantities are for a little over a pound of fish. Increase the proportions for more fish, but keep in mind the thickness of your fillets. The fish itself shouldn't get lost.

The toppings can be prepared ahead and kept in the fridge in small bowls covered with plastic wrap.

The whole baking dish can be assembled ahead and refrigerated. Bring it out to "unchill" about 15 minutes before baking.

JAMBALAYA

- 2 tablespoons butter
- 1 large Spanish onion, finely chopped
- ½ medium green pepper, finely chopped
- 2 cloves garlic, finely chopped
- 2 bay leaves, crumbled
- ¼ teaspoon thyme
- 2 tablespoons freshly chopped parsley
- ½ teaspoon freshly ground black pepper
- ⅛ teaspoon each: cayenne, cloves, nutmeg
- 1 tablespoon flour
  Salt to taste
- 3 large ripe tomatoes, peeled, cored, seeded, and chopped
- 1 teaspoon chili powder
- 4 cups strained fish stock (a recipe for the stock follows)
- ¾ to 1 cup rice
- ¾ cup cooked ham, cut in 2 x ½-inch strips
- ¾ cup cooked chicken, cut in 2 x ½-inch strips
- 2 pounds raw shrimp, shelled and deveined
- 1 or 2 hot Italian sausages, cooked and sliced in ½-inch lengths (optional)
- 1 or 2 sweet Italian sausages, cooked and sliced in ½-inch lengths (optional)

Sean and his catch of lowly
blowfish before they're transformed
into delicious sea squabs

Melt the butter in a large, heavy casserole, and sauté the onions, green pepper, and garlic, until the onion wilts. Stir frequently. Add the bay leaves, thyme, parsley, pepper, cayenne, cloves, nutmeg, and sprinkle with the flour. Stir to blend, and add salt to taste. Cook for 2 or 3 minutes over moderate heat, stirring constantly. Then add the tomatoes, chili powder, fish stock, and blend. Taste for seasoning and add more salt if necessary.

Bring the pot to a boil, and gradually stir in the rice, ham, chicken, shrimp, and optional sausages. Cover, and simmer gently for 35 to 40 minutes, or until the rice is tender.

> *This serves 6 to 8, but the recipe happily doubles, triples, etc.*

> *It reheats well. If it seems dry the second time around, add a little more fish stock. Or chicken broth.*

FISH STOCK

1 pound inexpensive white fish — head, bones, and all
1 tablespoon butter
1½ quarts water (or half water and half dry white wine)
1 onion, coarsely chopped
2 sprigs parsley
10 peppercorns
1 bay leaf
1 clove garlic, peeled
¼ teaspoon thyme
1 stalk celery with leaves, cut up
Salt to taste

Wash the fish and bones in several changes of water until very clean. Melt the butter in a large, heavy saucepan, and add the onion, fish, and water. Cook, stirring, a few minutes, and then add the remaining ingredients.

Bring to a boil, and simmer 45 minutes. Strain the stock through a cheesecloth-lined colander.

> *Leftover stock may be frozen for future use.*

SAUTÉED SHRIMP

1½ pounds shrimp, shelled and deveined
3   to 4 tablespoons butter
2   tablespoons finely chopped shallots or scallions (with the green)
2   cloves garlic, finely chopped
1   tablespoon finely chopped fresh parsley
½ cup dry vermouth
¼ cup blanched slivered almonds
Salt and freshly ground black pepper

Toast the almonds under the broiler. Shake them a lot, and turn with a spatula, being careful not to burn them. Turn off broiler and keep the almonds warm in the oven.

Melt the butter in a heavy skillet. Add the shallots and garlic and sauté briefly. Add the shrimp and cook, stirring, until they turn pink all over. Add the parsley and stir to mix. Pour in the vermouth, bring to a boil, and then simmer until the shrimp are done, about 5 minutes. Season to taste with salt and pepper. Just before serving, add the toasted almonds. Very good over rice.

This recipe also works well with bay scallops.

BROILED SCAMPI

30   jumbo shrimp
½ cup butter, softened
6   cloves garlic, minced (8, if they're small cloves)
5   teaspoons chopped fresh parsley
3   teaspoons Worcestershire sauce
1   teaspoon salt
½ teaspoon paprika
¼ teaspoon freshly ground black pepper

Remove the shells from the shrimp, all except the last segment and tail. Wash well under the cold water tap, and devein. With a sharp knife, split each shrimp evenly at the underside curve without cutting through, and spread them open so they lie flat. Dry thoroughly, and place them in one layer on a foil-lined shallow baking pan.

Blend the butter, garlic, parsley, Worcestershire sauce, salt, paprika, and pepper thoroughly. Spread the mixture over each shrimp.

Broil 10 to 12 minutes, until the shrimp are thoroughly cooked and the tails begin to blacken. Serve immediately on a bed of hot, cooked rice, dribbling the remains of the melted butter from the pan over the shrimp. Serves 4 to 6.

SHRIMP AND CHEESE CASSEROLE (Cathleen Schurr)

     6 slices white bread, crusts removed
     1 pound cheese (Gruyère or Old English)
     1 pound cooked shrimp (1¼ to 1½ pounds raw) — use
          cooking instructions on page 207, the second method
     ¼ cup melted butter
     3 eggs, beaten
     ½ teaspoon dry mustard
          Salt to taste
     2 cups milk

Cut or break the bread into quarter-sized pieces. Cut or break the cheese into bite-sized pieces. If your shrimp are large, cut them in half. Butter a deep casserole that has a lid. Arrange the bread, shrimp, and cheese in several layers. Pour the melted butter over the mixture.

Beat the eggs, add the mustard, and salt to taste. Add the milk and blend well. Pour the mixture over the shrimp, cheese, and bread in the casserole.

Let it stand in the fridge, covered, a minimum of 3 hours, preferably 6 hours or overnight.

Take from the refrigerator and let stand at room temperature for ½ to 1 hour before baking. Preheat the oven to 350°, and bake for 1 hour, covered. Serve with a tossed green salad and garlic bread (see page 345).

> *As is, it serves 4 to 6, but the casserole doubles and triples well.*

CREAMED TUNA FISH (McMenamin)

      2   tablespoons oil
      ¼ cup chopped onion
      3   tablespoons butter
      3   tablespoons flour
    1½ to 2 cups milk
      ½ teaspoon salt
      ½ tablespoon chopped fresh basil, or ½ teaspoon dried
      ¼ teaspoon nutmeg
      1   tablespoon chopped fresh parsley
      1   teaspoon Worcestershire sauce
      2   (7-ounce) cans tuna fish, drained, and flaked with a fork
      1   boiled potato, diced
          Buttered toast — 4 to 6 slices
      1   hard boiled egg, finely chopped
          Freshly chopped parsley
      4   to 6 paper-thin lemon slices
          Paprika

Heat the oil in a small skillet and sauté the onion until golden. Remove the onions with a slotted spoon and set aside.

In the top of a double boiler, over direct heat, melt the butter and stir in the flour. Stir until the flour begins to take on color.

Heat water to boiling in the bottom of the double boiler.

Add the milk gradually to the butter-flour mixture, stirring constantly. (Add enough milk so the sauce is not too thick. The potato will thicken it further.) When blended and smooth, put the pot over the boiling water and add the onions, salt, basil, nutmeg, 1 tablespoon parsley, and Worcestershire sauce. Bring to the boiling point, stirring.

Add the flaked tuna fish and the diced, boiled potato. Cook very gently for 15 minutes, stirring occasionally.

Spoon the creamed tuna fish over thin, buttered toast. Garnish with sprinkles of chopped egg and freshly chopped parsley. Add a lemon slice on top of each portion, sprinkle with paprika, and serve immediately.

SHRIMP CURRY (adapted from Pearl Phipps' recipe)

  1½ pounds shrimp, shelled and deveined
  2   medium-small onions
  1   clove garlic, finely chopped
  2   tablespoons butter
  1   (8-ounce) can tomato sauce
  ⅛ teaspoon cayenne pepper
  ¼ teaspoon paprika
  ¼ teaspoon freshly ground black pepper
  3   tablespoons curry powder, or to taste (preferably Malaysian-type)
  1   cup water
    Salt to taste

Heat the butter in a skillet. Thinly slice the onions, separate into rings, and sauté gently with the garlic for 15 minutes. Add the tomato sauce and the spices. Stir to blend.

Now add the shrimp and stir for about 5 minutes, or until they turn pink all over. Add the water, and salt to taste. Cover the skillet and simmer on medium-low heat for about 20 minutes.

Serve with rice, and chutney.

Cathleen Schurr at home on Barrow Street in the early 1950's — with husband Joe Skelly and son Chris

311

> Two Chiles Rellenos recipes... one is fairly
> traditional, the other is an adaptation, both delicious.
> Mabel de Rose was a high school chum of Bob's in
> Monterey, and his first dancing partner...
> performing for the public, that is. She still lives in the
> old home town. Irene McMenamin is married to
> Bernie, Bob's cousin. They now live in Hawaii.

CHILES RELLENOS (Mabel de Rose)

2   (7-ounce) cans Ortega whole green chiles
2   tablespoons olive oil
1   medium onion, chopped extremely fine
1   (28-ounce) can solid-pack tomatoes, chopped very fine
½ teaspoon salt, or more to taste
¼ teaspoon basil
1   tablespoon finely chopped fresh parsley
4   ounces sharp Cheddar cheese
3   eggs, separated
3   tablespoons flour
    Salt
    Sifted flour
    Olive oil

Drain 1 can of the chili peppers, and try to remove the seeds and membrane with your fingers without tearing them open. If it's impossible to keep them whole, better just to split them down one side to do it, rather than tearing them in shreds. Then rinse under cold water and drain the peppers on paper towels.

Heat the 2 tablespoons olive oil in a skillet, and sauté the chopped onions on very low heat until tender, about 20 to 30 minutes. Drain the other can of chiles, seed them, rinse under cold water, and chop very fine. Add the chopped chiles, tomatoes, salt, basil, and parsley to the onions. Simmer 20 minutes.

Meanwhile, cut slices of the cheese (approximately ¼-inch thick) to stuff the whole chiles. Trim the slices to fit, and fill each pepper entirely. (If you've had to split them open, slice the cheese to fit one half of the pepper, and fold the other half over.)

Beat the egg whites with the 3 tablespoons flour, and add a couple of pinches of salt. Beat the yolks, and fold them into the beaten whites. Pour the mixture into a pie plate. Put a cup or two of sifted flour on a platter. Roll the stuffed chili peppers in the flour, coating them thoroughly. Then roll them in the egg batter, again coating thoroughly. Shake off the excess batter.

Heat ½ inch (at least) olive oil in a heavy skillet. Gently drop the peppers into the hot oil, a few at a time. Cook over moderately high heat until they're a light, golden brown on both sides.

Spread a little of the sauce (or salsa) on the bottom of an 8 x 12 x 2-inch baking dish and place the fried peppers on top, in one layer. Pour the rest of the salsa (or sauce) over the chiles.

Grate the remaining cheese coarsely, and sprinkle over the sauce. Bake at 350° for 20 minutes, or until the cheese is melted and the casserole is thoroughly hot and bubbling. Serves 3 to 4.

Two of the McMenamin ladies — Bob's sister-in-law Marge and his mother Agnes

CHEESE

CHILES RELLENOS CASSEROLE (Irene McMenamin)

2 (4-ounce) cans Ortega green chiles, whole
3 eggs, separated
 ½ cup milk
 ¼ cup flour
 ½ teaspoon salt
 ¼ teaspoon freshly ground black pepper
 ½ pound grated sharp Cheddar cheese or Tillamook
2 scallions, chopped with the green
1 (10-ounce) can Ortega salsa (enchilada sauce)
4 ounces mozzarella cheese, grated

Butter an 8 x 12 x 2-inch baking dish. Slit each chile lengthwise, and then rinse under cold water and remove the seeds. Dry on paper towels.

Beat the egg yolks with the milk, and mix in the flour, salt, and pepper until smooth and well-blended. Beat the egg whites until stiff, but not dry, and fold them into the yolk mixture.

Pour half the batter on the bottom of the casserole. Layer the chiles flat over the egg mixture, and sprinkle lightly with salt. Distribute the grated cheddar cheese over the chiles, and sprinkle the chopped scallions on top. Pour on the rest of the egg batter to cover.

Bake at 325° for 20 minutes, or until set. (Test with a silver knife.) Remove the baking dish from the oven and cover the top with a light layer of the salsa. Distribute the grated mozzarella on top of the sauce, return the dish to the oven, and bake 10 minutes longer.

Meanwhile, heat the remaining salsa in a saucepan. To serve, cut the portions in squares, and pass the extra sauce in a gravyboat. The casserole will serve 5 or 6.

CHEESE STRATA (Grace Stebbins)

This is from Mother's recipe collection, attributed to Amy Tomlison, whoever she may be.

- 12 slices white bread, crusts removed
  - Butter
- 6 or 7 slices Old English cheese
  - Cooked chicken or turkey, sliced (enough to cover 6 slices of bread generously)
- 6 or 7 eggs
- 3 ⅓ cups milk
- 1 can cream of mushroom soup, undiluted
  - Paprika

Generously butter a baking dish that will just hold 6 slices of bread in one layer. Butter all the bread slices, and place 6 of them in the dish, buttered side up. Arrange cheese slices on top, and the sliced chicken or turkey on top of that. Place the remaining bread slices on top, buttered side down. Beat the eggs with 3 cups milk and pour over all. Let stand overnight in the fridge, covered.

Remove from fridge to reach room temperature, and bake uncovered at 350° for 1 hour. Dilute the mushroom soup with ⅓ cup milk and heat thoroughly. Pour the sauce over each serving, and sprinkle paprika on top.

Bernie and Irene McMenamin

315

CHEESE ENCHILADAS (Marge McMenamin)

*Marge is wife to Bob's older
brother, Emmet, Jr.*

FILLING (for 1 dozen)

6 hard boiled eggs (one-half, chopped, for each enchilada)
2 or 3 large onions, chopped, and cooked in a very small
   amount of water, covered tightly, then thoroughly drained
1½ pounds Tillamook or sharp Cheddar cheese, grated
1 large can ripe olives (not pitted, and small)

SAUCE

2 (10-ounce) cans Las Palmas red chili sauce (if unavailable,
   any good brand of enchilada sauce can substitute)
2 cans water
 ½ cup flour
1 teaspoon salt
 ⅓ cup shortening

Brown the flour in a large skillet, and add the salt. Add the
shortening, stirring to make a smooth paste. Slowly add the chili
sauce, stirring constantly to keep smooth. Add the water, stirring.
Cook a few minutes until the sauce is thickened. This makes a
medium gravy. Keep warm until ready to use.

TORTILLAS

4 cups flour, unsifted
1¼ teaspoons salt
1 cup shortening (Crisco or Snowdrift)
1 cup ice water, approximately

Cut the shortening into the flour mixed with salt, and add enough
water to hold the dough together, as for pie crust. Divide the dough
into 12 balls. Roll out each ball to the shape of a circle, no thicker
than 1/8 inch, thinner if you can handle it. Fry the tortillas on an
ungreased griddle, or electric fry pan (375°), until there are golden
flecks on both sides. (You don't want to get them crisp.) Place
tortillas between towels to keep warm until ready to use.

TO ASSEMBLE AND BAKE

Have ready a large baking pan with 1-inch sides (to hold in the sauce). For each enchilada, dip a tortilla into the sauce, then place in the pan. From end to end, down the center only, distribute grated cheese, chopped hard boiled egg, about 1 or 2 tablespoons cooked onion, and 2 olives. Fold each side over the filling so they overlap like an envelope. Put on a little more sauce, sprinkle with more cheese, and top with another olive for garnish.

Bake at 350° for 15 minutes, or until the cheese melts and the enchiladas are thoroughly heated. Serve hot, and pass any leftover sauce.

Hélène Stewart

Another view of our renovated kitchen

<u>WELSH RAREBIT</u> (Florence Butterworth)

*Canadian-born "Aunt" Florence was a
long-ago friend of Mother's in Detroit.*

1   tablespoon butter
1   pound mild Cheddar cheese, grated
½ teaspoon dry mustard
½ to ⅔ cup beer
1   egg, slightly beaten
    Cayenne pepper
    Salt to taste
    Bread or split English muffins, lightly toasted and buttered
    Paprika

Melt the butter in the top of a double boiler. Add the cheese and mustard. As the cheese melts, gradually add the beer, stirring constantly. When blended and smooth, add some of the hot mixture to the beaten egg, and then turn it all back into the pot, stirring vigorously. Add a dash or two of cayenne and salt to taste.

Pour over the buttered toast or muffins, garnish with paprika, and serve immediately. Serves 4 to 6.

This, along with Chili and Eggs, is a favorite after-theatre snack.

Mother's house in Encino

WOODSTOCK STEW (Lois Seibel)

Lois is daughter to a dietician,
and mother to a vegetarian.

2   cups soy beans
1   clove garlic, crushed

Pick over the soy beans, wash, and soak overnight in water to cover. Cook early the next day in the soaking water with the garlic. Add more water to cover. It will take about 3 hours until they're tender.

⅓ cup light vegetable oil
1   cup finely chopped green or sweet red pepper (red is higher in protein content)
2   cups finely chopped onions
1   or 2 garlic cloves, minced
2   cups mung bean sprouts
1   package frozen chopped kale, collards, or spinach (listed in order of highest protein content)
1   or 2 teaspoons curry powder
    Salt to taste
2   vegetable cubes, or 1 heaping teaspoon vegetable essence
    Soy sauce (optional)

Put the frozen vegetable out to thaw.

Heat the oil in a large casserole and sauté the peppers for 10 minutes. Add the onions and garlic and sauté 30 minutes more. Add the drained, cooked soy beans, and all remaining ingredients (except the soy sauce). Bring the casserole to a simmer, and partially cover. Simmer for 30 minutes, stirring occasionally.

Serve with buttered brown rice and a side vegetable.

The soy sauce is for sprinkling at the table, if wished.

Woodstock Stew freezes well. It's particularly useful to freeze in individual portions when there's only one vegetarian in the family.

See the Pasta section for Lois' Baked Ziti, *another of her vegetarian concoctions. (Page 327.)*

VEGETARIAN CASSEROLE

1   cup thinly sliced carrots
1   cup green beans, cut diagonally in 1-inch slices
½ cup celery, cut diagonally in ¼-inch slices
1   large tomato, peeled, cored, seeded, and cut in 1-inch cubes
1   yellow squash, cut in ½-inch slices
1   zucchini, cut in ½-inch slices
1   medium onion, cut in half, and then in ¼-inch slices
3   scallions, cut in ½-inch slices, including the green
½ head cauliflower, cut into flowerets
¼ cup sweet red pepper, cut in thin strips
¼ cup green pepper, cut in thin strips
½ cup fresh green peas

Combine all the vegetables in a casserole that has a top. Mix them gently but thoroughly.

1   cup vegetable broth
⅓ cup olive oil
3   cloves garlic, finely chopped
1   tablespoon chopped fresh parsley
2   teaspoons salt, or to taste
½ bay leaf
¼ teaspoon thyme
½ teaspoon rosemary
½ teaspoon chili powder
1   teaspoon sesame seeds
   Freshly grated Parmesan cheese
   Thinly sliced cheese — imported Swiss, Monterey jack, or Cheddar

Heat the broth in a saucepan and add the oil, garlic, parsley, salt, chili powder, and sesame seeds. Crush the bay leaf with the thyme and rosemary in a mortar, and add. Bring the mixture to a boil and pour over the vegetables in the casserole. Cover tightly, using a layer of foil between the casserole and its top.

Bake at 350° for about 1 hour. Gently mix the vegetables once or twice during the cooking, and re-cover the pot.

At the end of the hour, remove the cover and foil. Sprinkle the vegetables generously with grated Parmesan, and cover completely with the sliced cheese. Place under the broiler until the cheese is melted, bubbly, and lightly browned. Serves 4 to 6.

If you wish, you may also add 1 cup diced potatoes to the vegetables.

Suggest serving the casserole with buttered brown rice, or with lentils.

Official United States Air Force Photograph

With Bill Holden in "Reconnaissance Pilot"

LEO'S EGGPLANT CASSEROLE (Leo Lotito)

*When Leo gave this to me, he said, you won't believe it doesn't have meat in it. He's right. It also totally fools people who are prejudiced against eggplant. He once saved the purple peelings to prove to a friend who swore he **never** ate eggplant that he just had. And had raved about it.*

4   medium-sized eggplants
2   large cloves garlic, finely chopped
1   large white onion, diced
 ½ large green pepper, diced
1½ to 2 tablespoons oil
2   (8-ounce) cans tomato sauce
1   teaspoon sweet basil ⎱ crush together in a mortar
 ¼ teaspoon oregano   ⎰ until powdery
    Salt and freshly ground black pepper to taste
    Flour
4   eggs, separated
    Oil, or fat, for frying
2   (4½-ounce) cans chopped black olives
1   pound medium Tillamook cheese, grated (or use a mild Cheddar cheese, if Tillamook is unavailable)

Slice the eggplants, peel them, and then cut into cubes. Put the cubes in a large pot, cover with boiling water, and cook until transparent. When the eggplant is done, drain thoroughly, and mash the cubes in a mixing bowl. (If a potato masher doesn't get all the lumps out, use an electric hand beater briefly.)

In the meantime, heat 1½ to 2 tablespoons oil in a heavy skillet, and add *half* the chopped garlic, onion, and green pepper. Sauté until soft, about 20 minutes. Add the tomato sauce, 2 cans of water, the basil, oregano, and salt and pepper to taste. Put the skillet on a back burner and let it simmer very slowly until ready to use.

Add the remaining chopped garlic, onion, and green pepper to the mashed eggplant, and blend. Add enough flour to thicken the mixture so it will hold a firm ball on a spoon.

Beat the egg yolks and blend into the eggplant mixture. Add salt and pepper to taste. Beat the whites until they form peaks, and then fold into the mixture.

Heat oil or fat in a large, heavy skillet, enough to come up the sides about half an inch. Drop heaping tablespoonsful of the eggplant mixture into the hot fat, 4 or 5 at a time, and mash them down with a spatula to make a patty. Fry them to a golden brown on both sides.

Using a slotted spatula, drain the patties well, and place them close together on an ovenproof platter (or on a 13 x 9 x 2-inch baking dish), in layers. Top each layer with the tomato sauce, chopped olives, and grated cheese. (2 to 4 layers, depending on the size of your eggplants.)

Bake at 350° for 30 minutes. The dish serves about 8.

> *The whole dish can be prepared a day ahead, ready to bake. Just refrigerate it. (Actually, it's better to do it ahead — the flavors have more time to blend.) Either remove from the fridge to reach room temperature before baking, or put it straight into the oven and add to the baking time. The casserole should be piping hot before serving.*

With Bill Macy, Julie Harris, and DeAnn Mears in "And Miss Reardon Drinks A Little"

SPANISH RICE VANCOUVER (Sean Emmett)

¾ cup oil (or enough to cover the bottom of a large, heavy
  skillet to ¼ or ½ inch)
2 cups short grain brown rice
2 (8-ounce) cans tomato sauce
2 medium-large onions, chopped
1 green pepper, chopped
2 cloves garlic, finely chopped
4 cups water (more if necessary)
1 teaspoon salt, or more to taste
   Freshly ground black pepper
1 tablespoon freshly chopped parsley
½ teaspoon paprika
½ teaspoon dill weed
¼ teaspoon oregano
¼ teaspoon basil
1 bay leaf
1 teaspoon sesame seeds

Heat the oil almost to smoking in a large, heavy skillet. Add the rice
and cook over high heat until gently browned. Shake and stir the
skillet so all the grains are equally toasted. Don't let them get too
brown.

Turn off the heat, and add the tomato sauce slowly, into the sides of
the skillet. (Stand back . . . the oil will splatter.) Add the onions,
green pepper, and garlic. Add 2 cups of the water, and stir. (Do not
stir from this point on!)

Sprinkle all the seasonings and sesame seeds over the surface evenly,
and add the bay leaf. Bring the skillet to a gentle simmer and cover.

At the end of 45 minutes, add another cup of water. (Do not stir.)
Re-cover the skillet, and continue simmering. Repeat with the fourth
cup of water in another half-hour or so. Total simmering time should
be approximately 3 hours.

Test by gently pushing the rice apart with a fork to see if the water is
absorbed, and tasting a couple of grains of rice. If the water absorbs
too soon, before the rice is tender, add a little more.

When done, fluff the rice with a fork and serve. As a vegetarian entrée, it serves 5 to 6. As a side vegetable, it will serve 8 or more.

Serve with Gomazio (page 334), a seasoning to sprinkle on at the table.

STUFFED ZUCCHINI — VEGETARIAN STYLE (See page 255.)

EGGPLANT PARMIGIANA (Bob Emmett)

    2   cloves garlic, finely chopped
    1   tablespoon grated onion
    ½   teaspoon salt
    ¼   cup olive oil
    ½   teaspoon lemon juice
        Large pinch of oregano
        Freshly ground black pepper
    1   medium eggplant
        Tomato Sauce, canned or homemade (p. 336)
        Mozzarella cheese, thinly sliced
        Freshly grated Parmesan cheese

Blend the first 7 ingredients thoroughly to make a marinade.

Wash the eggplant, trim the ends, and slice it crosswise in ¾-inch slices. Brush both sides of the slices with the marinade. Line a shallow pan that will fit under the broiler with foil, and arrange the eggplant slices on it in one layer.

Broil about 5 inches from the flame for 5 minutes, basting once. Turn the slices, brush with marinade again, and broil another 3 minutes, or until tender.

Spread the slices with Tomato Sauce, sprinkle generously with Parmesan, and cover completely with the mozzarella slices. Broil until lightly browned and bubbly.

> *I don't know how this adds up in calories, but it's a great dish for low-carbohydrate diets.*

SPAGHETTI WITH BEEF AND SAUSAGE SAUCE

4   tablespoons olive oil
2   cups finely chopped onions
4   large garlic cloves, finely chopped
2   links hot Italian sausage
1   pound lean ground beef
2   (1-pound, 12-ounce) cans Italian plum tomatoes
1   (6-ounce) can tomato paste
1   bay leaf
¼ cup chopped fresh parsley
½ teaspoon salt, or more to taste
¼ teaspoon freshly ground black pepper
½ cup water, or beef broth
½ teaspoon oregano
½ teaspoon basil
1   pound No. 9 spaghetti
Freshly grated Parmesan cheese

Heat the oil in a heavy casserole. Add the onions and garlic and cook over medium heat, stirring frequently, until they begin to brown.

Remove the sausages from their casings and add to the onions. Cook, stirring, about 2 minutes. Add the ground beef and cook (still on medium heat) until all the red is gone. Mush it up with a wooden spoon so the lumps of meat aren't too large.

Add the tomatoes and mash them over the meat with the spoon. Add the tomato paste, bay leaf, parsley, pepper, salt, and water. Mix thoroughly. Bring the pot to a boil, turn down heat, and simmer gently, uncovered, about an hour. Stir occasionally. After the hour, adjust the seasoning, adding more salt if necessary. Add the oregano and basil. Simmer another 15 minutes. Discard the bay leaf.

Prepare the spaghetti according to package directions, adding 1 tablespoon olive oil to the water. Drain thoroughly and serve immediately, topped with the sauce. Pass the Parmesan.

This will make about 2 quarts sauce. It freezes well.

BAKED ZITI (Lois Seibel)

    1   pound ziti (Buitoni's is best for vegetarians)
    1   cup (8-ounces) Ricotta cheese
    2   cups Tomato Sauce (see recipe following)
     ½ pound cubed mozzarella cheese
     ¼ cup grated Parmesan cheese
        Thin slices mozzarella cheese
        Grated Parmesan cheese
        Soft butter

Prepare the Tomato Sauce. Cook the macaroni according to package directions and drain. Mix the Ricotta with the Tomato Sauce. Pour over the macaroni. Add the cubed mozzarella and the ¼ cup of Parmesan. Mix well.

Turn into a buttered oblong baking dish. Top with slices of mozzarella and sprinkle lavishly with grated Parmesan. Dot generously with butter.

Bake in a preheated 350° oven for 30 minutes, or until the mozzarella is melted and the top is nicely browned.

TOMATO SAUCE

    1   (28-ounce) can tomato puree
    3   onions, finely chopped
    1   or 2 cloves garlic, minced
     ⅓ cup olive oil
     ½ (6-ounce) can tomato paste (optional)
     ¼ teaspoon sugar
     ½ teaspoon basil
     ½ teaspoon oregano
        Salt and pepper to taste

Sauté the onions and garlic in the oil until very soft. Add the tomato puree (and paste) and all the other ingredients and cook at least 30 minutes, stirring occasionally.

Don't bother to measure . . . add it all to the pasta.

FISHERMAN'S FETTUCINI

½ pound shrimp in the shell
2 cups water
1 stalk celery, cut up in 1-inch lengths
1 small onion, coarsely sliced
¼ teaspoon thyme
4 peppercorns
½ small bay leaf
1 clove garlic, minced
¾ pound fillet of sole
5 tablespoons butter
⅓ cup white wine
1 leek finely chopped (white part only)
¼ to ½ teaspoon salt
2 tablespoons flour
2 cups half-and-half
Salt and freshly ground black pepper to taste
Pinch nutmeg
Dash cayenne pepper
1 to 2 tablespoons lemon juice
8 ounces fettucini (narrow noodles, about ¼-inch wide)
½ cup freshly grated Parmesan cheese
6 tablespoons melted butter

Wash the shrimp in their shells in several changes of water, and drain. Put 2 cups water, the celery, onion, thyme, peppercorns, bay leaf, and garlic in a heavy saucepan and bring to a boil. Simmer for 12 minutes, and then add the shrimp. Return to a boil quickly and then simmer 3 to 5 minutes, depending on the size of the shrimp. Remove shrimp from the liquid and shell them. Return the shells to the pot and boil over high heat until the liquid is reduced by half. Strain it and reserve ¾ cup. Devein the shrimp and cut them up coarsely. Put in a bowl, salt lightly, and set aside.

Rinse and dry the fillets of sole, and cut them into ¾-inch cubes. Melt 2 tablespoons of the butter in a skillet and add the fish cubes, the wine, ¾ cup of the strained shrimp stock, the chopped leek, and salt to taste. Simmer until the sole is just tender, about 4 to 5 minutes. Remove the fish cubes with a slotted spoon, and set aside in a bowl. Then cook the poaching liquid over medium heat until reduced by half. (See comments following.)

In a saucepan, melt 2 tablespoons butter and add the flour. Cook, stirring, 3 to 5 minutes, until well blended. Gradually add the half and half, stirring constantly. When smooth and hot, add salt and pepper to taste and a generous sprinkling of nutmeg. Then add the reduced poaching liquid, cayenne, and more salt if necessary, stirring constantly. When the sauce is smooth and piping hot (but not boiling), take off heat and stir in lemon juice to taste.

Cook the pasta al dente according to the package directions, adding salt and 1 tablespoon olive oil to the water. Do not overcook. Drain thoroughly and toss with the remaining tablespoon of butter.

Butter a medium-sized baking dish and layer ⅓ of the pasta in the bottom. Sprinkle ⅓ of the fish and ⅓ of the shrimp on top. Pour a third of the sauce over, and sprinkle with ⅓ of the Parmesan. Dribble ⅓ of the melted butter on top. Repeat the layers 2 more times, and bake covered at 350° for 15 minutes. Remove the cover and continue baking another 15 minutes, or until the casserole is piping hot and bubbly. Toss gently and serve immediately.

The recipe can be prepared a day ahead up to beginning the sauce. Cover the fish and shrimp bowls with plastic wrap and refrigerate. Refrigerate the reduced poaching liquid as well, tightly covered, but be sure to bring it to room temperature before continuing with the recipe.

The recipe serves 4 generously, perhaps more, and doubles well. I haven't tried tripling it, but see no reason why it couldn't be done.

LASAGNE

 ½ pound sweet Italian sausages
 ½ pound hot Italian sausages
 1½ pounds lean ground beef
  Salt and freshly ground black pepper
 ½ pound mushrooms, chopped coarsely
 2 cloves garlic, finely chopped
  Fresh Marinara Sauce (see recipe p. 332)
 3 tablespoons butter
 3 tablespoons flour
 1¼ cups milk
 1 cup heavy cream
 ¼ teaspoon nutmeg
 12 ounces lasagne
 ½ pound mozzarella cheese, cut into ¼-inch cubes
 ¾ to 1 cup freshly grated Parmesan cheese
 6 tablespoons melted butter
  Ricotta (see recipe p. 332)

Prepare the Marinara Sauce first.

Stab the sausages all over with a fork, and cook them until lightly browned in a large, heavy skillet, about 20 to 30 minutes. Remove the sausages to paper toweling to drain, and pour off almost all the fat from the skillet.

Add the beef to the skillet, and break it up into bite-sized chunks with a wooden spoon. Add salt and pepper, the mushrooms, and garlic, and cook over medium heat until the meat loses its red color. Stir gently and frequently, trying not to break up the meat chunks too much.

Skin the sausages, and slice them into ½-inch chunks. When the beef begins to brown, add the sausages and the Marinara Sauce. Partly cover the skillet, and simmer about 30 minutes, stirring occasionally.

Melt the 3 tablespoons of butter in a saucepan, and add the flour. Stir constantly for 3 to 5 minutes, until the mixture is well blended and the flour begins to brown slightly. Add the milk gradually, stirring constantly. When it's smooth and blended, add the cream, salt and pepper to taste, and the nutmeg. Stir the sauce until it's hot (but not boiling), and then add to the meat sauce.

Cook the lasagne al dente, adding salt and 1 tablespoon olive oil to the water. Drain, rinse under cold water, drain again, and as soon as you can handle it, lay the pasta strips out on sheets of waxed paper. Prepare the Ricotta.

Assemble the dish in a large, lightly buttered lasagne pan (a rectangular baking dish with at least 3-inch sides). Spoon a layer of sauce on the bottom. Add one layer of lasagne. Spread a third of the Ricotta over the pasta. Spoon meat sauce on next. Then sprinkle with a third of the mozzarella cubes, and a third of the Parmesan. Dribble 2 tablespoons of the melted butter on top. Start again with the pasta and continue the layers in the above order, ending with mozzarella, Parmesan, and melted butter. 3 layers in all. (You may not be able to, or want to, use all the pasta.)

Bake the dish at 375° for 45 minutes, until it's piping hot and bubbling throughout. Serves 8.

It's a good idea to prepare the meat sauce a day ahead. Actually the whole thing can be assembled a day ahead and refrigerated. If you do, take it out of the fridge an hour or so before baking, and be sure you give it enough time in the oven to get thoroughly bubbly.

If, by any chance, you find yourself with more sauce than the size of the pan can hold comfortably (I frequently do), here's a suggestion. Get most of the chunks of meat and sausage into the lasagne, and save the leftover sauce for a very tasty chicken dish. Sauté a 2½- to 3-pound cut-up chicken in oil until nicely browned all over. Drain the chicken pieces on paper towels, and then sprinkle both sides with salt and pepper. Pour off the oil and wipe out the pot. Then return the chicken pieces, and pour the lasagne sauce over. (I recommend scraping the top layer of solidified fat from the sauce after it's been refrigerated, before adding it to the chicken.) Bake, covered, in a 300° oven for 1 to 1¼ hours. Unless you have enough sauce to cover the chicken, turn the pieces in the sauce every now and then. It goes very nicely with rice.

MARINARA SAUCE

½ cup olive oil
4   cups coarsely chopped onions
½ cup finely chopped carrots
3   to 4 teaspoons finely chopped garlic
2   (2-pound, 3-ounce) cans peeled Italian plum tomatoes
    Salt and freshly ground black pepper
4   tablespoons butter
2   teaspoons oregano
2   teaspoons basil
1   teaspoon parsley

Heat the oil in a large, heavy skillet, and add the onions, carrots, and garlic. Cook over moderately high heat, stirring, until the vegetables are golden brown. About 20 to 30 minutes.

Put the tomatoes through a sieve, pushing the pulp through with a wooden spoon, and discard the seeds. Add the pureed tomatoes to the onions, stir, and season with salt and pepper to taste. Bring the sauce to a boil, partly cover the skillet, and simmer gently for 10 minutes.

Put the sauce through a sieve, and push the solids through with a wooden spoon. Return the sauce to the skillet and add the butter, oregano, basil, and parsley. Stir to blend, partly cover the skillet, and simmer another 30 minutes.

RICOTTA

1   pound Ricotta cheese
3   eggs
½ cup freshly grated Parmesan cheese
2   tablespoons chopped fresh parsley
    Salt and freshly ground black pepper

Beat the eggs, add the Ricotta, Parmesan, and parsley, and blend thoroughly   Add salt and pepper to taste.

LINGUINE WITH GARLIC BUTTER

¼ pound butter
4   large garlic cloves, finely chopped
1   pound linguine
   Freshly grated Parmesan cheese

Sauté the garlic in 2 tablespoons of butter for 5 minutes, stirring constantly. Add the remaining butter to melt, and blend. Keep warm.

Meanwhile, prepare the linguine according to package directions, adding 1 tablespoon olive oil to the water. Drain thoroughly, and return to the pot. Add the hot garlic butter and toss to thoroughly coat the pasta.

Serve immediately, with plenty of grated Parmesan cheese to pass.

Backstage "on the road." William Hansen joins us for Julie Harris' birthday party in Hollywood.

GOMAZIO (Sean Emmett)

Toast ⅓ cup sesame seeds over medium-low heat in a small, heavy skillet until an even, rich brown. Shake the pan a lot. (No oil is needed. The seeds will exude their own oil.)

Place the seeds in a mortar, small quantities at a time, and grind thoroughly with salt ... approximately 1½ tablespoons salt to ⅓ cup sesame seeds. As a seasoning, Gomazio should be salty, but not so salty one loses the toasty flavor of the sesame seeds. Store in a tightly covered jar. (A Spice Islands jar with a perforated under-cap is perfect.)

> *Gomazio is good over almost anything, including salads. Sprinkle as you would salt.*

CHINESE MUSTARD (See page 281.)

MORNAY SAUCE

- 2 tablespoons butter
- 3 tablespoons flour
- 1½ cups milk
- ½ cup heavy cream
    Salt and white pepper to taste
- ¾ to 1 cup grated Swiss cheese
- ¼ cup grated Parmesan cheese
- ¼ teaspoon nutmeg
    Dash cayenne pepper
- 1 egg yolk
    Paprika (optional)

Melt the butter in a saucepan, and add the flour. Blend well, and cook over low heat, stirring, about 2 to 3 minutes. Gradually add the milk, stirring constantly, and then the cream. When blended and smooth, add salt and pepper to taste.

When the sauce is hot (but not boiling), add the grated cheeses and stir until they're melted. Add the nutmeg and cayenne, and taste for seasoning. You may want to add more salt and/or pepper.

Bring the sauce to just under boiling, and add the egg yolk, stirring rapidly. (A wire whisk is best to use at this point.) When smooth and blended, remove the saucepan from the heat. The paprika is for a bit of color when serving.

The sauce can be made early and reheated in a double boiler. Beat it smooth again with a wire whisk before serving. The recipe makes 2 to 3 cups.

CURRY SAUCE FOR LEFTOVER MEAT OR FOWL

- 3 tablespoons butter
- 1 to 2 medium onions, chopped
- 2 cloves garlic, minced
- 1½-inch slice whole ginger
- 1 to 2 tablespoons flour (depending on how thick you like the sauce)
- 1½ to 2 tablespoons curry powder (preferably Malaysian)
- ¼ teaspoon freshly grated nutmeg
- 2 cups chicken, beef, or vegetable broth
  Salt and freshly ground black pepper to taste
- 2 to 3 cups cooked lamb, beef, chicken, turkey . . . cubed

Melt the butter in a heavy skillet, and sauté the onions, garlic, and ginger until the onion is wilted. Add the flour, blend thoroughly, and cook until the flour begins to brown, stirring constantly. Add the curry powder and nutmeg, blend, and continue cooking and stirring over low heat for about 5 minutes.

Add the broth gradually, stirring constantly. Bring the sauce slowly to a boil, and then simmer very gently for about 10 minutes. Stir occasionally. Season to taste with salt and pepper.

Remove the slice of ginger, add the cooked meat or fowl, and continue to simmer until it is thoroughly heated.

Serve over rice, and pass the chutney.

CURRY ACCOMPANIMENTS (See page 297.)

TOMATO SAUCE

¼ cup olive oil
2 cups onions, finely chopped
4 cloves garlic, finely chopped
2 green peppers, finely chopped
4 bay leaves
4 vegetable cubes (or 4 teaspoons vegetable essence)
1 (46-ounce) can tomato juice
1 teaspoon salt
½ teaspoon rosemary
½ teaspoon thyme
1 teaspoon oregano
1 teaspoon basil
3 (6-ounce) cans tomato paste

Heat the oil in a large, heavy pot. Sauté the onions, garlic, and green peppers about 30 minutes. Add the bay leaves, vegetable cubes, and tomato juice. Simmer 15 minutes.

Pound together in a mortar, the salt, rosemary, thyme, oregano, and basil. Add to the pot.

When the onions and green peppers are thoroughly tender, add the tomato paste, and simmer another hour, very gently.

Remove the bay leaves before serving (or storing).

This recipe makes approximately 2 quarts. Freeze what you don't plan to use in the near future.

The sauce can be used as a topping for the Stuffed Zucchini recipes (pages 254 and 255), or in any recipe that calls for tomato sauce.

It also makes a good sauce for spaghetti. Add sautéed ground beef or mushrooms coarsely chopped for variation.

MOTHER'S CRANBERRIES (Grace Stebbins)

1 pound cranberries
2 heaping cups sugar (approximately 2¼ cups, slightly more
   or less, depending on how many of the cranberries have
   to be discarded)

Pick over the cranberries carefully, discarding any imperfect ones, and wash well. Put the berries, still wet from the washing, into a 10-inch stainless steel skillet (or a 10-inch enamel pan with 2½ to 3-inch sides). Add a touch more water to the berries, no more than to make a thin film on the bottom of the skillet. Mother taught me to hold the pan near the cold water tap and use my fingers to flick the extra cold water over the berries. Hard to gage how *many* flicks — but the point is to get by with as little water as possible.

Add the sugar, distributing evenly as you pour, and turn on the heat. Bring the berries slowly to a simmer over medium-low heat. Use a spatula and work the sugar gently into the berries. Fold, don't stir, or the berries will get mushy. Scrape the sides and bottom of the skillet occasionally with the spatula, to get the sugar thoroughly into the berries. (Regulate the heat as they cook, so they simmer gently and don't boil.)

Cook the berries until they pop, and then a little longer. The berries should be tender but not mushy. When they're done, in 10 to 15 minutes after they begin to simmer, the sugar will be thoroughly dissolved and syrupy.

Remove the pan from the stove and let cool. Spoon the berries and syrup into a jar and cover tightly. Refrigerate.

> *If you like them juicier, add more sugar, but be very cautious about adding more water.*
>
> *The cranberries freeze well, but if tightly covered, will last months and months just in the fridge.*
>
> *One pound at a time is quite enough to handle, but during the cranberry season, I make several batches so they will last the family until the next season.*
>
> *Serve them with almost anything, not just turkey or chicken. Good with Flank Steak (page 260), pork, ham, pot roast, even over vanilla ice cream. Marvelous on Party Pancake (page 340) in place of the jam or jelly.*

RHUBARB COFFEE CAKE (Tillie Cole)

½ cup butter (¼ pound), softened

1½ cups brown sugar, packed

2 eggs

2 cups flour, sifted before measuring

1 teaspoon baking soda

1 cup buttermilk, or sour milk

To make sour milk, add 4 teaspoons vinegar to 1 cup sweet milk, stir, and let stand 5 minutes or more.

1 teaspoon vanilla

2 cups floured rhubarb cut in ½-inch pieces (use part of the 2 cups flour)

½ cup chopped walnuts (optional)

Butter and lightly flour a 9 x 13 x 2-inch baking dish. Preheat the oven to 350°.

Cream the butter and sugar until very smooth and creamy. Add the eggs, one at a time, and beat well after each addition. Add the vanilla and blend.

Use as much flour as you need to flour the rhubarb, and sift the rest again with the soda. Add the flour and the buttermilk alternately to the butter-sugar-egg mixture, beating well after each addition. Add the rhubarb and the nuts, and blend thoroughly. Pour the batter into the baking dish, and sprinkle the following topping evenly over the batter. Bake at 350° for 45 minutes.

TOPPING

6 tablespoons flour

½ cup sugar

1 teaspoon cinnamon

4 tablespoons cold butter

Mix the flour, sugar, and cinnamon together, and cut it into the butter until thoroughly blended and crumbly.

BRAN MUFFINS (Tillie Cole)

> ¾ cup bran buds (or Kellog's All-Bran)
> ½ cup milk
> 1 egg
> 3 tablespoons soft butter
> ¾ cup flour, sifted before measuring
> ¼ cup sugar
> 1½ teaspoons baking powder
> ½ teaspoon salt

Butter a six-cup muffin tin. Preheat the oven to 400°.

Combine the bran and the milk. Let stand about 5 minutes. Then add the egg and the butter, and beat until well blended.

Sift the flour again with the sugar, baking powder, and salt. Add to the bran mixture, *stirring only until combined.*

Bake in the greased muffin tin at 400° about 20 to 25 minutes, or until lightly browned.

For 12 muffins, double all the ingredients, but still use only 1 egg.

Reheat the muffins as you would the blueberry muffins (p. 342, in NOTE).

All the muffins ... plain, blueberry, nut, and bran ... are also good split and toasted under the broiler.

CRÉOLE PANCAKES (Lloyd and Dorothy Bridges)

4   eggs
1   cup sour cream
1   cup cottage cheese
1   tablespoon sugar
½ cup flour
¼ teaspoon baking soda
⅛ to ¼ teaspoon salt, to taste

Beat the eggs lightly with a rotary beater, and then beat in the sour cream until blended. Stir the remaining ingredients in until mixed.

Lightly grease a griddle (or skillet) with butter or oil. When hot, drop the batter by the tablespoonful, approximately two to a pancake. Cook over moderate to high heat, regulating it as you go. When bubbles appear to break on top of the pancakes, turn them with a wide spatula. They're done when lightly browned on both sides. (Wipe off the griddle before re-greasing for the next batch.)

Serve immediately with butter and syrup. The pancakes are very light, but sufficient for 4 people.

PARTY PANCAKE

½ cup flour
½ cup milk
2   eggs, lightly beaten
    Pinch of nutmeg
4   tablespoons butter
2   tablespoons confectioners' sugar
    Juice of half a lemon
    Jelly, jam, marmalade, or Mother's Cranberries (see p. 337)

Combine flour, milk, eggs and nutmeg in a mixing bowl. Beat lightly, leaving the batter a little lumpy. Melt the butter in a 12-inch skillet, and when it is very hot, pour in the batter.

Bake in a 425° oven 15 to 20 minutes, or until the pancake is golden brown. Sprinkle with confectioner's sugar and return to the oven for a few minutes.

Sprinkle with lemon juice and serve immediately, with jelly, jam, marmalade or Mother's Cranberries on top. Serves 2 to 4.

BAKING POWDER BISCUITS (Grace Stebbins)

      2   cups cake flour, sifted before measuring
      ¼ teaspoon salt
      5   level teaspoons baking powder
      3   tablespoons Crisco, very cold
    1½ tablespoons butter, very cold
      ½ to ⅔ cup cold milk, enough to hold the dough together

Preheat the oven to 475° and lightly butter a cookie sheet.

Sift the flour again with the salt and the baking powder. Work the cold shortening and butter into the dry ingredients, using a pastry blender, two knives, or your fingertips, until it is the consistency of coarse cornmeal. (Work with dispatch if using your fingers, to avoid body heat warming the shortening.)

Add milk cautiously, using only enough to make a soft dough. Toss the dough onto a floured board and knead slightly (very slightly). Pat the dough with your hands (don't roll) to a thickness of ¾ inch. Cut in rounds with a biscuit cutter and put them on the cookie sheet. If the dough is too sticky to handle easily, dip your cutter in flour first, shaking off the excess. Shape the last biscuit with your fingers.

Bake in the 475° oven for 10 to 12 minutes, or until lightly browned.

Serve hot, with butter, and if you're like me, with honey.

The recipe makes approximately 8 biscuits with a 2½-inch biscuit cutter.

Easy to reheat, using the same method as for the muffins on page 342.

BLUEBERRY MUFFINS (Grace Stebbins)

2   cups cake flour, sifted before measuring
½ cup sugar
5   teaspoons baking powder
1   egg, beaten
¼ cup melted butter
1   cup milk
1   cup blueberries, fresh . . . or well-drained, if canned
    Flour

Wash the fresh blueberries, drain, and dry gently on paper towels. (If using canned, dry them after draining on paper towels, too, or they'll get quite gummy when floured.) Lightly flour the berries. Butter your muffin tins, at least 15 cups. Preheat the oven to 425°.

Sift the flour again with the sugar and baking powder. Combine the beaten egg with the melted butter and the milk until well blended.

Stir the liquid ingredients into the dry ingredients quickly, using only about 10 to 15 strokes. Make no attempt to stir or beat out the lumps. Ignore them.

Fold in the floured blueberries gently and quickly. Pour the batter at once into the greased muffin tins, filling the cups about ⅔ full. Bake for 15 to 20 minutes at 425°, or until the muffins are lightly browned.

Tip the muffins onto their sides in the tins immediately, and serve while still warm or hot.

> *15 is an odd number, but that's approximately what the recipe yields. I fill two 6-cup muffin tins (the cups measure 2 ⅝ inches in diameter at the top, 2 inches at the base) and 3 foil baking cups. If you use all tins, and have leftover cups unfilled, half-fill the empties with water before putting the pans in the oven.*

> **To reheat** *the muffins, dash them under the cold water faucet, shake off the excess water, and either wrap in foil or put in a brown paper bag in a 425°. oven for 5 to 10 minutes.*

These muffins are also great plain. Make exactly the same . . . just eliminate the blueberries.

You can also substitute ¾ cup chopped nutmeats for the blueberries. Not bad, either.

SPOON ROLLS (Tillie Cole)

1   cake or 1 package dry active yeast (if compressed yeast is used, it would be approximately 1⅗ ounces)
¼ cup warm water
¼ cup sugar
⅓ cup butter, softened
1   teaspoon salt
¾ cup scalded milk (heated until wrinkles form)
½ cup cold water
1   egg
3½ cups unsifted flour

Dissolve the yeast in the warm water. Heat the milk to scalding, and add to the sugar, butter, and salt in a mixing bowl. Stir until thoroughly combined, and then add the cold water to cool the mixture.

Blend in the egg and the dissolved yeast. Add the flour and mix until well blended.

Place the dough in a large, greased bowl and cover with a cloth. Let it rise in a warm place until double in size — 45 to 60 minutes. Stir down the dough. Then spoon it into well-greased muffin tins, filling them half full. (Two dozen.) Let rise again in a warm place until the batter has risen to the edge of the muffin cups and is rounded in the center. About 30 to 45 minutes. (This time, covered or not. Covered makes for a slightly softer crust.)

Bake at 400° for 15 to 20 minutes, or until nicely browned on top. The rolls are at their best hot. If serving later, reheat them as you would the muffins. (See page 342.)

SOURDOUGH FRENCH BREAD (Bob Emmett)

Starter:
- 1 package dry active yeast
- 2 cups warm water
- 2 cups unbleached, unsifted flour

Using a glass or ceramic bowl, dissolve the yeast in the warm water. Add the flour, and mix until well blended. Let the bowl stand, uncovered, in a warm place at least 48 hours, preferably 72 hours. Stir occasionally, and add more warm water if it begins to dry out. A yellowish liquid may rise to the surface. That's normal. Stir before using.

After removing some of the starter to make bread, replenish the remainder in the bowl with equal quantities of warm water and flour. Let the bowl stand in a warm place until it bubbles well, and then store loosely covered in the fridge. It should be used and replenished about once every two weeks, if not oftener.

Bread:
- 11 to 13 cups unbleached, unsifted flour
- 4 cups warm water
- 1½ cups starter
- ¼ cup sugar
- 2 packages dry active yeast
- 4 teaspoons salt
- Cornmeal

Combine 4 cups of the flour with 4 cups of warm water, 1½ cups starter, and the sugar in a large glass or ceramic bowl. Beat until smooth. Cover the bowl with a cloth or plastic wrap, and let stand in a warm place at least 20 hours, preferably 24, stirring occasionally. The longer it stands, the sourer it gets.

Combine the yeast with the salt and 2 cups of flour, and add to the bowl. Beat until well-blended, and then gradually add enough of the remaining flour to make a fairly stiff dough.

Knead the dough on a floured board until it's smooth and satiny, a good 15 minutes. Divide the dough into 3 parts, and shape each into a loaf . . . either round or long.

Lightly grease a large baking sheet, and then sprinkle it lightly with cornmeal. Shake the cornmeal around so it covers the baking sheet evenly. Place the loaves on the sheet with space between them, and score the tops with diagonal slashes or in a lattice pattern. Cover them with a cloth, and let rise in a warm place until doubled in bulk, about 1½ hours.

Preheat the oven to 400°, and place a pan of boiling water in the bottom. Brush the tops of the risen loaves with water, and bake on a rack over the boiling water for 40 to 45 minutes. Brush them with water twice more during the baking. The loaves are done when they have a slightly hollow sound if you tap them on the bottom. Remove from the pan to cool.

GARLIC BREAD

Melt 4 to 8 tablespoons butter with 3 to 6 cloves of garlic, crushed. Slice a loaf of French or Italian bread at about ¾-inch intervals, not quite all the way through. With a pastry brush, paint all the cut surfaces with the garlic butter. Wrap the loaf in foil and put in a 350° oven for 10 to 15 minutes, or until thoroughly hot.

Alternative: Cut the bread all the way through. Paint on one side with the garlic butter and toast on a foil-lined pan about 4 inches from the heat in the broiler. Turn the slices, paint the other side, and toast again. You can also sprinkle with grated Parmesan cheese before toasting on the second side.

NUT BREAD (Grace Stebbins)

    1   egg
    1   cup milk
    2   cups flour, sifted before measuring
    1   cup sugar
    1   level teaspoon salt
    4   level teaspoons baking powder
    1   cup walnuts, finely chopped but not powdery

Beat the egg and add the milk. Blend well.

Sift together the flour, sugar, salt, and baking powder. Add this to the egg and milk gradually and beat well to blend. Stir in the walnuts until thoroughly blended.

Pour the batter into a buttered loaf pan and let sit in a warm place for 30 minutes.

Bake in a 300° oven for 60 minutes. Let the bread cool in the pan for 15 minutes, and then turn out to cool completely.

> *Mother would sometimes turn the recipe into Date-Nut Bread by adding ½ to 1 cup cut-up dates along with the walnuts. It's delicious.*

BANANA BREAD (Grace Thompson)

> *A friend of Mother's from the Florida years. Her son, Russell, taught me to fly a seaplane. I emigrated to California before I was ready to solo. And that was that.*

    ½ cup butter, softened
    1   cup sugar
    2   eggs, beaten
    1½ cups flour, sifted before measuring
    1   level teaspoon soda
    ½ teaspoon salt
    4   bananas, crushed
    ¼ cup chopped walnuts

Cream the butter and sugar until very light and fluffy. Add the beaten eggs and blend thoroughly. Sift the flour, soda, and salt together and add to the butter-sugar-egg mixture alternately with the crushed bananas. Stir in the nuts.

Pour the batter into a buttered loaf pan and bake at 350° for about 50 minutes, or until browned, and the top rebounds slightly when pressed gently in the center.

Let cool in the pan about 20 minutes before turning it out to cool completely.

CRANBERRY NUT BREAD (Maryesther Denver)

½ cup butter
1¼ cups sugar
1 egg, slightly beaten
1 cup milk
2½ tablespoons grated orange or lemon rind
½ teaspoon vanilla
2 cups flour, sifted before measuring
½ teaspoon salt
2 cups chopped cranberries
½ cup chopped nutmeats

Cream the butter and sugar until very light and fluffy. Add the egg, milk, and orange or lemon peel. Beat vigorously until well blended. Add the vanilla and stir.

Sift the flour again with the salt, and fold into the mixture. Stir in the cranberries and nuts, and pour into a buttered loaf pan. (Ordinary bread size.)

Bake at 350° for 1 hour, or until a wooden pick inserted in the center comes out clean. (Watch closely toward the end of the hour so as not to burn the edges. If it starts to get too brown, lower the oven temperature to 300°.)

Run a sharp knife around the edges, and remove the bread to a rack. Cool thoroughly before slicing.

STUFFED FRENCH ROLLS (Jack Barron)

½ cup chopped olives
½ teaspoon sugar
½ cup oil
1   pound grated cheese, sharp or mild
1   small can tomato sauce
2   chopped hard boiled eggs
3   chopped scallions, with the green
3   tablespoons vinegar
½ teaspoon salt
6   French rolls (approximately) (I prefer crusty type)

Mix all the ingredients together. Cut the rolls near the top, but not all the way through. Pull out all the soft dough so only a shell remains. Fill each roll with the stuffing and bake 20 to 30 minutes at 325°.

OPEN-FACED SHRIMP

½ cup mayonnaise
1   teaspoon curry powder
Pinch of salt
Cooked baby shrimp
White bread of the sturdy sort, such as Pepperidge Farm
Paper-thin slices lemon
Thin slices cherry tomato
Chopped chives

Combine the mayonnaise with the curry powder and season with salt to taste.

Trim the crusts from each slice of bread. Spread generously with the curried mayonnaise. Top with as many baby shrimp as the bread will accommodate, pressing them gently into the mayonnaise. Then add another, scattered, layer of shrimp. Garnish with a paper-thin slice of lemon in the center, topped by a thin slice of cherry tomato, and a dab or rosette of the mayonnaise. Sprinkle the whole thing with chopped chives.

Serve on a plate with fork and knife.

TUNA FISH

Drain well one can tuna fish, and put in a bowl. Flake the tuna. Add a tablespoon of mayonnaise and mix. Chop finely half a celery stalk, 1 or 2 scallions including the green ends, and mix with the tuna. Season with salt, pepper, and paprika. Add more mayonnaise, according to your taste . . . gently . . . don't get it too moist. Make a sandwich with the bread of your choice, toasted or not, with or without butter, lettuce, tomato slice, etc.

Good on saltines for a snack.

Hot Version: Spread the tuna mixture generously on buttered bread, add a slice of tomato on top, and on top of that a smidgeon of melty cheese. Broil slowly until lightly browned and bubbly.

GRILLED CHEESE AND SCALLIONS

To slices of Cheddar cheese, add sprinkles of chopped scallions and Taco Sauce. Surround with bread and grill as usual in butter. (Put a heavy plate or flat-bottomed pitcher on top of the sandwich as each side is browning in the skillet.)

PEANUT BUTTER AND JELLY

1 slice white bread, preferably the doughy kind
Soft butter
Smooth peanut butter
Jelly, jam, or preserves — your favorite kind (jelly is the hardest to spread)

Butter the slice of bread. Carefully spread about ⅛-inch peanut butter over the butter, making sure it reaches evenly to the crust edges of the bread. This is a little tricky, as the butter makes the peanut butter skid. Finally, spread jelly on top, again taking care to completely cover the peanut butter to the EDGES.

> *Other than using only one slice of bread, that is really the main point . . . getting everything out to the BRINK, so the WHOLE sandwich is equally goopy. Use as thick a layer of peanut butter and jelly as you like.*

BEEF JERKY (Jack Stone)

- 2 pounds boneless sirloin or round steak
- 4 tablespoons Wright's or Colgin's liquid smoke
  Salt and freshly ground black pepper

This recipe requires a gas oven . . . important to know before you start.

Carefully trim *all* fat from the meat. This is not a personal idiosyncrasy . . . it is essential to make good Jerky. Live profligately and lose some of the beef rather than goof. Then divide the meat into its natural sections, and trim fat further, if necessary.

Marinate the sections in the liquid smoke for about 30 minutes, turning the meat frequently to absorb most of the liquid.

Cut the meat into strips, about ¼-inch thick, and lay out on cookie sheets in one layer. Salt and pepper each piece individually, on one side only. (Garlic salt or onion salt may be used if you prefer.)

Put the cookie sheets into the oven, pilot heat only, for three days. After 24 hours, turn each piece to expose the underside.

The Jerky is done when thoroughly dry. But *not* crisp. It should be tough, chewy, sort of leathery.

> *If you have to use your oven for other purposes, remove the cookie sheets and return them only after the oven has cooled completely. Add to the timing slightly.*

**My brother Gordon and me —
being ever so proper**   *. . . aviation became his career.*

PEACH SOUFFLÉ (Marilyn Weitz)

  2   pounds peaches
  ¼ cup lemon juice
  1   cup sugar
  1   envelope unflavored gelatin
  4   eggs, separated
  ½ teaspoon salt
  ¼ teaspoon almond extract
  1   cup heavy cream (or 2 cups prepared Dream Whip)
  1   or 2 extra peaches for garnish
      Toasted slivered almonds (optional)

Peel the peaches and slice them into a bowl. Squeeze ¼ cup lemon juice, remove 1 tablespoon for later, and pour the rest over the peaches. Add ½ cup sugar and let stand at room temperature for 2 hours.

Put the peaches through a strainer or sieve and mash all the liquid out of the pulp with a wooden spoon. Save the pulp *and* the liquid.

Put ¾ cup of the liquid in the top of a double boiler. Sprinkle with the gelatin. Beat the egg yolks lightly and stir into the gelatin mixture. Cook over hot water, stirring, until the gelatin dissolves, about 5 minutes.

Remove from heat, and stir in the 1 tablespoon lemon juice, salt, and almond extract. Cool, and then refrigerate about 30 minutes.

Combine the reserved peach pulp with the remaining liquid and blend well.

Beat the egg whites until soft peaks, add the remaining ½ cup sugar, and then beat until stiff and shining.

Remove the gelatin mix from the fridge and beat until smooth. Add the pulp mixture and blend well. Fold into the egg whites. Whip the cream until stiff, and fold in lightly.

Pour into a 1½-quart soufflé dish, and refrigerate at least 4 hours.

Peel and slice the extra peaches and decorate the soufflé before serving. Pass toasted almond slivers at the table to sprinkle on top of each portion, if desired.

DESSERTS

COFFEE SOUFFLÉ

*Not to be confused with Coffee **Mousse**. This is a confection developed for the days we want a sweet, but are watching calories. It's not **exactly** low-calorie, but almost.*

- 2 tablespoons instant coffee powder (*not* freeze-dried type)
- ½ teaspoon cinnamon
- 1 cup hot water
- ½ cup sugar
- 1 envelope unflavored gelatin
- ¼ teaspoon salt
- 1 cup milk (made from non-fat dried, if you're really conscientious)
- 3 eggs, separated
- ½ teaspoon vanilla

Blend the coffee powder with the cinnamon and stir into the hot water. Blend 4 tablespoons of the sugar with the gelatin and salt in the top of a double boiler. Add the hot coffee mixture and stir until the gelatin and sugar are dissolved. Add the milk.

Beat the egg yolks slightly and blend into the coffee mixture. Cook over hot water, stirring, until the custard coats a metal spoon. Remove from the stove, stir in the vanilla, and cool. Then chill in the fridge until it's slightly thickened.

Beat the egg whites until foamy. Gradually add the remaining sugar, beating thoroughly after each addition, until the meringue holds stiff, shiny peaks. Fold into the gelatin mixture. Turn into a 1-quart soufflé dish and chill at least 3 hours.

Don't worry about "blending" the egg whites into the gelatin mixture. The finished product is supposed to have chunks of meringue throughout.

LEMON SOUFFLÉ (Jane Warwick)

1 envelope unflavored gelatin
¼ cup water
6 egg yolks
1 cup sugar
⅔ cup lemon juice
2 tablespoons grated lemon rind, or a little more
4 egg whites
2 cups heavy cream

Soften the gelatin in the water.

Beat the egg yolks with the sugar until thick and light. Stir in the lemon juice, and cook over low heat, beating until thick and hot but not boiling.

Mix in the gelatin and stir until dissolved. Add 1 tablespoon lemon rind. Remove from the heat and cool, stirring occasionally.

Beat the egg whites until stiff, but not dry, and fold into the lemon mixture.

Whip 1½ cups of the heavy cream and fold into the lemon mixture. Pour slowly into a 1½-quart soufflé dish. Refrigerate overnight.

Before serving, whip the remaining ½ cup heavy cream and decorate the top of the soufflé. (Either spread it on top meringue-like, or use a decorating tube to make designs.) Then sprinkle the extra grated lemon rind all over.

The soufflé freezes very well. It's a grand summer dessert to make on a rainy day and freeze for serving on a gorgeous day. Or any kind of day. Few desserts I know have received as many compliments as this one.

PINEAPPLE MOUSSE PIE (Nadine Korman)

Note that the chocolate leaves for the topping should be prepared first. Then the crust. They can be kept in the freezer for days until you're ready to make the filling and put it all together.

THE CRUST

1½ cups graham cracker crumbs
¼ cup granulated sugar
¼ cup crushed pistachio nuts (unsalted)
¼ pound sweet butter, melted

Combine all the ingredients and blend well. Using a 10-inch springform pan, firmly press the crumb mixture up the sides and on the bottom of the springform. (Leave ½ inch at the top of the pan free of crust, and go around it with your fingers to make the crust edge even.) Chill the crust in the freezer for an hour or more.

THE FILLING

1   large package (6-ounce) lemon Jello
1   cup boiling water
1½ cups pineapple juice (drained from the cans of pineapple)
8   ounces cream cheese
½ pint sour cream
1   cup powdered sugar
2   cans (1 pound 4 ounces each) Dole pineapple chunks, drained, and diced
2   cups heavy cream
4   tablespoons powdered sugar
1   teaspoon vanilla

Dissolve the Jello in the boiling water. Add the pineapple juice. Cool, and refrigerate for about an hour, or until it's almost gelled.

Place half the gelatin mixture into a blender, with half of the cream cheese, half of the sour cream, and half of the cup of powdered sugar. Mix until well-blended. Repeat with the remaining gelatin, cream cheese, sour cream, and sugar. Combine and return the mixture to the fridge.

Chill a bowl and whip the cream. After 30 seconds, add the 4 tablespoons powdered sugar and the vanilla, and continue whipping until thick.

Fold the whipped cream into the gelatin mixture, and then fold in the diced pineapple. Pour it all into the crust and chill thoroughly. Overnight is best.

THE TOPPING

- **8** ounces white chocolate
- **12** camellia leaves
- **½** pint heavy cream
- **2** tablespoons confectioners' sugar
  Unsalted pistachio nuts

Melt the white chocolate in the top of a double boiler. Wash and dry the camellia leaves, and spread the melted chocolate on the dull, under-side of each leaf. Lay them out on a cookie sheet covered with waxed paper, and place gently in the freezer. Chill at least a couple of hours, or until the chocolate is thoroughly solid again.

When the mousse pie is completely chilled, whip the cream with the sugar in a chilled bowl. Using a pastry bag, pipe double rosettes all around the edge of the mousse, and one double rosette in the center. Put pistachio nuts on top of each whipped cream puff. Peel the leaves from the chocolate, and decorate the mousse with the chocolate leaves between the rosettes.

The Pie serves 12. It freezes beautifully, but be sure to begin defrosting at least 12 hours before you plan to serve it. 18 to 20 hours may not be too long, depending on how cold your freezer is. Then bring it out of the fridge altogether the last hour before serving.

RASPBERRY MOUSSE PIE (Nadine Korman)

See note at the beginning of the Pineapple Mousse Pie recipe.

THE CRUST

1   package Nabisco's Famous Chocolate Wafers
¼ pound sweet butter, melted

Crush the wafers in a blender or food chopper until very fine. Add the melted butter and mix well. Use a 10-inch springform pan, and firmly press the crumb mixture up the sides and on the bottom of the springform. (Leave ½ inch at the top of the pan free of crust, and go around it with your fingers to make the crust edge even.) Chill in the freezer for an hour or more.

THE FILLING

1   large package (6-ounce) raspberry Jello
1   cup boiling water
1½ cups raspberry juice (boil 1½ cups water with ¾ cup granulated sugar. Add one basket of fresh, washed raspberries, and cook slowly until soft. Pour the mixture through a sieve, pressing down on the raspberries, and reserve 1½ cups of the juice.)
2   baskets fresh raspberries (in addition to the above basket used to make the juice)
1   cup powdered sugar
1   pint heavy cream
4   tablespoons powdered sugar
1   teaspoon vanilla
3   egg whites, at room temperature
⅛ teaspoon cream of tartar
     Pinch salt

Dissolve the Jello in the boiling water. Add the raspberry juice. Cool, and put in the fridge for 1 hour, or until almost gelled.

Wash the 2 baskets of raspberries, and crush them through a sieve to get rid of the seeds.

Put the gelatin mixture in a blender and whip with the cup of powdered sugar. Chill a bowl and whip the cream. After 30 seconds, add the 4 tablespoons powdered sugar and the vanilla, and continue whipping until thick.

Use a warmed bowl, and whip the egg whites with the cream of tartar and salt. Beat until they're stiff, not dry.

Fold the seeded raspberries into the gelatin mixture, then the whipped cream, and then the egg whites. Pour into the crust and chill, overnight if possible.

THE TOPPING

- 8 ounces Baker's semisweet chocolate
- 12 camellia leaves
- ½ pint heavy cream
- 2 tablespoons powdered sugar

Melt the chocolate in the top of a double boiler. Wash and dry the camellia leaves. Spread the melted chocolate on the dull, under-side of the leaves, and put them on a cookie sheet covered with waxed paper in the freezer. Chill for several hours, or until the chocolate is completely solid again.

Chill a bowl and whip the cream with the sugar. Using a pastry bag, pipe double rosettes all around the edge of the mousse, and a double rosette in the center. Peel the leaves off the chocolate, and decorate the mousse with the chocolate leaves between the rosettes.

> *The Pie serves 12. If you prefer, you can melt 8 ounces of* white *chocolate to make the leaves, and either leave them au naturel, or add a few drops of red food coloring to the melted chocolate.*
>
> *It freezes beautifully, but allow 12 to 20 hours for defrosting. Bring out of the fridge an hour before serving.*

STRAWBERRY MOUSSE PIE (Nadine Korman)

Follow the directions for the Raspberry Mousse Pie, with the following exceptions:

Use strawberry Jello.

Use one basket of fresh (washed and stemmed) strawberries to make the fruit juice for the Jello.

Put one basket of strawberries in the blender with the gelatin and powdered sugar, to crush.

Slice a third basket of strawberries to *fold* into the mousse before adding the whipped cream and egg whites.

FRUIT COMPOTE (May Katz)

1	pound crisp apples, peeled, cored, and sliced
3	bananas, sliced
2	thick slices pineapple, core removed and cut in chunks
3	tablespoons white raisins
2	tablespoons pignola nuts
2	tablespoons pistachio nuts
1	cup sugar
2	cups water
1	box strawberries, washed, stemmed, and cut in half
	Mock Devonshire Cream (see recipe page 387)

Mix the apples, bananas, pineapple, raisins, and nuts gently in a large bowl. Sprinkle the strawberry halves with sugar, and refrigerate in a separate bowl.

Put 1 cup sugar and 2 cups water in a saucepan and bring to a boil over moderate heat. Stir occasionally. Let it continue to boil for about 4 minutes. Stir, remove from the stove, and cool. When thoroughly cooled, pour the syrup over the fruit in the large bowl. Chill in the fridge at least 2 to 3 hours.

When ready to serve, add the halved strawberries to the rest of the fruit and mix gently. Top each portion with a dollop of Mock Devonshire Cream. Serves 8.

COFFEE MOUSSE (Carl Van Vechten — Saul Mauriber)

1   package unflavored gelatin
½ cup water
1   cup milk
1¼ cups confectioners' sugar
2   tablespoons instant coffee (*not* freeze-dried)
1   tablespoon heavy rum (preferably Myers' Dark Jamaica)
2   egg whites
2   cups heavy cream
¼ envelope gelatin (¾ teaspoon)
1   jar brandied peaches, coarsely chopped
     Whipped Cream Sauce (see page 387)

Prepare a 2-quart mold (see NOTE below) by coating it thinly with vegetable oil. Turn it upside down to drain on paper towels.

Soak the gelatin in the water. Heat the milk, sugar, and instant coffee in the top of a double boiler, stirring until both sugar and coffee are dissolved. Add the gelatin, and stir until thoroughly dissolved. (Don't let it reach the boiling point.)

Remove from the heat, and pour into a large mixing bowl to cool. When it's cool, add the rum, stir, and refrigerate briefly.

When the gelatin mixture is cold, and before it starts to set, beat the egg whites until stiff but not dry. Fold them into the mixture until it's pretty well blended.

Whip the pint of cream with the ¼ envelope gelatin, and fold it into the mixture. Pour into the prepared mold and refrigerate at least 4 hours, preferably overnight.

Immediately before serving, invert the mold onto a platter. Serve the Mousse topped with chopped brandied peaches and a dollop of Whipped Cream Sauce.

> *A ring mold is very convenient. When the mousse is on the platter, put the chopped peaches in the center, and the sauce in a serving dish on the side.*

MOUSSE KIM HUNTER (Coleman Dowell)

        4   squares semisweet chocolate
        4   squares bitter chocolate
        ½ cup honey
        1   tablespoon instant Expresso coffee
        3   tablespoons Kahlua
        2   cups heavy cream

Dissolve the instant coffee in the Kahlua.

Melt the 8 squares of chocolate with the honey in a double boiler over hot water. (See NOTE.) Stir the coffee-Kahlua mixture into the chocolate and let cool slightly.

Beat the heavy cream until it holds peaks, and then fold into the chocolate. Pour into a 1½-quart mold and chill for several hours.

> *As Coleman's own note added, this is also very interesting if the chocolate is not entirely melted. A few lumps form a sort of cakelike base for the mousse.*

FRUIT YOGHURT DESSERT (Bob Emmett)

        4   cups fruit (fresh or frozen, all one fruit or in combination.
            If frozen, defrost and strain off the syrup)
        1   cup plain yoghurt
        2   to 3 tablespoons honey
        2   teaspoons lemon juice
        ⅛ to ¼ teaspoon nutmeg
            Pinch cinnamon

Blend the yoghurt with the last four ingredients, then mix gently with the fruit. Chill thoroughly before serving.

> *If the fruit is fresh, and not as sweet as you would like, sprinkle it with a little sugar and refrigerate a couple of hours before combining with the yoghurt mixture. Don't overdo the sugar, as the honey will add to the sweetness.*

FRUIT FLUMMERY (Grace Stebbins)

3   tablespoons unflavored gelatin
½ cup cold water
1½ cups boiling water
1   cup orange juice
    Grated rind of 1 lemon
¼ cup sugar
¾ cup dessert wine, such as port, sauterne, cream sherry, etc.
½ pint heavy cream
2   (10-ounce) packages frozen sliced strawberries, raspberries, or fresh berries well-sweetened

Soak the gelatin in the cold water about 5 minutes, then dissolve it with the boiling water. Let cool to room temperature. Add the orange juice, lemon rind, sugar, wine, and blend well. Chill in the refrigerator until the mixture begins to gel.

Whip the cream. Then whip the gelatin mixture and add the whipped cream, beating until it's smooth. Turn into a mold or dessert bowl and chill until thoroughly set.

Serve topped with the thawed berries, or the sweetened fresh berries. The dessert will serve 6.

"Flummery" simply means a kind of custard. This one gets its sweetness from the berry topping. If you should ever want to serve it plain, add another ¼ cup sugar (or slightly more) to the gelatin mixture.

DESSERTS

SPANISH CREAM (Grace Stebbins)

1   envelope unflavored gelatin
4   cups milk
5   extra large eggs, separated
1   cup sugar
2   teaspoons vanilla
    Freshly grated nutmeg (optional)

Put the milk and gelatin in the top of a large double boiler set over water. Turn on the heat. As the milk begins to warm, stir occasionally until it scalds (until wrinkles form on the surface). *Do not let it boil.*

Beat the egg yolks with the sugar until very light and thick. When the milk is scalded, pour a little into the eggs, stirring. Then add more, a little at a time, stirring, until it's all blended and smooth. Turn it all back into the top of the double boiler and stir constantly over hot water until the mixture masks a metal spoon. *Never let it boil.*

Remove from the fire, add the vanilla, and pour the mixture into a large mixing bowl to cool to egg-white consistency. Stir occasionally as it cools.

> *It shouldn't curdle, but if it does, all is not lost. Just beat with a rotary egg beater until smooth again before folding in the whites.*

Beat the egg whites until stiff, not dry, and fold them into the cooled egg-yolk mixture. Pour gently into a 2-quart mold or dessert bowl and refrigerate until thoroughly set, at least 4 or 5 hours. (Overnight is best.)

Serve plain, or sprinkle with freshly grated nutmeg, or top with sweetened fresh fruit, such as sliced strawberries, or whole raspberries.

> *Ideally, there should be a layer of gelatin at the bottom, and fluffy fluff the rest of the way up. Mother always managed that. Mine seems to be more fluff than gelatin, if I have gelatin at all. But either way, it's scrumptious.*

362

APPLE PUDDING (Bellevernon Shapiro)

8   small, hard and crispy Delicious apples (approximately),
    peeled, cored, and sliced — about 1 quart when sliced
1   teaspoon cinnamon
½ cup water
1   cup sugar
¾ cup flour
6   tablespoons cold butter, cut up

Mix the apples, cinnamon, and water together, and pour into a buttered baking dish, 8 x 12 x 2-inch.

Work the sugar, flour and butter together with your fingertips until crumbly and no lumps of butter remain. Sprinkle the mixture evenly over the apples.

Bake uncovered at 400° for 30 minutes, or longer. It should be well-browned on top, and bubbly.

Serve hot or warm. It's super plain. But if you wish, top with Whipped Cream Sauce (p. 387) or a dab of vanilla ice cream. Serves 4 to 6.

DATE PUDDING (Florence Butterworth)

2   cups dates, cut up in small pieces with scissors
½ cup chopped walnuts
2   eggs, beaten lightly
¾ cup honey
½ cup flour, sifted before measuring
1   teaspoon baking powder
½ cup bran (Kellogg's All-Bran will do, but Pure Bran is best)

Put everything together at once in the electric mixer bowl and beat together until blended. Pour into a well-buttered 8 x 8 x 2-inch pan. Bake at 375° for 20 to 30 minutes, or until nicely browned. Serve warm with Whipped Cream Sauce (p. 387), or vanilla ice cream. It's also good cooled.

QUEEN OF PUDDINGS

As classic an English pudding as Trifle.

5 cups diced fresh bread (crusts removed and loosely measured, not packed)
3 cups milk
Rind of 1 lemon, cut carefully so no white membrane is included
¼ teaspoon salt (to go with milk)
3 tablespoons butter, softened
½ cup sugar
3 eggs, separated
1 teaspoon vanilla
½ teaspoon freshly grated nutmeg
¼ cup tart preserves or jelly, melted
⅛ teaspoon salt (to go with egg whites)
6 tablespoons sugar
½ teaspoon vanilla

Put the milk and lemon rind in a saucepan and heat gently to just under scalding. Discard the rind and add the milk with ¼ teaspoon salt to the bread crumbs in a large mixing bowl. Stir gently. Soak the bread crumbs about 15 minutes.

Preheat the oven to 350°, and put a large pan containing ½ inch water on the middle shelf.

Cream the butter with the ½ cup sugar till well blended and fluffy. Beat the egg yolks until lemony-colored. Add the yolks to the butter and sugar with 1 teaspoon vanilla and the nutmeg. Beat until well blended. Pour egg yolk mixture over the soaked bread crumbs and stir lightly with a fork. Turn the mixture into a 1½-quart soufflé dish. Place the dish in the pan of hot water in the oven and bake 45 minutes, or until set. Test with a silver knife. Cool the pudding for an hour or two at room temperature. (See NOTE.)

Preheat the oven to 300°

Spread the top of the pudding with the melted preserves or jelly. Beat the egg whites with the salt until foamy. Add the 6 tablespoons sugar gradually, then the ½ teaspoon vanilla, and continue beating till the whites are stiff and shiny. Spread the pudding with the meringue and bake at 300° for 15 to 20 minutes, until the top is set and lightly browned.

Serve the pudding hot, or warm.

> *I suggest completing the first step early in the day, and timing the baking of the meringue so the pudding comes out of the oven as you sit down to eat dinner. It will still be warm enough to serve when dessert-time arrives.*

BREAD PUDDING (Bellevernon Shapiro)

     3   eggs
     ½ cup sugar
     ¼ teaspoon each: nutmeg, allspice, and cinnamon
     1   quart milk
     1   teaspoon vanilla
     6   slices stale bread, cut or torn into quarter-sized pieces (do
           not remove crusts)
     1   cup raisins
     4   tablespoons butter

Beat the eggs until light, and gradually add the sugar. When lemony and thick, add the spices and blend. Then gradually add the milk. When thoroughly blended, add the vanilla. Stir in the bread cubes and raisins.

Melt the butter in a 9 x 9 x 2-inch baking pan in the oven, pour the bread mixture in gently, and bake 1 hour at 350°. Serve hot, warm, or cold.

DESSERTS

HER CAKE (Grace Stebbins)

I prepare this cake one of two ways: in three 9-inch round tins for a frosted layer cake; or our favorite family way, in two 8 x 8 x 2-inch pans. The portions are then cut into squares, and topped with hot chocolate or hot butterscotch sauce. (Another favorite way is heating the cake portions too, and topping with hot vanilla sauce . . . a sort of "Cottage Pudding.")

1   cup butter, softened
2   cups sugar
4   eggs, separated
1   teaspoon vanilla
3   cups cake flour, sifted before measuring
4   teaspoons baking powder
1   cup milk

Choose the baking tins you're going to use, and generously butter the bottoms and sides. Preheat the oven to 350°.

Cream the butter and sugar together until thoroughly blended, pale in color, and so light and fluffy it's practically a soufflé.

Beat the egg yolks until quite thick and lemony-colored. Stir them into the butter-sugar mixture, and then beat until they're thoroughly blended. Stir in the vanilla and mix well.

Sift the measured flour 2 more times. Then add the baking powder and sift again. (4 siftings, total.)

Beginning and ending with the flour, add the flour and milk to the batter alternately, a little at a time. Beat well after each addition with a wooden spoon. (Stir first, so the flour doesn't fly or the milk slurp . . . and then beat vigorously with an upward motion until well blended each time. Get to the very bottom of the bowl and beat upward, so lots of air mixes with the batter, scraping constantly around the sides so all the batter gets the same treatment.)

Have the egg whites at room temperature, and whip them until they're stiff but not dry. Fold very gently into the batter, using no more strokes than necessary. Better to leave bits of egg-white unmixed than over-handle at this stage.

Divide the batter evenly into the buttered baking tins, and put in the preheated 350° oven. Three tins will take approximately 30 minutes. Two tins will take 40 minutes or so. Tread softly, and don't open the

366

oven door for at least 20 minutes in any case. When the cakes begin to brown and come ever so slightly away from the sides of the pans, test for doneness with a flat toothpick, sticking it through the center of the cake to the bottom of the pan. If no moist batter clings to the pick, the cake is done.

Put the pans on racks so air circulates underneath, and cool for about 15 minutes. Then place the rack on top of the pan, invert the two together, and turn the cake out onto the rack. Give it a gentle rap on the table if it doesn't come out by itself immediately.

When the cakes are thoroughly cooled, they're ready to frost. Or store in covered cake containers for serving later with your choice of sauce. Or eat plain. If you don't give a hoot about calories, ice cream between the cake and the sauce isn't bad either.

A Chocolate Frosting recipe is on page 388. The Sauces are on pages 387, 388 and 389.

I learned to make Mother's Cake by hand and with a rotary beater. My KitchenAid mixer does much of it better than my arm can today . . . but I still revert to the manual method when it comes to the beating-in of flour and milk. I may be unduly "hung-up," but I'm convinced the cakes wouldn't turn out as light and gorgeous without that vigorous "upward" beating with the wooden spoon. The results are well worth an exhausted arm and sore muscles. Of course, the egg whites must be folded in by hand, with the spoon or with a spatula.

STRAWBERRY SHORTCAKE (Grace Stebbins)

   3   quarts fresh strawberries
       Sugar
       Whipped Cream Sauce (see page 387)

Remove the stems from the strawberries and wash gently but thoroughly. Cut them up over a bowl so you don't lose the juice. Add sugar to taste and refrigerate for several hours. Stir gently once or twice. Take the bowl out of the fridge as you start to mix the biscuits, so they have time to lose their chill.

BISCUITS

   2   cups cake flour, sifted before measuring
   4   tablespoons sugar (¼ cup)
       Pinch of salt
   5   teaspoons baking powder
   6   tablespoons cold, hard butter
   ½ to ¾ cup half-and-half

Lightly butter a cookie sheet and preheat the oven to 475°.

Sift together the flour, sugar, salt, and baking powder. Cut up the cold butter and add. Blend with a pastry blender, two knives, or your fingertips, until the mixture is the consistency of coarse cornmeal.

Add the half-and-half gradually, and mix with a fork. Add just enough to hold it together in a soft dough.

Put the dough on a floured board and knead briefly until the stickiness is subdued. Pat the dough, do not roll, to a thickness of ¾ inch. Cut rounds with a biscuit cutter and place them on the cookie sheet. (Dip the cutter in flour if necessary to keep it from sticking to the dough.)

Bake for 10 to 12 minutes at 475° or until the biscuits are lightly browned.

ASSEMBLING

Split the biscuits in half and butter the inside surfaces. Put the bottom half in an individual dessert bowl, buttered side up. Top with a generous portion of strawberries and add a dab of Whipped Cream Sauce. Place the rest of the biscuit on top, buttered side up, and add more strawberries. Top the whole thing with a large spoonful of Whipped Cream Sauce. Serve immediately.

The recipe should serve 6 to 8, with a few biscuits left over.

The shortcake is at its best when the biscuits are buttered and assembled while still hot. If you make the biscuits ahead of time, put them in a brown paper bag (run them under water first, and shake off the excess) and heat 5 to 10 minutes in a 425° oven.

Fresh peaches cut up and sweetened make a splendid shortcake, too.

And, of course, frozen fruit will do in a pinch.

CHOCOLATE CAKE (Tillie Cole)

This makes a very small cake, but it's very rich and moist, and a little goes a long way.

4   ounces semisweet chocolate
6   tablespoons butter
3   eggs, separated
½ cup sugar
2   tablespoons flour, sifted before measuring

Melt the chocolate and butter in the top of a double boiler, over hot, not boiling water. Stir to blend, and cool. Beat the egg yolks, add the sugar gradually, and beat well to the ribbon stage. Add the cooled chocolate mixture and blend. Then add the flour, gradually, and beat to blend thoroughly. Whip the egg whites stiff, not dry, and stir about ¼ of the whites into the batter to loosen it slightly. Fold in the rest of the whites quickly and gently. The batter may seem oddly lumpy, but that's all right.

Pour into a buttered 6 x 6-inch cake pan, or a small loaf pan, 8½ x 4½-inch. Bake at 350° for 35 minutes. The cake won't seem thoroughly cooked inside, but it gets firmer as it cools. Cool in the pan 10 minutes, and then turn out to cool completely. You may either spread the top with Whipped Cream Sauce (page 387), or ice the cake all over with Chocolate Frosting (the small recipe, page 388).

RAW APPLE CAKE (Tillie Cole)

2   cups sugar
1   cup butter, softened
4   eggs, beaten
3   cups cake flour, sifted before measuring
 ¼ teaspoon cloves
2   teaspoons soda
2   teaspoons cinnamon
1   teaspoon nutmeg
1   cup cold coffee (Instant may be used if cooled)
3   cups raw, peeled, cored, diced apples (approximately 5
      apples)
1   cup raisins
1   cup chopped walnuts

Cream the butter and sugar until light and fluffy. Beat the eggs separately and add to the butter-sugar mixture. Beat well.

Sift the flour, cloves, soda, cinnamon, and nutmeg together. Add to the batter alternately with the cold coffee. Beat well after each addition. (See HER CAKE beating instructions, page 366.) Stir in the apples, raisins, and walnuts.

Pour the batter into a buttered 9 x 13 x 2-inch baking dish. Bake at 350° for 1 hour.   While the cake is still warm, spread the following topping on, and brown slightly under the broiler. (This burns quickly, so keep it far enough away from the flame.)

TOPPING

2   tablespoons butter, melted
3   tablespoons light cream
 ½ cup brown sugar, packed
 ½ cup coconut, shredded.

Mix it all together thoroughly.

CHOCOLATE CHEESE CUPCAKES (Tillie Cole)

1   cup (8-ounce package) cream cheese, softened
⅓ cup sugar
⅛ teaspoon salt
1   egg, unbeaten
1   cup semisweet chocolate morsels
1½ cups + 2 tablespoons cake flour, sifted before measuring
1   cup sugar
¼ cup cocoa
1   teaspoon soda
½ teaspoon salt
1   cup water
⅓ cup cooking oil
1   tablespoon vinegar
1   teaspoon vanilla

Beat the cream cheese until soft and smooth. Gradually add the ⅓ cup sugar mixed with ⅛ teaspoon salt. Add the egg, and beat until well blended. Stir in the chocolate bits and set aside.

Sift together the flour, 1 cup sugar, cocoa, soda, and ½ teaspoon salt. Combine with the water, oil, vinegar, and vanilla in a mixer bowl and beat until well blended.

Line 1½ to 2 dozen muffin cups with paper baking cups and fill ⅓ full with the chocolate batter. Top each one with a heaping teaspoonful of the cream cheese mixture. Distribute evenly any remaining cream cheese mix. Bake at 350° for 30 to 35 minutes.

If you wish, before baking you can sprinkle the tops with sugar and chopped blanched almonds.

If you have empty muffin cups in your tins, half-fill them with water before putting in the oven.

LEMON BUNDT CAKE (Bellevernon Shapiro)

 1   package Duncan Hines' Lemon Supreme cake mix
 1   package lemon pudding (regular)
 1   cup water
 ½ cup oil
 4   eggs
 1½ cups sifted confectioners' sugar
 ¼ cup lemon juice

Put the cake mix, pudding, water, oil, and eggs in the mixer bowl and beat 6 minutes on medium speed until it is thoroughly mixed. Butter a Bundt pan *lavishly,* and pour the batter into the pan. Bake at 350° for 35 to 55 minutes, or until done. Use a long cake tester. Cool in the pan 10 minutes, then turn out to a cake platter. While the cake is still warm, stab it all over with a fork. Blend the sugar with the lemon juice until smooth, and pour into the holes.

CARAMEL SUPREME BUNDT CAKE (Bellevernon Shapiro)

 1   package Duncan Hines' Caramel Supreme cake mix
 1   package butterscotch pudding (regular, not instant)
 4   eggs
 ½ pint sour cream
 ½ cup oil
 1   cup chopped dates (cut up with scissors)
 1   cup walnuts, chopped loosely
     Sifted confectioners' sugar

Preheat the oven to 375°, and *lavishly* butter a Bundt pan.

Put the cake mix, pudding, eggs, sour cream, and oil in a large mixer bowl and beat for 6 minutes on medium speed. Stir in the dates and nuts, and mix thoroughly.

Pour the batter into the pan and bake 40 to 50 minutes. Do not cook too long or the cake will be dry. It should be done, but moist. (Use a long cake tester, and take the gooeyness of the dates into consideration.)

Cool in the pan for 10 minutes, and then turn out to cool completely. Dust with sifted powdered sugar, while still a little warm.

> *The reason for the "lavishly butter" is the crevices of a Bundt pan, particularly around the tube. It makes a very attractive cake, but not if some of it stays stuck to the pan.*

CHOCOLATE DATE CAKE (Tillie Cole)

  1   cup chopped dates (use scissors)
  1   cup hot water
1¾ cups cake flour, sifted before measuring
  1   teaspoon soda
  1   tablespoon cocoa
  ½ teaspoon salt
  1   cup butter, softened
  1   cup sugar
  2   eggs
  1   teaspoon vanilla
  1   cup semisweet chocolate morsels
  ½ cup chopped walnuts
     Confectioners' sugar (optional)

Soak the dates in the hot water, and cool. Sift the flour again with the soda, cocoa, and salt. Cream the butter with the sugar until light and fluffy, and beat in the eggs, one at a time. Beat well after each addition. Add the vanilla, and blend.

Add the dates and flour mixture alternately, and beat well as for HER CAKE (see directions, page 366). Stir in ½ cup of the chocolate morsels.

Pour the batter into a buttered 9 x 13 x 2-inch pan. Sprinkle the remaining chocolate bits and the nuts on top of the batter. Bake at 350° for 35 to 40 minutes, or until done. (Use a cake tester.) Sprinkle confectioners' sugar over the top of the warm cake if desired.

CHOCOLATE ROLL (May Katz)

- 7 eggs at room temperature, separated
- 1 cup sugar
- ½ pound semisweet chocolate, broken up
- 4 tablespoons instant coffee (not freeze-dried)
- 1 cup heavy cream

Preheat the oven to 350°. Melt the broken up chocolate with the instant coffee in a double boiler, and cool.

Beat the egg yolks until a lemon color, then add the sugar slowly and beat until it reaches the ribbon stage. Add the cooled chocolate. Beat the egg whites stiff. Stir a couple of spoonsful of beaten egg-white into the chocolate mixture to unstiffen, then fold in the rest of the egg-whites.

Butter a large cookie sheet that has 1-inch sides, and place parchment paper to measure on the sheet. Pour the batter on the sheet, and when evenly distributed, give the pan a rap on the table. Bake about 20 minutes at 350°.

Cover with a damp towel for 1 hour. Then turn out on aluminum foil. Whip the cream and spread on top of the cake. Then roll, as for a jelly roll, using the foil to help you as you go. Refrigerate. Before serving, remove the cake roll from the fridge for an hour or so. Cut in slices to serve.

GINGERBREAD (Grace Stebbins — Jeannette Obenauer)

Mrs. Obenauer was our nextdoor neighbor in Detroit.

- 1 cup sugar
- 1 cup butter, softened
- 2 eggs, not beaten
- 1 cup molasses
- 1 cup sour milk (to make: add 4 teaspoons vinegar to lukewarm sweet milk, stir, and let stand 5 to 10 minutes before using)
- 1 level teaspoon soda
- 1 tablespoon ginger
- ½ teaspoon salt
- 2 cups all-purpose flour, sifted before measuring

Preheat the oven to 350°, and generously butter a 9 x 13 x 2-inch baking dish.

Sift the flour once more, and then again with the soda, salt, and ginger.

Cream the butter and sugar until very light and fluffy. Add the eggs, one at a time, and beat well after each addition. Stir in the molasses and blend well. Add the flour mixture alternately with the sour milk, beating vigorously after each addition (as in HER CAKE, p. 366).

Pour the batter into the pan and bake at 350° approximately 40 minutes. Use a cake tester. Cool in the pan at least 20 minutes before removing. Or don't remove at all, and cut portions from the pan. Serve the Gingerbread topped with Whipped Cream Sauce, page 387.

The original recipe called for "clabbered" milk. I haven't been able to get milk to clabber for 30 years. Homogenized is grand . . . but!

WALNUT MERINGUE (Cathleen Schurr)

Easy and special. Need I say more?

3   egg whites
1   cup sugar
1   teaspoon vanilla
1   teaspoon baking powder
14   unsalted soda crackers, 2 x 2-inch, coarsely crumbled
   ¾ to 1 cup chopped walnuts
1   cup heavy cream
      Chocolate shavings made with dark chocolate, or semi-
         sweet, for garnish

Beat the egg whites to soft peaks, and gradually add the sugar, then the vanilla, beating until the whites are stiff and shiny. Combine the crumbled crackers, walnuts, and baking powder, and fold into the egg mixture. Spread in a 9-inch pie plate and bake at 350° for 30 to 35 minutes. Cool.

Whip the cream and spread lightly over the torte. Decorate the top with the shaved chocolate, and refrigerate about 2 hours before serving.

SOUR CREAM PIE (Bellevernon Shapiro)

 2 (8-ounce) packages cream cheese, softened
 3 eggs, well beaten
 ½ lemon, juice and rind (grated)
 ½ cup sugar
 2 pints sour cream
 1 teaspoon vanilla
 3 tablespoons sugar
 1 Graham Cracker Crust (recipe on page 381) in a 9½-inch
     pie plate (2 inches deep)

Set the prepared pie plate in the fridge at least one hour before you'll be ready to fill it.

Beat the cream cheese until light and fluffy, and add the eggs, lemon juice and grated rind, and ½ cup sugar. Blend thoroughly. Fold in 1 pint of the sour cream. Pour into the crust, and bake 25 minutes in a 270° oven. Cool 15 minutes.

Mix the remaining sour cream, sugar, and the vanilla. Spread evenly on top of the pie. Bake at 450° about 7 minutes, or until the top bubbles. Cool the pie, and then chill a couple of hours.

Take out of the fridge 1 hour before serving.

CARROT CAKE (Tillie Cole)

 2 cups sugar
 1½ cups oil
 4 eggs
 1 teaspoon vanilla
 1 ounce brandy (optional)
 2 cups cake flour, sifted before measuring
 1 teaspoon cinnamon
 2 teaspoons soda
 ½ teaspoon salt
 ⅛ teaspoon allspice (optional)
 3 cups shredded carrots
 ¾ cup finely chopped walnuts (chopped, not ground)

Put the sugar and the oil together in a large bowl and beat until thoroughly blended. Add the eggs, one at a time, beating well after each addition. Add the vanilla (and optional brandy) and blend.

Sift the flour again with the cinnamon, soda, salt, and optional allspice. Gradually add the sifted ingredients to the sugar-oil-egg mixture and beat well until blended. Stir in the carrots and walnuts, and then beat (as in HER CAKE, p. 366) until they are thoroughly mixed with the batter.

Pour the batter into a well-buttered 10-inch springform cake pan, and bake at 350° approximately 60 minutes. Insert a silver knife in the center of the cake to test. If it comes out "clean," the cake is done. Let it cool in the pan at least 30 minutes, and then turn out to cool completely. When cooled, spread all over with the following icing.

ICING

6   ounces cream cheese (two 3-ounce packages)
4   tablespoons butter, melted
1   teaspoon vanilla
2½ to 3 cups sifted confectioners' sugar

Put the cream cheese out to soften. When very soft, beat it until it's light and fluffy. Gradually add the melted butter, beating until it is thoroughly blended. Add the vanilla.

Add the sugar gradually, beating well after each addition so the icing will be smooth. Use as much sugar as you need for the icing to reach a good spreading consistency.

POLISH CAKE (Jane Warwick)

    8   eggs, separated
    1¼ cups sugar
        Rind of 1 lemon, grated
    2   tablespoons lemon juice
    ½ pound shelled walnuts, finely chopped or put through the
        meat grinder

Beat the egg yolks. Gradually add the sugar, and beat well until thick and lemony-colored. Add the lemon juice, rind, and walnuts, and beat until well blended.

Whip the egg whites until stiff but not dry. Scoop one-fourth of the beaten whites into the yolk mixture and stir to loosen it. Then fold in the rest of the whites.

Pour the batter into a buttered 10-inch springform cake pan, and bake in a 350° oven 50 to 60 minutes. If the cake seems to be getting very brown and looking as if the top may be done early, open the oven door partially and continue baking. Use a cake tester after 50 minutes.

When done, turn off the oven and let the pan sit in the partially opened oven about 30 minutes or longer. Then remove from the oven and cool completely before frosting.

> *The cake will sag as it cools, much like a soufflé.
> Don't worry . . . the icing covers the funny look (sort
> of), and the whole thing's too good to care.*

ICING

    1   cup heavy cream
    ¼ cup sifted confectioners' sugar
    1   tablespoon cocoa
    1   tablespoon instant coffee
    1   egg yolk, beaten

Whip the cream and add the sugar gradually. Add the cocoa, instant coffee, and beaten egg yolk, and continue beating until everything is thoroughly blended and the mixture is smooth and thick.

MOTHER'S PUMPKIN PIE (Grace Stebbins)

  1   large cup canned pumpkin
  1   scant cup sugar
  2   eggs, lightly beaten
  ½ teaspoon cloves
  ½ teaspoon ginger
  ½ teaspoon nutmeg
  ½ teaspoon cinnamon
  1   teaspoon vanilla
  1   cup half and half
  1   eight-inch pastry pie crust, slightly pre-baked (see page 380 for 1-crust instructions — prick the crust all over with a fork, top it with an 8-inch lightweight tin or aluminum pie plate, and bake at 375° for 8 to 10 minutes)

Put all the ingredients into a mixer bowl and beat until well blended and smooth. Pour into the pre-baked crust gently, almost to overflowing. Place a cookie sheet on the center rack of the preheated 450° oven. Lift the pie plate ever so carefully to the oven. Bake at 450° for 15 minutes, then turn the oven heat down to 375° and bake another 30 minutes. It's done when a silver knife inserted about 2 inches from the edge comes out clean. Refrigerate the pie when it's cooled.

Serve each slice topped with a dab of Whipped Cream Sauce (see page 387).

Double all *the ingredients when making 2 pies.*

STREUSEL TOPPING FOR FRUIT PIES (Tillie Cole)

  ½ cup sugar
  ¾ cup flour
  ⅓ cup butter

Use your fingers to mix into fine crumbs, working the mixture until all lumps of butter disappear. Sprinkle over the top of the pies. This should make enough for two 9-inch pies.

PASTRY PIE CRUST (for two 9-inch crusts)

2½ cups unsifted flour (don't pack or shake down; use a scoop to fill the measuring cup and level off with a knife)

1 teaspoon salt

2 sticks (½ pound) Fleischman's or Mazola Oleomargarine, *cold and hard*

½ cup *cold* water, approximately (have ice cubes in the water while you work)

Add the salt to the flour in a bowl, and cut the cold oleo in until it's the size of peas. Pour ¼ cup cold water into the mixture, and use a fork to pull the dough together as much as possible. Then take another ¼ cup cold water and sprinkle where needed, usually near the bottom where flour accumulates. Remove what holds together, and continue sprinkling and pulling together the remainder with a fork. (Use a bit more water if necessary.) Put it all back together in the bowl, and use your hands to press together. The dough may be wrapped in waxed paper and refrigerated at this point until ready to use.

Divide the dough in half. Roll out one half at a time on a lavishly floured board, into a circle quite a bit larger than the pie plate. Flour the rolling pin as well. (It may also be rolled out between two sheets of lightly floured waxed paper, which makes it a bit easier to lift the crust to the pie plate.) Roll out as thin as possible without making it difficult to transfer to the pie plate.

For a 1-crust pie: Butter the pie plate and cover with the crust, pressing it gently but well into the corners and up the sides, allowing it to hang over the edges. (Start from the center of the bottom, work out, and avoid stretching the dough.) Use a sharp knife to cut off the overhang at the *bottom* of the outside rim. (The crust will shrink a little as it bakes.) Crimp the dough around the rim to make a neat, fluted edge.

If baking a cream pie, such as pumpkin, cut off less of the overhang and push the edging up, about ½ inch high around the rim, and make a doubled-over fluting with the crust to form a sort of "gallery." A pumpkin filling in particular should be piled high in the crust, as it will shrink as it cools.

If you are to bake the crust *before* adding the filling, stab the bottom and sides with a fork all over so the crust doesn't buckle or bubble up.

<u>For a 2-crust pie</u>: Butter the pie dish and put the bottom crust on as for a 1-crust pie, trim the excess dough with a knife the same way, but don't flute. Pour or spoon in the filling, and cover *loosely* with a rolled-out top crust. Trim the excess dough around the edges, leaving enough extra to be able to press a fluted edging to the rim on top of the bottom crust. Dip your fingers in water as you do this if the crust isn't moist enough to stick. Stab the top crust all over with a fork, so steam can escape.

> *The secret of a good crust is not so much in the amount of water used, although that's important, too — not to use more than necessary to hold the dough together — it's the* speed *with which it's made. The less handling with hands, the better.*

GRAHAM CRACKER CRUST

    1½   cups graham cracker crumbs
    ¼   cup confectioner's sugar
    6   tablespoons melted butter

Crumble the crackers and grind until very fine before measuring. (Or put in the blender.) Stir in the sugar and melted butter until well blended.

Put the mixture in a 9-inch pie plate, distribute as evenly as possible, and pat firmly against the bottom and sides of the dish, covering the rim as well. Try to keep the thickness even throughout. Press it in firmly. (Using a slightly smaller pie plate to help you press in the crumbs is a useful trick.)

Chill the crust thoroughly before filling, at least an hour or two. The alternative is to bake in a 375° oven for 15 minutes to set. If the crust is chilled, it may, but need not be baked.

> *For the Sour Cream Pie on page 376, increase the recipe to:*
> > *2¼ cups crumbs (scant measurement)*
> > *⅓ cup confectioner's sugar*
> > *8½ tablespoons melted butter*
>
> *You may have a little left over, which you can use to sprinkle on top of the pie as garnish if you wish. Don't use more than you need for the crust.*

APPLE PIE (Tillie Cole)

Her variations follow.

5　to 7 apples, peeled, cored, and sliced (the hard, juicy, *tart* apples are best, such as Grannies, Jonathans, Cortlands, or MacIntosh — *not* Delicious)
1　tablespoon lemon juice (optional)
¾　to 1 cup sugar
2　tablespoons flour
　　Dash of salt
　　Dash of nutmeg
1　teaspoon cinnamon, or to taste (probably less, not more)
2　tablespoons butter (if making a 2-crust pie)
1　nine-inch pastry crust (see page 380)
1　top pastry crust (p. 381), or ½ recipe Streusel Topping (p. 379)

Add the lemon juice to the apples if they aren't tart enough. Mix the sugar, flour, salt, and spices together and pour over the sliced apples. Stir or fold all together. Spoon the filling into the pie crust. If you're making a 2-crust pie, dot the apples with butter before adding the top crust.

Bake the 2-crust pie at 450° for 10 minutes, then lower the oven heat to 350° and bake 40 minutes longer, or until the crust is nicely browned. If using the Streusel Topping, follow the same baking directions, but sprinkle the crumb mixture over the pie for the last 10 minutes only.

CARAMEL APPLE PIE (Tillie)

Prepare as for the regular Apple Pie, except use 1 full cup of light brown sugar, packed. Omit the nutmeg, and go easy on the cinnamon.

SOUR CREAM APPLE PIE (Tillie)

2　tablespoons flour
　　Dash of salt
¾　cup sugar

1   egg, beaten
1   teaspoon vanilla
2½ cups finely chopped apples
1   cup sour cream
1   nine-inch pastry pie crust (p. 380)

Sift the dry ingredients together, then add the beaten egg, sour cream, and vanilla. Beat until smooth. Fold in the apples, and spoon the mixture into the pie crust. Bake 15 minutes at 400°, lower the oven heat to 350° and bake another 30 minutes. Make the following topping while the pie is in the oven.

TOPPING

⅓ cup sugar
⅓ cup flour
1   teaspoon cinnamon
¼ cup butter

Mix everything together thoroughly with your fingertips. Sprinkle the mixture over the top of the pie and bake 10 minutes longer at 350°

Jack Barron, my makeup artist for "Escape from the Planet of the Apes"

LEMON MERINGUE PIE (Bob Emmett)

1 cup sugar
Pinch salt
¼ cup flour
1 tablespoon cornstarch
2 cups water
3 eggs, separated
1 tablespoon butter
⅓ cup lemon juice
Grated rind of 1 lemon
1 baked 9-inch pastry pie shell (see **NOTE** following Chocolate Cream Pie, page 385)
6 tablespoons sugar
¼ teaspoon cream of tartar

Combine the 1 cup sugar, pinch of salt, flour, and cornstarch in the top of a double boiler, and gradually stir in the water. Cook over boiling water, stirring constantly, until mixture thickens and is smooth.

Beat the egg yolks in a separate bowl. Gradually add the hot mixture to the yolks, stirring all the while, and then return mixture to the double boiler. Cook just a minute or two longer, stirring constantly Take off heat and stir in the butter, lemon juice, and lemon rind. Cool slightly, then pour into the pie shell and cool completely.

Beat the egg whites until foamy, and add the cream of tartar. Keep beating until the whites hold soft peaks, and then gradually add the 6 tablespoons sugar until the whites are stiff and shiny.

Spread the meringue on top of the cooled lemon filling, and decorate the surface with your spatula, making swirls and peaks of the meringue. Make sure the meringue covers the edges of the pastry. (It will shrink slightly in the baking.)

Bake the pie at 425° for about 5 minutes, or until the top is lightly browned. Let the pie cool completely before serving.

CHOCOLATE CREAM PIE

1 cup semisweet chocolate morsels
2 tablespoons sugar
2 tablespoons milk
1 teaspoon vanilla
4 eggs, separated
1 baked 9-inch pie shell (see **NOTE**), or graham cracker crust
(p. 381) that's been refrigerated 2 hours
Whipped Cream Sauce (see recipe page 387)
Dark Chocolate shavings for garnish

Combine the chocolate morsels, sugar, and milk in the top of a double boiler, and heat over boiling water until the chocolate is melted and the sugar is dissolved. Add the vanilla and cool to lukewarm. Beat the egg yolks into the chocolate mixture one at a time, blending well after each addition. Beat the egg whites until just stiff, and gently fold into the chocolate mixture. Pour into the pie shell and refrigerate 3 or 4 hours.

When firm, spread the sweetened whipped cream lightly over the top, and decorate with the chocolate shavings.

See the instructions, page 380, for a 1-crust pie. After pricking the crust, lay a 9-inch lightweight aluminum pie pan on top and bake at 450° for 10 minutes. Remove the top pie plate and continue baking another 5 to 10 minutes, until the crust is golden brown.

SWEET POTATO PIE (Doris Shaw)

Doris, our housekeeper, has been my savior more than once . . . coming up with right answers to the mysteries of cooking when I'd been in great trouble if left on my own. This is just one of her very delightful personal creations. We exchange . . . a lot.

1½ cups cooked sweet potatoes
1 cup brown sugar, packed
1 teaspoon cinnamon
⅛ teaspoon nutmeg
½ teaspoon salt
1 cup milk
2 tablespoons melted butter
2 tablespoons bourbon
3 eggs
1 unbaked 9-inch pastry pie shell (p. 380)

Mash the sweet potatoes until they're free from lumps. Then add the sugar, cinnamon, nutmeg, salt, milk, and melted butter. Beat until thoroughly blended. Stir in the bourbon.

Beat the 3 egg yolks with 2 of the egg whites, and add to the mixture. Beat until blended. Whip the remaining egg white until stiff, not dry, and fold into the mixture.

Pour the filling into the pie crust, and bake at 425° for 10 minutes. Reduce the heat to 350°, and then continue baking another 30 minutes.

VANILLA SAUCE

- ¾ cup sugar
- 2 tablespoons cornstarch
  Pinch salt
- 2 cups boiling water
- 4 tablespoons butter, softened
- 1 teaspoon vanilla
- 1 teaspoon grated lemon rind

Mix the sugar, cornstarch, and salt in a saucepan. Over low heat, add the boiling water gradually, stirring constantly. Turn the heat up to medium and bring to a rolling boil. Boil 5 minutes, stirring occasionally.

Remove from heat and add the butter, vanilla, and lemon rind. Stir to blend. Serve hot over squares of HER CAKE (p. 366).

WHIPPED CREAM SAUCE

- 1 cup (½ pint) heavy cream
- 2 tablespoons sifted confectioner's sugar
- 1 teaspoon vanilla

Whip the cream until it begins to thicken slightly. Add the sugar gradually, and then the vanilla. Continue to whip until it's thick.

MOCK DEVONSHIRE CREAM (May Katz)

- 1 (3-ounce) package cream cheese, at room temperature
- ½ cup sour cream
- 1 tablespoon sifted confectioner's sugar
- ½ cup heavy cream, whipped

Cream the cheese. Blend with the sour cream and the sugar until smooth. Fold in the whipped cream and chill.

Yields about 2 cups.

CHOCOLATE FROSTING

For a 9-inch layer cake:

 1½ cups sugar
 ⅔ cup half-and-half
 ½ cup corn syrup
   Pinch salt
 1 (12-ounce) package chocolate morsels
 1 teaspoon vanilla

For a small cake:

 6 tablespoons sugar
 2 tablespoons + 2 teaspoons half-and-half
 2 tablespoons corn syrup
   Small pinch salt
 ½ (6-ounce) package chocolate morsels
 ½ teaspoon vanilla

Combine the sugar, half-and-half, corn syrup, and salt in a saucepan. Bring just to a boil over low to moderate heat, stirring constantly. Remove from the stove and stir in the chocolate morsels and the vanilla. Keep stirring until the chocolate is thoroughly melted. Let cool, 30 minutes to an hour, until the frosting is thick enough to spread. As it cools, beat it with a wooden spoon occasionally.

CHOCOLATE SAUCE I

 1 ounce (2½ squares) unsweetened chocolate
 ½ cup cold water
 ¾ cup sugar
   Pinch salt
 1 tablespoon butter, softened

Break up the chocolate in pieces and combine with the water in the top of a double boiler. Cook over hot water, stirring occasionally, until the chocolate is melted. Add the sugar and salt, and stir constantly until the sugar is dissolved and the sauce is smooth, about

5 minutes. Off heat, add the butter and stir until it's melted and blended.

Makes approximately 1¼ cups, and will keep in the fridge indefinitely if stored in an airtight jar. Serve either hot or cold. (Always reheat in a double boiler — chocolate has a tendency to burn easily.)

Chocolate Sauce I (hot) is designed to top HER CAKE squares, but can be used for anything. Chocolate Sauce II is really too thick for the cake, but is super when heated for a Hot Fudge Sundae. (Topped with toasted nut meats and a dab of Whipped Cream Sauce?)

CHOCOLATE SAUCE II

    2   ounces (5 squares) unsweetened chocolate
    1   can (5 ⅓ ounces) evaporated milk
    1   cup confectioner's sugar, sifted before measuring
    1   tablespoon butter, softened
    ½   teaspoon vanilla

Put the chocolate, milk, and sugar in the top of a double boiler. Heat over hot water until the chocolate is melted and the sugar is dissolved. Cook, stirring, about 5 to 10 minutes until smooth and beginning to get thick. Take off heat and stir in the butter and vanilla. Serve immediately, or reheat in a double boiler when ready to use.

BUTTERSCOTCH SAUCE

    3   tablespoons butter
    1   cup light Caro Syrup
    1   cup brown sugar, packed
    ½   cup milk
    ½   teaspoon vanilla
    ¼   teaspoon salt

Combine all the ingredients in a saucepan and bring to a rolling boil over medium heat. Continue boiling 5 minutes, stirring occasionally.

PECAN BALLS (Bellevernon Shapiro)

    ½ pound sweet butter, softened
    ½ cup sugar
    2   teaspoons vanilla
    1   cup all-purpose flour, sifted before measuring
    2   cups shelled pecans, ground through the meat grinder
           Confectioners' sugar (to which you may add a vanilla stick
            if you wish)

Cream the butter and sugar until thoroughly blended and fluffy. Add the vanilla, nuts, and flour. Blend well. (It can all be done with the electric mixer.)

Roll the dough into balls, about ¾-inch in diameter.

> *Add a little more flour to the dough if it sticks too much to your hands while rolling into balls.*

Bake on an ungreased cookie sheet at 300° for 25 to 30 minutes, until lightly browned. While the balls are still warm, roll them in the powdered sugar.

> *If the cookies cool faster than you can roll them in the sugar, put them back in the oven briefly to warm. The sugar doesn't cling properly if the cookies aren't warm.*

> *One batch makes approximately 2 pounds or more of balls. If you find you like them as much as we do, I suggest it's wise to at least double the recipe each time you make them. They disappear shamelessly.*

MELBA'S COOKIES (Tillie Cole)

1½ cups brown sugar, packed
1 cup shortening (half butter, half Crisco)
3 eggs, beaten
3 tablespoons jelly or fruit juice
3 cups flour, sifted before measuring
½ teaspoon cloves
1 tablespoon cinnamon
1 teaspoon soda, dissolved in 1 tablespoon boiling water
1 cup dates, cut up with scissors
1 cup nutmeats (walnuts or pecans)
1 cup raisins (optional)

Cream the sugar and the shortening. Add the beaten eggs and blend well. Stir in the jelly or fruit juice and blend. Sift together the flour, cloves, and cinnamon. Add to the mixture along with the soda, dates, and nuts (and optional raisins). Blend well.

Drop by a teaspoon onto a greased cookie sheet. Bake at 350° for 12 minutes, or until lightly browned. If the first batch spreads too much, put the batter in the fridge for a while so it will be thicker.

When Gordon and Tillie were first married, she flew, too.

DATE COOKIES (Tillie Cole)

DATE FILLING

1½ cups dates, cut up with scissors
⅓ cup water
½ cup sugar

Put the dates, water, and sugar in the top of a double boiler and cook over hot water until the mixture is thick, stirring constantly. Remove from the fire and cool.

COOKIE DOUGH

1   cup Crisco or Spry
2   cups brown sugar, firmly packed
2   eggs, unbeaten
1½ teaspoons grated orange rind
1½ teaspoons salt
3⅓ cups all-purpose flour, sifted before measuring
1½ teaspoons soda
2   tablespoons milk

Cream the shortening and brown sugar until well blended and fluffy. Add the eggs, one at a time, and beat well. Add the salt and orange rind and blend.

Sift the flour and soda together. Add ½ of the flour to the creamed mixture and blend. Then add the milk and blend. Then the remaining flour, mixing thoroughly.

TO ASSEMBLE

Divide the dough in half. Roll each half out on a sheet of waxed paper, into rectangles about ¼ inch thick (approximately 14 by 6 inches). Spread a thin layer of the cooled date mixture all over each rectangle of dough. Using the waxed paper to help you, roll them up like a jelly roll, lengthwise (each roll will be about 14 inches long and

2 inches in diameter). Wrap the rolls in waxed paper and chill thoroughly, overnight if possible, or until the dough is firm enough to slice.

Cut into ¼-inch slices and bake on a greased cookie sheet in a 375° oven, about 12 minutes, or until lightly browned.

The recipe makes approximately 6 dozen cookies.

BROWNIE DROPS (May Katz)

   2   packages Baker's German Sweet Chocolate
   1   tablespoon butter
   2   eggs
   ¾ cup sugar
   ¼ cup unsifted all-purpose flour
   ¼ teaspoon baking powder
   ¼ teaspoon cinnamon
   ⅛ teaspoon salt
   ½ teaspoon vanilla
   ¾ to 1 cup finely chopped walnuts

Melt the chocolate and butter in a double boiler over hot water. Stir to blend, and cool.

Beat the eggs until foamy, and then gradually add the sugar. Beat the eggs until thick, about 5 minutes on the electric mixer. Blend in the cooled chocolate. Add the flour, baking powder, cinnamon, and salt. Blend thoroughly. Stir in the vanilla and the nuts.

Drop by a teaspoon onto a greased baking sheet. Bake in a 350° oven until the cookies feel almost but not quite "set" when lightly touched . . . about 8 or 9 minutes. Unless, of course, you prefer them crispy rather than slightly chewy. Then wait until they are set, about 10 minutes.

Let them cool a few minutes before removing from the cookie sheet with a spatula. The recipe makes about 3 dozen cookies.

This Book Typeset by
Pat Volz and Gloria Doty
of Aalpha Typesetting